RENAISSANCE
AND
REVOLUTION

The Remaking of European Thought

JOSEPH ANTHONY MAZZEO

RENAISSANCE AND REVOLUTION

The Remaking of European Thought

PANTHEON BOOKS

A DIVISION OF RANDOM HOUSE

NEW YORK

Acknowledgments

I would like to thank the following for permission to quote from various works: Longmans, Green and Co., Ltd. and McGraw-Hill, Inc., for John Plamenatz, *Man and Society;* Routledge and Kegan Paul, Ltd., for C. D. Broad, *Ethics and the History of Philosophy* and Karl Vossler, *The Spirit of Language in Civilization;* Sheed & Ward, Inc., for H.-I. Marrou, *A History of Education in Antiquity;* Washington University Press for R. F. Jones, *Ancients and Moderns;* Basil Blackwell, Ltd., for Michael Oakshott's introduction to his edition of Hobbes, *Leviathan;* International Universities Press, Inc., for Ernst Kris, *Psychoanalytic Explorations in Art.* The chapter on Machiavelli in this book is based entirely on studies I published earlier in *Renaissance and Seventeenth-Century Studies* (Columbia University Press, New York, and Routledge and Kegan Paul, London, 1964).

Preface

I have written this book primarily for laymen, whether students or adults, although I allow myself to hope that scholars interested in the Renaissance may also find it useful. A work of this kind, in which the author has to reach out from his more or less specialized interests into other disciplines and into the realm of large generalizations, must depend more heavily on the labors of other scholars than a work of specialized character. Nevertheless, none of us is entirely a specialist, nor do we refrain, in thought or conversation, or even in print, from drawing large conclusions from a finite store of particular knowledge or from speculating about what conclusions might be drawn from other intellectual disciplines over which we possess no authoritative command. In this respect we are all laymen and must try to pass from those things we know well and are certain of to others, more encompassing and more important, perhaps, but less precise. The whole can, in fact, be glimpsed from the part, but only if one's knowledge of the part is deep enough and if one can apprehend what others, who start with different interests or from different points of departure, have made of it. Then perhaps the final vision may not be too obscure.

Thus the scholar will recognize my debt in this work, not only to great figures of the past like Jacob Burckhardt or J. B. Bury, but to distinguished contemporaries as well. I have, in the text, given many specific acknowledgments, but I would like to state here how much my own thinking was stimulated and my own investigations guided by the work of R. F. Jones and F. J. Anderson on Bacon, of Michael Oakshott on Hobbes, of John Plamenatz on the idea of progress, of P. O. Kristeller and Erwin Panofsky on the Renaissance and humanism, of Marjorie Hope Nicolson on the relations between seventeenth-century literature and science, of Felix Gilbert on Machiavelli and H.-I. Marrou on classical education and its ideals.

A brief book on the intellectual backgrounds of the literature of the Renaissance could easily become a *catalogue raisonné*. The Renaissance was a European movement to which many men and several nations contributed. So much seems to demand inclusion, so many generalizations demand qualification, that the task seems endless if it is not to result in a superficial treatment of an era whose great complexity equals its importance. Moreover, it is the kind of subject no man can hope truly to command, the kind of work which cries out for lots of space and collaboration on the scale of the Cambridge histories. On the other hand, as I have already suggested, those of us who have worked extensively on this period of our culture, whether as historians or as students of the art, literature, or thought of the era, do finally come to have some sense of what in the Renaissance was new and of enduring importance.

In this book, then, I have tried to isolate some of the great new themes, the revolutionary shifts in thought, taste, or perception as they manifest themselves in the work of crucial writers and thinkers. My own sense of the civilization of the Renaissance, insofar as it is concrete and specific, has come about largely through a number of studies in depth, and this is the only way I can hope to convey it to my readers without an excess of abstraction and generalization. My discussion, therefore, is anchored in the extensive treatment of a few selected authors, who are magisterial and comprehensive as well as somehow typical: Machiavelli, Castiglione, Bacon, and Hobbes. I have, moreover, tried to enrich my analysis of their work by relevant allusion to the related work of others, in England and elsewhere. The reader will thus find, for example, some pages on Galileo and Descartes in the chapter on Bacon, and on Montaigne in the chapter on Castiglione.

Obviously, other figures could have been chosen to bear the weight of my discussion. My excuse can only be that my authors are important and rich, that they lend themselves admirably to the use I wish to put them to, and that I know their works better than those of some others I could have chosen. I might, too, have chosen to delineate the intellectual "background" through the literary "foreground," so to speak. A chapter on the historical and political plays of Shakespeare instead of one on Machiavelli would have permitted me to say many of the same or similar things and to make abundant reference to the "Machiavelli" of the Elizabethans. Such a procedure has sometimes been followed, and with success, in books on a theme like the one I have chosen. I have, however, rejected this alternative for what I take to be important reasons. An artist will always make a personal diffraction of the surrounding culture. He may respond only to some limited aspects of thought in his time, or he may make a quite personal and idiosyncratic use of those ideas which capture his imagination. And to the extent that he is a great artist, his diffraction will probably be untypical, his work will transcend the "ideas" and "attitudes" one can find in it. Also, works of the poetic imagination of the order of *Don Quixote* or *Henry IV* cannot really be wisely or tastefully used entirely as documents. There is often a peculiar irrelevance, both scholarly and aesthetic, in ripping allusions and ideas out of a dramatic and literary context and using them to develop the "world-view" of the author or his age. Philosophical poets like Dante can lend themselves to a careful modification of this procedure, but few poets were either philosophical enough or systematic enough in dealing with ideas to withstand such treatment. Where, as in Dante, the ideas are, in some sense, the poetry itself or a large part of it, the "background" is the "foreground" and we do not really need to go beyond him very much in order to elucidate him.

I have also tried to exercise my and the reader's historical imagination by contrasting various currents of thought and taste in the Renaissance with their medieval counterparts or forerunners. It cannot make much sense, to the uninitiated reader at least, to talk of Bacon and the "new philosophy" unless the reader has some grasp of the "old philosophy." At times, too, I have reached back into classical antiquity for illustrations, parallels, and precedents, since again it is not very helpful to talk of revivals of classical ideals in the Renaissance without conveying some idea of what those ideals were. Much that was revolutionary in the culture of the Renaissance has become so deeply woven into the fabric of thought and feeling of our culture that only by such a process of continual comparison between the Renaissance and the medieval or classical past can we hope to experience again something of the bold adventure of that age.

Moreover, the reader who wishes to understand the literature of the Renaissance must bear in mind that the older images of order and ideals of life did not immediately disappear and give way to the new—whether original or classical revivals—but coexisted with them. Indeed, some of the peculiar richness of the literature of the Renaissance derives from the availability of alternative, imaginatively compelling ways of organizing experience. In the evolution of thought as in the evolution of life, the emergence of a new phylum does not immediately drive out its forerunner, even if it is so much better adapted to life and so successfully competitive that its ancestors are doomed to become fossils. Indeed, quite often the new and the old coexist contentedly, and every now and then, even in our own time, one uncovers a "living fossil," ideas and attitudes which really had no business surviving but which somehow managed to do so.

Two of the chapters of this book are not focused on the work and thought of a single individual but on cultural movements and general ideas. The very concept of the Renaissance needs description and definition. Like all historical categories it is inevitably ambiguous, a brief way of referring to a complex set of events. The Renaissance as a cultural and historical category has been subject to such varying interpretations and evaluations that no book purporting to introduce the reader to the intellectual life of this period can ignore some consideration of the history of the term and its varying fortunes.

Humanism, the intellectual movement which more than any other marks the beginning of the Renaissance, cannot, I think, be satisfactorily discussed in terms of a single figure. It was too varied and heterogeneous a movement and, although it was of crucial

importance and had its great men, there is for humanism, in my
opinion, no figure as paradigmatic as Galileo for science or Machiavelli for political and historical thought. Humanism was less a
matter of spectacular intellectual "breakthroughs," or comprehensive intellectual syntheses, than a program of education. It was the
work of many teachers and scholars unified by a fresh kind of enthusiasm for the classical past and the determination to make a
fresh kind of use of it. In all else, humanists possessed widely differing opinions, interests, and abilities.

If anything in the sphere of thought can be said to mark the end
of the Renaissance it is the spread of the idea of progress. It marked
the appearance on the scene of history of a radically new orientation toward human life and human destiny, and changed the character of our hopes, attitudes, and aspirations. Like humanism, it
was not a single cultural "achievement" but a general, diffuse, cultural change, a change in sensibility or outlook and in the nature
of human expectations. It, too, was the slow work of time and of
the labors of many men. The last chapter of this book is devoted
to an examination of that idea and to a description of its gradual
emergence from the culture of the Renaissance. In the final pages
I have tried to indicate how the legacy of the Renaissance is still at
work in our own thought defining some of our critical intellectual
and cultural problems. Through a consideration of what I call, in
a broad sense, "science and poetry," the artistic and the scientific
ways of looking at the world, I have tried to suggest how some of
our intellectual dilemmas have arisen from the past and perhaps,
in perspective, how our knowledge of the past may suggest some
solutions.

J. A. M.

Contents

RENAISSANCE AND REVOLUTION

The Remaking of European Thought

I

RENAISSANCE AND HUMANISM:

The New Education

The category of the Renaissance in historical thought is an ambiguous one. There are as many interpretations of the period as there are patterns of history or social, political, and cultural ideals. There is a pagan Renaissance and a Christian one, a Renaissance which liberated the individual from the coercive collectivities of the Middle Ages, and a Renaissance which drowned him in all the confusions and complexities of modern civilization. It has been pushed back in time, and we now have a twelfth-century Renaissance, one in the eleventh century, and even a ninth-century Carolingian Renaissance.

The tendency to medievalize the Renaissance or, what amounts to the same thing, to push it further and further back into the Middle Ages, was not very widespread among scholars until the decades just before and after World War I, and it typified a good deal of Renaissance scholarship until the opening of World War II, when embattled nations found other, less innocuous, pursuits for scholars than restructuring the past.[1]

However much the term may have been criticized, no one has quite been able to dispense with it since it was first introduced to describe a general historical period by Michelet in the seventh volume of his *Histoire de France* (1855). Five years later Jacob Burckhardt used it in the title of his famous study, *Die Kultur der Renaissance in Italien,* and it has since formed part of the intellectual equipment of educated men.

The idea of a rebirth of the arts, or of letters and learning, goes back to the fourteenth century and was part of the consciousness of the very first generation of Renaissance humanists and artists. The term "Renaissance," however, as used to refer to the totality of events occurring during a crucial period in the history of Europe, dates from the work of Michelet. The historiographical problem of the Renaissance derives from the widespread adoption of his generalized use of the term and the subsequent attempt to synchronize all the particular "rebirths" of one kind or another which presumably took place in this era. It is not difficult to detect the Hegelian *Zeitgeist* hovering over this kind of historical thinking, the notion that there is a common spirit of the times discernible in all the activities of a culture, and if such a unified approach to a period of history has often been fruitful, it has also generated problems. The historian of art may wish to date his Renaissance with Giotto, but the political historian cannot find the most distinctive features of the modern state quite that early, and some historians of science, overwhelmed by Galileo, were tempted to write off much of the Renaissance as a generally unproductive time for the sciences.

If it is difficult to find a beginning for the Renaissance agreeable to scholars from different disciplines—assuming the improbable, that all the scholars from even a single discipline would agree—it is almost as difficult to find the end. Most historians would agree that the Renaissance is over in Italy by 1600, but the historian of English literature, reflecting on the monumental achievement of Milton, for example, would have to push the date forward some sixty years, for the work of the great poet is unintelligible except in terms of the literary ideals and achievements of the Renaissance.[2]

We can say, then, that the Renaissance spans the period from about 1300 in Italy to about 1660 in England. At least the cultural, social, and political events that scholars of the European Renaissance are interested in took place more or less within this span of time, with varying birthdays and expiration dates for the Renaissance depending on the particular country or field of inquiry.

Perhaps the best way of clarifying this problem is to give some specific examples of how and why scholars from different disciplines define the Renaissance in the way they do. The political historian, for example, will look for the crucial stages in the transition of Europe from medieval forms of political and social organization to those characteristic of the modern world. He will note the critical stages in the decline of the medieval empire and Papacy as the primary antagonists in the quest for temporal power, and the parallel rise of powerful independent monarchies or city-states with new polities and social structures which bear a closer resemblance to ancient or modern analogues than to anything distinctively medieval.

This process was well under way by the later Middle Ages, but our political historian will detect real novelties, or the re-creation of ancient forms, in the growth of a civil bureaucracy, the decline of feudal military and economic structures, the rise of professional and mercenary armies, the development of advanced forms of diplomacy including the use of resident ambassadors, the keeping of permanent administrative records in government, the secularization of political theory, and the more candid recognition among rulers of something like what we would call *raison d'état,* in theory as well as in immemorial practice. He will note, too, at what point men and their rulers quite consciously began to relinquish that ideal of a hierarchically structured, spiritually and politically unified international order which was in theory, if not always in practice, the fundamental axiom of the most sophisticated philosophical thought of the Middle Ages. He will thus look for the critical signs of the clear emergence of a pluralistic Europe composed of sovereign, autonomous states, with a fundamentally secular orientation, in spite of all the religious intensities and medieval survivals so conspicuous during the fifteenth and sixteenth centuries in Europe. According to one distinguished historian, this process of change, defined in terms of the characteristics here enumerated, did not reach a crucial character much earlier than 1400 in Italy and about one hundred years later in the rest of Europe.[3]

Art historians have obviously used other criteria for describing their Renaissance. The theme of "rebirth" of the arts was contemporary with the great Italian artists of the Renaissance and it should come as no surprise that among the most brilliant interpreters of the period we should find art historians, or those cultural historians like Burckhardt and Symonds who responded deeply to works of art. They have drawn some of the most important lineaments of our vision of the Renaissance, and many features of their interpretations of the period are less vulnerable to criticism simply because they are based on what the artists of the Renaissance thought about themselves and their work, or because their insights are rooted in the description of perfectly obvious changes in pictorial and architectural techniques.

There is, for example, little question that the medieval painters thought of paintings as composed upon a flat surface which was, so to speak, impenetrable to light. The medieval picture was, visually, on the surface of a substratum, and this effect obtained even when, as in stained-glass windows, the substratum was transparent. With Giotto and the other great Italian masters of the fourteenth century, there begins that gradual mastery of the representation of space which transforms the surface of the painting into a transparent plane *through* which the observer sees the object extended in three dimensions. By the beginning of the fifteenth century the whole theory of perspective is complete both philosophically and mathematically, and a great revolution in the approach of the educated eye to the representation of the visual world has been completed. This transformation of pictorial technique which took place between 1300 and 1400 cannot be understood merely as some external, more or less technical, process. On the contrary, it corresponds to a revolution in perception which goes hand in hand with the rational conquest of methods of representing reality.[4]

Another important development in the art of Western Europe which marks the beginning of the Renaissance for art historians is visible in the difference between the medieval and Renaissance treatment of classical themes. Both in medieval art and in much of medieval literature there was a pervasive separation of classical form from classical subject matter. Thus the figures of classical myth and legend, whether gods or heroes, were universally represented as knights if they were warriors, or as "clerks" if they were given to more intellectual pursuits. On the other hand, the figures of biblical story could be delineated, and frequently were, by modeling them on what remained of classical art. This remarkably un-historical treatment of classical material produced strange icono-graphic results whereby pagan gods could look like contemporaries while the prophets or the Virgin could look like pagan figures.[5]

This peculiar manner of treating classical material ended about the fourteenth century when classical myths and classical artistic and visual motifs began to be reintegrated. As is the case with the development of perspective, the reintegration of these elements of classical culture is much more than a change in technique or crafts-manship. It signifies the existence of a different historical conscious-ness, a realization that certain cultural facts belong together be-cause they were so created at a particular moment of time past and constitute therefore a single cultural event. The earliest great exam-ple of the reintegration of classical meaning with classical motif is given to us not by a painter but by a poet. However medieval Dante may have been in much of his thought, his Virgil is a stupendous example of this process of reintegrating the past into the present in a historically authentic way. The Virgil of the Middle Ages had been, at best, a kind of medieval sage and, at worst, a necroman-cer. In either disguise, the Virgil of medieval legend and story is virtually unrecognizable. In Dante's great poem he is again an an-tique Roman whose sentiments are recognizably "Virgilian." Of course, Dante was not dealing with a mythological figure, but that great act of the historical imagination which went into the creation of his Virgil is analogous to the act whereby, in time, it became possible to paint a figure like the Venus of Botticelli and call her Venus.

It is clear that ancient art in one way or another exerted a con-tinual influence throughout the Middle Ages even if ancient artistic motifs were, at least from the twelfth to the fourteenth centuries, detached from their classical substance. What then was the special character of the influence of ancient art on the Renaissance artists? In some degree the difference is ideological. The early humanists confronted with the work of Giotto, Duccio, and their successors, of Dante and Petrarch, articulated and brought to a highly self-conscious level the idea of a renovation of the arts and of learning.

Adopting a cyclical view of history, they saw their own times as engaged in a reconquest of the heights of the creative achievement of classical times. The cycle, having reached a trough in the Middle Ages, had turned up again.

The artists themselves adopted this conception and turned to antiquity not merely to learn various techniques but to incorporate its total achievement. Nor were they slavish imitators. On the contrary, they made an extraordinarily free and imaginative use of the art of antiquity. At least this was true of the greatest artists of the Renaissance. Moreover, different aspects of ancient art were appropriated at different times. Thus, in the early fifteenth century artists were attracted to the skill of the ancients in representing natural forms, and especially forms in motion. By the end of the century they had shifted their attention to the idealizing tendencies in ancient art and its achievements in the heroic and monumental vein.[6]

The achievement of Renaissance artists was not simply the conquest of a realistic vision of the world, for medieval art had had its consummate realists. But the realism of the sculptured figures on a Gothic cathedral, or of the details in a manuscript illumination, was "particularizing." The medieval craftsman was inclined to represent the individual, "warts and all." The artists of the Italian Renaissance sought, on the other hand, to convey the general mathematical proportions, the ideal structure, which in their view shone *through* the particular. Like the great Greek artists they portrayed the "concrete universal," that unity of general truth with particular experience which in Aristotle's view made poetic representation a "higher" thing than history or philosophy.

The classicism and naturalism of the Renaissance Italian masters is so palpable that it is surprising to discover that many of them thought about art in the allegorical and heavily didactic terms characteristic of the Middle Ages, in spite of their utterly different powers of vision and representation. The amount of allegorical freight which Botticelli, for example, tried to paint into some of his greatest canvases would have done credit to the most ingenious of medieval allegorizers.[7] Nevertheless, the allegorical paintings of

Renaissance artists seldom seem positively to demand exegesis, and this is a measure of what in fact they were actually doing, whatever they may have thought they were doing with some more traditional part of their minds.

From the point of view of the historian of education and of learning, the Renaissance presents a picture in striking contrast to that of the Middle Ages, and not simply because there was a greater amount of knowledge in the later period. The character of Renaissance intellectual movements is decidedly different, and they are marked both by syncretism and by the attempt to synthesize and relate disparate subject matters and disciplines. The medieval intellectual had inherited, and even expanded upon, the whole of the rigorous Aristotelian morphology of knowledge. His thought abounded in distinctions and separations, whether between faith and reason or between one branch of learning and another. Medieval intellectual life was compartmentalized not only in terms of subject matter but in terms of methodological principle. Each discipline was separated from another because each was defined as governed by a distinct method. Each field of inquiry was characterized by its own special kind of result and its own degree of exactitude. The medieval thinker possessed an ideal order of knowledge and being, and the whole of reality, social, political, economic, and intellectual, was, in principle, a hierarchical system of clearly defined, minute subordinations and superordinations. Thus to the seven liberal arts there corresponded seven planets and seven metals, not to mention seven virtues, and all were arrangeable in an ascending order of dignity and worth. Moreover, this order was comparable to an analogous system of order observable in the ecclesiastical, angelic, and feudal hierarchies.

A Renaissance thinker like Ficino, on the other hand, conflates theology with philosophy, faith with knowledge, pagan thought with Christian belief to a truly extraordinary degree, and tries to bring the most disparate ideas together into a unity—a unity, to be sure, which remains rather loose and which, often enough, is the result of analogical and metaphorical ingenuity rather than logical rigor. Ideas from Plato, Aristotle, Plotinus, the Hermetic writings, the ancient magicians and astrologers, patristic and medieval theologians—all find a place in his ardently imagined but weakly articulated system. With a thinker like Paracelsus or, late in the Italian Renaissance, Tommaso Campanella and Giordano Bruno, this urge to mix subjects and disciplines led at times to remarkable intellectual obscurity. The modern reader of their works will sometimes feel that he has entered an intellectual twilight world illuminated at uncertain intervals by bright flashes of light.

The controlling medieval images of order survived into the Renaissance. Men did not shake off the great models of thought such as hierarchy, universal analogy, symmetrical correspondences between orders of being, with ease, or without conflict and suffering. Indeed, some of them, like the principle of universal correspondences between things, were even more widely employed by thinkers like Paracelsus and Bruno than they were by St. Bonaventura, although with less control and in a different metaphysical framework. Nevertheless, they were weakened, and had to coexist along with new, alternative ideas of order. One of the peculiar qualities of the Renaissance skeptics such as Montaigne or John Donne (in one of his moods) is their power to apprehend imaginatively the viability of alternative and mutually exclusive ways of organizing experience. The old may have been dying, but it was still usable alongside the new.

It is clear, however, that the weakening or, in some cases, the complete breakdown of the medieval schemes of organizing experience and thought went *pari passu* with the decompartmentalization of thought. Indeed, it was a precondition for the Renaissance confluescence of the different streams of knowledge, and for the flooding of those streams by the rapidly expanding quantity of knowledge and skill which was being recovered from the libraries of Europe, in the *botteghe* of artists, and in the shops of artisans and craftsmen. If the result of this process was, in part, intellectual confusion, premature syntheses and methodological cul-de-sacs, the rich mixture of disciplines and skills also led to fruitful amalgamations of ideas. Ficino's eclectic Platonism and Lipsius' heterogeneous Stoicism frequently had little enough to do with their assumed classical prototypes, but they were enormously influential in their times and served at least to saturate the minds of the literate with new ideas and to suggest new interrelationships between them.

Another sign of this breakup of traditional disciplines is the emergence of a new type of intellectual hero, the "universal man," usually an artist but also, in another tradition of universalism, the magician or "scientific" wonder-worker. In the case of the artist, we must recall that the new art of painting demanded of its practitioner that he be a mathematician, if he was to master perspective, and a careful observer of nature, especially of human anatomy, if he was to paint things the way they are in reality. Leonardo, the most famous example of the artistic *uomo universale,* did not think of himself as other than an artist, however many-faceted his interests. He simply defined the artist, along with his contemporaries, as also and *necessarily* an anatomist, naturalist, physicist, and mathematician. This vastly broadened definition of the artist shattered the medieval distinction between the liberal arts and the so-called "mechanical" arts. It served to bring the artist, the skilled artisan, even the "tinker" into a closer relationship with the philosopher or man of letters, whose dignity he henceforth claimed, and prepared the way for that amalgamation of theory with technology, exhaustive observation, and experimentation which Bacon predicted as the necessary condition for the advancement of scientific learning.

Paracelsus is the second type of intellectual hero, and the controlling discipline of his multifarious activities was not art but magic, magic as the prototype of scientific knowledge, as the kind of knowledge of the mysteries of things, of their hidden properties and structures, which can give one power over nature. Interest in magic was widespread during the Renaissance and after, and it attracted the attention of some of the greatest minds of the age, Ficino, Pico, Bruno, Cardano to mention only a few. In spite of some of the charlatanry inevitably involved, magic was a serious pursuit and its practitioners were often men of the highest ethical character. Moreover, the Renaissance magus did not seek power over nature merely to exploit it. Rather, the power he achieved was a sign that he truly understood the nature of things, and this power was thus of a quasi-sacred sort.

We are perhaps most familiar with the great figure of the Renaissance magus in the form in which he entered the European literary imagination, as Dr. Faustus. The most sublime and the most trivial features of the great Renaissance magi such as Paracelsus entered into the Faustus legend. If the figure of Faustus from Marlowe to Goethe cannot refrain from magical tricks and charlatanry, his highest impulse is to experience the natural world as an intimate intellectual and spiritual possession, to appropriate and unite with that object of the understanding which is both natural and divine at the same time. Faustus, sick of bearing knowledge as mere intellectual baggage, wants knowledge of the sort that will divinize him, knowledge as a mode of ultimate action.

It is remarkable how many of the traits of Paracelsus went into the Faustus legend. He was enough of a charlatan to be Faustus the trickster and enough of a genius to inspire the portrait of the demonic intellectual hero. His reputation as a physician was fabulous, comparable only to that of Freud in our own time. He not only claimed to have made lead from gold but to have used the "quintessence" or elixer crucial in the alchemical process to cure all kinds of illness and even to make men, "homunculi," out of semen. Paracelsus, in fact, was actually able to cure syphilis, for example, by using mercurials, and his most important contribution to the history of medicine and science lay in his advocacy of drugs made from chemicals and minerals. While it is a little frightening to think of the fantastic mixtures with which Paracelsian physicians dosed their patients, there was little value in the herbs which were the total pharmacopeia of physicians trained in the tradition of Galen.[8]

We can observe in both of these figures, Leonardo and Paracelsus, not only what is new about some important features of intellectual life in the Renaissance, but also something which is traditional as well. Like the greatest of medieval thinkers, they are impelled by a belief in the unity of knowledge and of being. A medieval thinker, however, would have understood universality of understanding as attainable in terms of "first principles," not in terms of great erudition, or the total experience of things, or the possession of a large number of skills and powers. Still less would he have conceived of the *human* universal knower as possessed of a commensurable power, a power which is the sign of his unity with nature and the measure of the depth of his understanding of it. The highest type of the medieval intellectual was, in short, a metaphysician or religious sage. In the Renaissance he is displaced by the magus and the artist. However different, they are both makers and doers who conceive of their very activities as acts of the understanding. For Leonardo, to paint an object truly was to understand it, which is perhaps one reason why he was less interested in finishing his works than in conceiving them. So for Paracelsus, to cure a disease is to understand nature that much more.

Interestingly enough, the kind of universality of thought characteristic of a Leonardo or a Paracelsus, because of its artistic or scientific affinities, fostered the development of new specialties. Lens grinders, watchmakers, new kinds of pharmacists, or other specialized technicians and artisans came into being to meet the demand for new materials or new instruments. Moreover, as knowledge increased and as the Renaissance investigators gradually realized their search for more sophisticated and certain methods in scholarship, art, and science, a new kind of specialization began to arise. This was of the modern variety, a compartmentalization of the mind imposed by the ever increasing amount of knowledge a single individual must possess if he is to make his own original contribution to the sum of what is knowable. Although this problem did not become gravely acute until relatively recent times, we can trace its origins to these developments.

However various the views on the great transformation of European civilization which took place between the fourteenth and seventeenth centuries, certain common notions appear in all of them. All students of the era would agree that it is marked by the process of the secularization of culture. This does not necessarily mean "paganization," although some scholars have thought so. It does mean that many activities which had once been carried on by the church and the feudal court were being carried on by the newly emergent middle classes, by men who were neither clerics nor knights, but citizens or subjects fully engaged in an urban mode of existence. Again all would probably agree that the Renaissance was a process of recovery of past achievements, a search for pristine ideals. Of course, much that was new was coming to birth during the Renaissance, but it was frequently presented to the world as a revival. The novelty was validated, not as a fresh creation but as the resurrection of some better ancient teaching, institution, moral, or aesthetic idea.

This process of recovery took two main forms: the classical humanist sought to revive the art, literature, and learning of antiquity, while the Christian humanist, using the new philological and historical disciplines created by the secular humanist, sought to return to the authentic pristine Gospel, unencumbered by the massive complexities of Scholastic theology. The scope and scale of this process of recovery of the past, in the context of a new society and, therefore, of new uses for the vastly increasing store of learning, marks off the humanism of the Renaissance from any of its medieval prototypes. Humanism, broadly defined and with due note taken of its variousness, is the master key to our comprehension of the civilization of the Renaissance.

The term *humanista* was widely current during the Renaissance but it meant no more than a teacher of Latin. However, since Latin was the vehicle of the revival of the learning of antiquity, and even Greek was approached for a long time largely through Latin versions and commentaries, the term always implied a good deal more than a simple reference to a language teacher. The term "humanism" was coined only during the nineteenth century to refer to the revival of classical learning which began in the fourteenth century, but the scholars who coined it were faithful to the connotations of *humanista* who, as the master of the Latin language, held the key to the treasures of ancient civilization. The modern term "humanities" is simply a translation of the Latin phrase *studia humanitatis*, and it was used during the Renaissance to refer to secular literature as distinct from "divine" literature, or to the new curriculum based on the ancient Greek and Latin culture as against the old professional Scholastic curriculum developed during the Middle Ages.

Humanism was, in fact, an educational movement in the broadest sense of the term. The great humanists of the Renaissance were impelled to revolutionize the curriculum out of the conviction that the classical world had been through a complete cycle of human experience, moral, intellectual, and imaginative, and that the ancients had given a luminously intelligent account of that experience, in perfect form, in imperishable works of thought, art, and literature. For them, the corpus of classical writings, including works of a scientific character as well as humanist ones, were the unique instruments for the extension of consciousness and for making moral agents out of raw men. One could learn from the ancients what one could not from texts of the medieval schools, how to live and how to take one's place in the world.

The term *studia humanitatis* was ancient, and the humanists adopted it from Cicero and other Roman authors. Under their spiritual aegis, the humanists chose a new set of subjects for study and teaching, and formulated a new version of the ancient curriculum based on grammar, rhetoric, poetry, history, and moral philosophy. In so doing the humanists deliberately and self-consciously altered the focus of intellectual and moral concern. They placed their emphasis on man, man as he is revealed in the written records, intellectual and imaginative, of classical antiquity, records which were exemplary for elegance, clarity, and in the profundity of their grasp of human nature and its vicissitudes. The humanists not only changed the style in which philosophical questions were discussed, they changed the questions themselves. In elegant literary structures modeled on the best authors of antiquity, they abandoned the logical rigors of Scholasticism and Aristotelian metaphysics and discussed more ambiguous but, they felt, more vital questions like the dignity of man, the conditions and possibilities of happiness in human life, the role of chance or fate in human affairs and the power of human effort and ability to counteract it, whether the highest human activity was to be found in contemplation or in a life of political and social action, the relative merits of different kinds of government, whether government by the one or by the many.

We can detect in this list of problems a practical pedagogical impulse quite different from the theoretical urgency and systematic rigor with which a medieval thinker might have considered questions of similar import. But humanistic thought was not simply pedagogical and interpretive, it was also scholarly and innovative. Indeed, both of these orders of intellectual activity were one. Humanists read the ancients as guides to the ambiguities of action and thought as they are experienced in daily life, but they also discovered, edited, and glossed more ancient texts for men to study and use as guides. They uncovered more and more of the diversity of ancient philosophical and moral thought during the course of the Renaissance and, moreover, in the original sources and languages. Even traditional authorities like Aristotle, known largely in stiffly literal translations during the Middle Ages, came to be seen in a new light after a nucleus of scholars began to read him in the original and with the aid of Greek rather than Arabic commentators. Fresh translations prepared on this new basis were greatly superior to anything which existed before, and if it took a long time before a good command of Greek became the common property of educated men, a truer knowledge of the familiar ancient authors as well as fresh knowledge of previously unknown authors like Plato and Herodotus became available through the great efforts of the humanist translators.

The influence of the humanistic movement, through their literary and scholarly activity, spread far beyond humanistic circles proper and their particular schools and academies. The Renaissance Platonists drew on the work of the humanists for texts or commentaries, for much of the style and manner of the discussion of intellectual problems, for certain emphases of their thought, although their concern with the magical pseudo-sciences of antiquity and their fondness for cosmological and metaphysical speculations were alien to the typical concerns of the humanists themselves. Above all, however, the humanists created that version of the clas-

sical curriculum which, for better and for worse, in all of its variations, became the basis of Western education and remained its
basis until our own time.[9]

I have already pointed out that humanism, although a secular
movement, was not conspicuously "pagan." Indeed, the objections
of Italian humanists like Petrarch to the Aristotelians of the Padua
school was based not only on their "inelegant" Latin but on their
presumed "atheism." Like Erasmus later on, Petrarch's criticism of
the Scholastic tradition was in the name of a purer and simpler
mode of piety and religious devotion. It may strike the reader as
peculiar that Petrarch should be so severe with the Aristotelians
after the great Scholastics of the thirteenth century had virtually
canonized him, but Petrarch, altogether anti-Aristotelian, was also
attacking features which were peculiar to Italian Aristotelianism.

There was, even in medieval times, a substantial difference between the Aristotelianism of France and England and the Aristotelianism of Italy. First of all, the Italian universities did not teach
theology or philosophy (at least until the late fourteenth century),
but confined their curriculum to rhetoric, law, and medicine. In
Italy, theology and philosophy were taught in the houses of study
directed by Dominicans and Franciscans. In the universities, on the
other hand, although Aristotle's writings did not go unread, they
were part of the medical and not the theological curriculum. In
Paris or Oxford, Aristotle was a propaedeutic to theology, in
Padua to medicine. This situation not only determined which particular works of Aristotle were most extensively studied and read,
but set the tone of the entire speculative tradition at each university. Italian Aristotelianism had a decidedly more scientific and
naturalistic character than the Aristotelianism of the Sorbonne.[10]

The secular character of the main currents of Italian Aristotelianism is paralleled by the secular character of the work of the major Italian humanists. Although humanism *per se* was neither religious nor antireligious, north of the Alps and especially in England
and Germany, humanism and religion were intimately associated.
We need not assume from this that the northern races were more
saintly, or that the Italians were necessarily indifferent to religious

values. The reason lies in the simple fact that, except in Italy, medieval intellectual life in Europe was virtually a monopoly of clerics and ecclesiastics, and that this monopoly, even after it was broken, exerted a powerful influence on the intellectual activities of the transalpine humanists. Germany alone developed early a strong tradition of lay humanism alongside Christian humanism, although the latter was perhaps the more vigorous and influential of the two, for there is little doubt that the intellectual roots of the Reformation lay in the work of German scholars in the field of biblical and patristic literature.

The contrasts between medieval Italy and the rest of Europe were not confined to the matter of classical learning. On the contrary, if we think of England or France as models, Italy lacks many of the characteristic features of medieval life and culture. We must bear in mind that Italy never suffered, in extreme degree, the process of feudalization and deurbanization which took place in the rest of Europe with the decline of the empire. Town life, for example, never died out and at times it even flourished. Italian intellectual life never fell under complete ecclesiastical dominance simply because, throughout the Middle Ages, there existed in Italy a secular class of literate laymen, many of them lawyers. Although Italy suffered numerous invasions and upheavals during the "dark" ages, this class never died out, and it managed to establish a continuous tradition of lay intellectual life. The characteristic economic and social arrangements of feudalism either did not survive long where they were introduced or were not introduced at all. The Guelph and Ghibelline struggles of the Middle Ages in Italy marked the steady rise of the independent cities over the power of both the empire and the Papacy, while the commercial vigor of Venice, Genoa, and other important centers of northern and central Italy made possible an urban style of life richer and more cosmopolitan than could have been found elsewhere, even in great cities like Paris and London.

Gothic art, the symbol par excellence of medieval civilization, never really took hold in Italy. The cathedral in Milan is not only quite late but the work of foreign architects and craftsmen. The masterpieces of Italian medieval architecture are Romanesque, and the great paintings of the same era are all in the Byzantine style. Indeed, the rebellion of the great Italian artists and architects of the fourteenth century against the medieval style was not against the elaborateness of Gothic but against the austere "unnaturalness" of the *maniera Bizantina*. In literature, Latin remained a living language so long in Italy, its prestige was so high, that Italian literature is the last of the great European literatures to develop, even though it made up for its late start with Dante. The rich medieval literature in German and French has no parallel in Italian, and we find in Italy none of the great cycles of epic and romance or of mystery and morality plays. However much war and the erosions of time may have obliterated, Italy still possessed what remained of the classical legacy, not simply as a collection of monuments and manuscripts but as a datum of consciousness, as a crucial element in the self-definition of educated Italians.

In view of the power and strength of the classical past in Italy, visible in the very stones of the Italian cities and echoing in the names of its towns and countryside, we should not be surprised to find signs of highly developed humanistic interest and pursuits quite early. By the second half of the thirteenth century there was a flourishing circle of humanists in the city of Padua and we have ample evidence that they were studying and interpreting a much wider and more varied range of classical Latin than was known anywhere else in Europe.[11]

Gradually this tradition of humanistic study and enthusiasm for the culture of classical antiquity spread elsewhere in Italy and prepared the soil for the first great humanist of modern Europe, Francesco Petrarca, known as Petrarch. In his life and work, in spite of many medieval survivals, we can discern "writ large" and fully matured the characteristic interests and attitudes of the humanist. Petrarch defined his life in terms of his literary ambitions and his literary ambitions in terms of two works, one an epic poem, the *Africa,* modeled on Virgil, whose subject was the Punic Wars and which he never brought to completion, the other, a historical work of biographical character, *De viris illustribus,* which he was still revising when he died in 1374. What is astonishing about this well-defined ambition is that Petrarch set as his task the continuation of classical Latin literature at that point, so to speak, where it had been interrupted. The Punic Wars was a classical subject the ancient epic poets had not treated and, with the exception of Suetonius and Nepos, there was very little in classical historical biography. Unlike Dante, Petrarch would write in Latin, and unlike the medieval Latin poets, his subject would be one which would have been appropriate to an ancient author.

Most of the rest of his literary output was based not simply on classical precedent—writers had been doing that for a long time—but on the personal appropriation of the language, content, and attitudes of classical authors. There are three quite Horatian books of epistles, eclogues in imitation of Virgil's *Bucolics,* treatises on moral philosophy in the Senecan vein, the *Secretum,* a spiritual autobiography in dialogue form with St. Augustine as his interlocutor, and two groups of prose letters modeled on Cicero, the *Ad familiares* in twenty-four books and the *Seniles* in eighteen. In the *Ad familiares* he performs a great humanistic act of the imagination and addresses his letters to the greatest writers of antiquity, Homer, Virgil, Livy, Cicero, and Seneca, as an equal writing to equals. The ease with which he talks to, and even chides, these ancient greats, and his extraordinary plan, however incomplete, to write in Latin and for his own time works in the major literary genres of classical literature, marks an unprecedented and unique kind of relationship to antiquity, different not only in range but in kind from anything that came before. The seeking of glory through literary greatness, the bold attempt to revive in his own person the whole of ancient literature through an act of appropriation and re-creation, made Petrarch the most famous man of letters in the Europe of his time.

And this reputation was first achieved in Petrarch's own terms, as a poet and moral philosopher in the Latin language, not as the great Italian lyric poet of subsequent generations. Indeed, he dismissed his vernacular poems as trifles, although we need not take this public statement too seriously. We have ample evidence that he worked on his Italian lyrics with infinite care, revising and polishing them over many years. These poems, of course, are the basis of his present-day literary reputation, his Latin works having suffered the fate of most of the ambitious humanistic exercises in latinity. Indeed, of all the volumes of Latin prose and poetry produced by several generations of humanists perhaps only the *Utopia* of Sir Thomas More has achieved the rank of a modern classic.

A similar fate overtook the work of Giovanni Boccaccio, Petrarch's friend, admirer, and fellow humanist, whose *Decameron* has long outlived his other works in Italian, his Latin biographies, and his studies of ancient mythology and geography. The latter, as works of erudition, were bound to become obsolete eventually, but they are of great historical importance as among the first major works of classical scholarship we possess. But even the biographical works of both Petrarch and Boccaccio are now of little interest. They are strikingly medieval in character, in spite of the humanistic ideals of their authors, and they have much of the moral and literary structure of exemplaristic moral tales and of hagiographical legends. Boccaccio's widely read work on famous women, *De claris mulieribus,* or his equally well-known work on the tragic fall of illustrious men, *De casibus virorum illustrium,* are scarcely to be distinguished from their medieval prototypes. His short life of Dante, really a public lecture, is perhaps an exception to this generalization, and it has been called, with some exaggeration the first modern biography in that it presents us with a convincing portrait of an individual and not with a type of the poet or sage.

The most influential figure in Italian humanism after the prodigious activity of Petrarch and Boccaccio was Coluccio Salutati (1331-1406), Chancellor of the Florentine Republic, who, not greatly gifted himself, nevertheless recognized the gifts of others such as Poggio Bracciolini (1380-1459) and Leonardo Bruni (1369-1444). Together with his disciples he did much to disseminate the humanistic legacy by encouraging the study and collection of ancient manuscripts. Indeed, he and his successors created the foundation of the great Florentine manuscript collections of both Greek and Latin classics.

The earliest phase of humanism was largely concerned with the recovery of "lost" Latin classics, but from the beginning there was a strong interest in going beyond them to their Greek predecessors. Petrarch was the proud possessor of a Greek manuscript of Plato and cherished it even though he could not read it. Boccaccio went a bit further and welcomed Leontius Pilatus into his home when the Greek came to stay in Florence in 1360. Boccaccio procured a teaching post for Pilatus at the University in Florence and encouraged him to make a Latin version of the Homeric poems and some plays of Euripides. Although Pilatus had some students, they were few and undistinguished, so that this first attempt to introduce Greek into the university came to nothing and Greek studies did not get a firm footing in Europe until Emanuel Chrysoloras began to teach in Florence in 1397. Pilatus' poor and inaccurate versions of the *Iliad* and the *Odyssey* were read and circulated for about a century after he first published them, a small indication of how slow Greek studies were in getting started.

In regard to the history of Greek learning in the West two remarkable myths have found their way into the literature on the Renaissance and they still have some currency. The first is that knowledge of Greek was utterly dead during the Middle Ages. This is so obviously not true that it is hard to understand how it started. All during the Middle Ages, in Ireland and England during the ninth century, in Sicily during the twelfth, in southern Italy throughout the Middle Ages, some translators were at work turning Greek works into Latin. But those works were entirely of a theological, scientific, or philosophical character. Competent Greek scholars were not in great supply, to be sure, but there were some to be found in just about every century after the decline of the empire somewhere in Europe. The point is that medieval interest in Greek was of a professional sort, so that the authors translated were those who would be of interest to "experts" of one kind or another, like theologians and physicians.

The second and related myth was that Greek learning was introduced into the West first when Byzantine refugee scholars flocked to Italy after the Turkish capture of Constantinople. There is no doubt that the refugees stimulated Greek studies by their presence and by introducing new texts and authors. Nevertheless, Greek studies had been firmly established in Italy by the time they arrived.

What distinguished the Greek revival of the Renaissance from all of its medieval forerunners was not simply the fact that Greek gradually came to be part of the general curriculum of studies, but that the focus of interest of the new Hellenism was in the literary and historical masterpieces of Greek literature. Scientific and theological writings were not neglected, to be sure, but professional and specialized interest in Greek was henceforth subordinated to the encompassing humanistic task of appropriating ancient civilization. This was a slow process, in the case of Greek, and the diffusion of a good command of Greek among educated Italians and Europeans took between one and two centuries. Even in Italy, it is not until the sixteenth century that it is no longer rare to find a good Hellenist, and then much of the popular knowledge of Greek works was through the medium of translations, some of them inadequate by any standards. Enthusiasm for Greek outstripped general possession by almost two hundred years.[12]

The recovery and dissemination of a wider and more accurate knowledge of the ancient authors, whether Greek or Latin, demanded the development of critical methods of philological and historical scholarship, and the creation of the "instruments" and procedures of what we can clearly call modern scholarship is one of the greatest accomplishments of humanism. They introduced new methods into the study of sacred as well as secular texts, and with Flavio Biondo's (1388-1463) reconstruction of the ancient city of Rome the modern science of archaeology began.[13] The most spectacular demonstration of the revolutionary power of the new methods and achievements of humanistic scholarship occurred when, in the fifteenth century, Lorenzo Valla (1406-1457) demonstrated that the famous Donation of Constantine on which some of the papal claim to temporal sovereignty rested was a forgery. He showed beyond dispute that its Latin was of a considerably later date than the Latin of Constantine's era, and that a number of towns mentioned in the document did not exist at that time.

As I have already suggested, the philological, historical, and interpretative labors of the humanists were intrinsically related to their interest in educational reform. The renewed and expanded interest in antiquity, the search by humanists for every scrap of what remained of the culture of ancient Greece and Rome—all this energetic activity was finally in the service of creating a new educational ideal. The recovery of antiquity was, in a broad sense, the recovery of the curriculum of antiquity, a curriculum whose highest intention was to make the liberally educated man, the citizen, fit to perform with distinction the duties of peace and war. Just how the humanists tried to make the new learning serve these ends, how they transformed tradition by adapting some parts of it to the new ideals, will shortly be our concern, but we should first consider ancient education itself. I would like, even at the risk of appearing digressive, to treat this subject at some length. Studies on the Renaissance are saturated, as they must be, with terms like "rebirth" or "revival," but all too frequently the reader is given very little idea of what, precisely, was revived or reborn. Moreover, nothing is ever reborn as exactly the same, and revivals are always the advent of something new as well as the reintroduction of something old. Perhaps, then, a fairly thorough treatment of ancient education will help us to a more precise estimate of the humanistic achievement.

H.-I. Marrou, in his *History of Education in Antiquity,* summarizes the history of Greek education as the story of the transformation of Greek culture from one in which the ideal type of education was the noble warrior to one in which the ideal type was really a scribe-civil servant, a master of writing and expression who served political and administrative functions.[14]

The Homeric poems, of course, contained the types of nobility, of *arete,* the peculiar excellence or "virtue" proper to leaders of men, whether it was prowess in battle or skill in speech or wisdom in counsel, whether it was the fierce military energy of Achilles, or the shrewd, ingenious prudent calculations of Odysseus. They afforded models of courage and sacrifice in war as well as models —as in the *Odyssey*—of the proper relations between members of the family, guests and hosts, rulers and their subjects. After they were read allegorically—and such a reading began quite early in

Greek civilization—they became veritable compendia of moral knowledge and social or political "know-how." They remained, until Socrates, the foundation of Greek education.

With Socrates and his followers the character of Greek education began to change. With them we detect a displacement of educational ideals from those of the citizen functioning in the *polis,* the city state, ideals of civic and military excellence, to more personal subjective and individualistic ideals of moral self-development. If in the older education the individual realized himself by fulfilling the duties of war and peace as a member of his *polis,* the new education called him to his self-realization in a strenuous philosophical discipline which aimed at the transformation of self and of consciousness. Of course, with Socrates and Plato, the individual still remains a citizen. The great crisis which overtook the Greek world with the Peloponnesian War and the Macedonian ascendancy had called into question the whole of the older political and moral traditions, and the philosophical disciplines they advocated were meant to provide firm standards of thought and action for citizens. Not until the Cynics and Neoplatonists do we find men fleeing the community or, indeed, the world itself.

The new values, as they were developed by the lesser Socratics, can be referred to by the Greek word *paideia.* The word is difficult to define and no English expression such as "civilization," "culture," "tradition," "literature," "education" can express more than one of its aspects. It can include all of these English renderings simultaneously and in unity, or it can include them in different combination and with different emphases.[15]

At its greatest and best, the notion of *paideia* comprehended a peculiarly Greek synthesis of ideals of public service with ideals of personal self-cultivation, a devotion both to the beauties of art and literature, and to the hard-won truths of science and philosophy. Nevertheless, the shift from the Homeric basis of education soon precipitated a crisis in Greek thought. The question was no longer whether Homer was enough as the basis of education but whether poetry itself was the proper instrument for molding future generations. The *locus classicus* of our knowledge of this crisis and the most powerful attack on poetry or the literary imagination ever made is in the *Republic* of Plato.

There, Plato made a famous two-pronged attack on poetry: on moral grounds, for telling immoral stories of the gods; and on metaphysical grounds, for being a representation of the world of "becoming." The world of change is, in Plato's thought, merely a poor copy of an immaterial, changeless, and transcendental reality to the apprehension of which the mind should direct itself. The poet's world, possessing less "reality" even than the world of becoming it represented, could merely lead the mind away from true Being. Only activities like mathematics and philosophy could lead the human intellect in the right direction and deliver it from the cloud of ignorance and mere opinion in which it habitually dwelt.[16] Poetry, however pleasurable, served to keep us ignorant and often to corrupt us.

With this argument, Greek culture first faced, in a simple form to be sure, a fundamental educational problem which is still with us. On its intellectual side, the Homeric basis of education had been literary and artistic. Plato demanded that it be philosophical and "scientific." Over and over again in the history of Western culture these two antithetical views have, in one form or another, been restated. Even in the Middle Ages we see the humanistic curriculum of Orléans and Chartres in the twelfth century replaced in the thirteenth by the professional curricula of Paris. Indeed, from one point of view, we can understand the humanistically oriented reforms in education during the Renaissance as a return, on a higher and richer level, to the great literary and rhetorical traditions of the twelfth century.

The reply to Plato came in the work of Aristotle and Isocrates, the great orator. Much of our opinion of classical rhetoric and its traditions has been formed by those within classical culture itself who attacked it, from Plato to St. Augustine. The excesses of that tradition are of course apparent enough, and few of us would quarrel with the notion that precision and honesty of thought are more important than elegance and elaborateness of style, although this is finally a false set of alternatives. Beauty and truth, complexity and honesty are not mutually exclusive. Both Aristotle and Isocrates, in different ways, defended the legitimacy of rhetorical training and practice against its detractors, and Isocrates formulated a conception of rhetoric which was broad enough and humane enough to be a comprehensive system of education. Aristotle retained the older conception of rhetoric as a training in the art of persuasion and defended imaginative literature in the *Poetics*. Isocrates, on the other hand, expanded the conception of rhetoric to include poetry itself.

He felt that the study of language and literature, of rhetoric in the more comprehensive sense of the word, would develop the kind of sensitive intuition and subtle powers of judgment which would permit men to act wisely amid the complexities of practical life. The Socratic and Platonic attempt to ground judgment and decision in a "science" of morality, in a rational structure which would give clear and certain precepts for the guidance of all action was, in his view, a blind alley. Decisions in real life, at least ethical and political ones, are made amid a mass of complexities, ambiguities, and imponderables which require qualities of mind and character quite different from those making a good philosopher or mathematician. Reason, in the sense in which a brilliant philosopher possesses reason, is by no means enough for the "virtuous" conduct of life. Men require a certain kind of gift, a kind of "know-how," which is best improved by the study of the art of rhetoric or, as we might say today, the study of literature.

The careful choice of words, the marshaling of thoughts and arguments in precise formal structures, the painstaking revisions required to find the *mot juste*—all these are not merely the tasks of craftsmanship. Such a discipline developed an awareness of shades of meaning, a power of making subtle discriminations, which was much more adequate to the nature of experience and action than that skill in manipulating abstractions and axioms which a scientific or philosophical education fostered. Thus, at its best, the ancient rhetorical tradition enshrined the profound intuition that life is lived amid particular problems and events, each one in some degree unique, and that men require sensitivity and flexibility of mind much more than iron-bound logical rigor if they are to have a decent chance of managing amid the instabilities of concrete existence. It is not only for metaphysical reasons, after all, that Plato placed true being in an unchanging world beyond space and time. If ethics and politics are to have a basis as exact as mathematics, if they are to have an infallibly lucid logical structure, they must be the ethics and politics of another world.

Of course, ancient rhetoric also fostered a kind of linguistic virtuosity and sterile argumentation which was rightly condemned. The attacks of St. Augustine and Plato were directed against a rhetorical practice which had little concern for truth or even justice, which not only was obsessed with trivial aestheticism and verbal artifice but even made "the worse cause appear the better." But the wars between logicians and rhetoricians, philosophers and the upholders of "humane letters," were also based on misunderstanding. Great literature is not the enemy of knowledge, whether scientific or moral. Indeed, Isocrates correctly viewed it as a mode of knowledge, as the way in which the mind takes account of the complexities of concrete experience and communicates them to other minds. It deals with truth of another order than the truths of the philosopher. Unfortunately, the philosophers who chose to dwell in an ideal rational order could only view the rhetoricians, even the best of them, as concerned with mere "opinions" and not with truth.

Both the decay of rhetoric and its development into a comprehensive system of education were profoundly influenced by the political history of antiquity. The old Greek city-state with its freewheeling democracy fostered rhetoric. Both legal and political processes depended on the free citizen and his skill in speech and powers of persuasion. The individual need of such skills was great enough to bring into being a class of experts, the much maligned Sophists, who earned their living by teaching the arts of language. In this classic period, political activity is intrinsically connected with rhetorical skill and training, and rhetoric in turn partakes of the comprehensive character of Greek political thinking. For the classic Greeks, politics was more than the art of making a state or an administrative unit. Politics also dealt with moral and cultural questions such as the effect of a man's work upon his character, the role of women in society, the nature of poetry and its social importance. Thus the all-encompassing claims of the great rhetoricians to deal with all knowledge are understandable in the light of the essentially political function of classical rhetoric.[17]

The old city-states were eventually swallowed up in the new world empires, first that of Macedon and then of Rome. As rule became more autocratic and impersonal, rhetoric lost its essentially political function and much of the effort of rhetoricians went into panegyric of divine monarchs, or virtuoso performances for the entertainment of a select public. On the other hand, rhetoric in an expanded sense became the basis of Hellenistic education. Poetry—we would say literature—was the core of the Hellenistic curriculum. Plato's massive attack on poets and poetry had gone unheeded, and there evolved a comprehensive canon of literary classics which were the legacy of every educated man and the basis of his intellectual and moral culture.

As something essentially *classical,* Hellenistic civilization was the opposite of those revolutionary, innovating cultures that are propelled forward by a great creative drive. It rested essentially on the peaceful possession of an already acquired capital. It is a mistake to say as it is often said by its detractors, that it was born with its head back to front. It is not autumnal, tormented with nostalgic regret for a vanished spring. On the contrary, it looks upon itself as firmly established in an unchanging present, in the full blaze of a hot summer sun. It knows what mighty reserves it possesses, what past masters it has. That these appeared at a certain moment of time, under the influence of certain historical forces, is unimportant; what matters is that they exist and can be rediscovered in the same way, again and again, by each successive generation, can be recognized and admired and imitated. A classical culture can be defined as a unified collection of masterpieces, existing as the recognized basis of its scale of values.[18]

The decay of the ancient city preceded by only a short period of time its incorporation into the newly growing empires. If this great change involved the loss of the valuable creative influences of local pieties and allegiances, the loss or weakening of the heroic and civic ideals of the old education, it also meant the fostering of the ideal of personal self-development and self-cultivation. The old axiom of Protagoras, that "man is the measure of all things," found a new and larger meaning in the civilization of Hellenistic times. Citizenship in great empires can lead to a loss of individuality, but what was also lost in the transition from city-state to universal empire, from *polis* to *oikoumene,* was regionalism, provincialism, and the petty coercions of small cities. At one time the *polis* served to free men from the tyrannies of tribal customs and archaic family clannishness, but in turn it developed some of the characteristic faults of small towns. Cultural pressures of a totalitarian character and strong tendencies to coerce uniformity of opinion were the characteristic vices of life in the city-state, and the ideals which Thucydides put into the mouth of his Pericles were short-lived. We must recall that social pressures and political control inevitably diminished in ancient times as more and more of mankind was politically unified. Only the stupendous resources of modern technology can make the modern totalitarian state. A modern analogy to the passage from decaying city-states to world-empire might be found in the flight of contemporary young people from small towns to the big city. One loses the conventions which make life secure and cozy and so is vulnerable to more anxiety, but one also has the opportunity "to find oneself" if one wishes.

The influence of certain romantic tendencies has prompted some scholars to view the Hellenistic civilization as a period of cultural decay, and it is of course true that it produced nothing quite comparable to the unique masterpieces of thought and art of the Periclean period. Nevertheless, it is more just to view it as a period of cultural consolidation devoted to the enjoyment and dissemination of the incomparable legacy of the past. If as Gilbert Murray thought, this period was accompanied by the beginnings of a "failure of nerve" and the quest for salvation from the world, it was also accompanied by the growth of a true personalistic humanism. Ecstatic and otherworldly cults were largely the treasure of the humble, and even when educated and intelligent men gave their ultimate allegiance to ideals of fulfillment which lay beyond personality and cultural self-cultivation, they did not do so by committing cultural and intellectual suicide. Even late in antiquity, the same Plotinus, blind and absorbed in inner vision, who saw the goal of life in the flight of the alone to the alone, also told his disciples that they must be like the coroplast, the maker of decorated statues, and assume as the task of life the transformation of themselves into works of art. The intellectual and moral discipline of education, starting with the unadorned clay of childhood, was to help man model his own statue, to become a harmony of parts and functions, a work of ideal proportions.

Thus education, *paideia,* early and late in Hellenistic times, meant that cultural and intellectual discipline which produces a true man, an example of true humanity, out of the biological raw material. It strips him too of his cultural and political provinciality and turns him into a citizen of the world. It is significant that when Cicero translated the Greek word into Latin he used the word *humanitas.*[19]

Paideia, in fact, became truly a religion, available, to be sure, only to the educated minority, but nevertheless a religion which was not extirpated until the conversion of the empire. There even developed in Hellenistic times an interesting doctrine that immortality was a gift of the muses, a gift of learning and culture. The man who shaped himself into a true exemplar of *humanitas* might hope to spend eternity in the Elysian fields where his philosophical discussions and his enjoyment of the pleasures of art and philosophy would go on forever.

An otherworldly beatitude available only to the highly cultured may strike our egalitarian age as a fearfully snobbish extension of temporal intellectual pride into eternity, as a most unjust way of separating the erudite sheep from the unlettered goats. Yet a cultural criterion of salvation is in some respects less arbitrary, and certainly far less vindictive, than the obscure criteria by which Christians managed for centuries to relegate those who disagreed with them to eternal torment. And if an eternity of unrelieved cultural refinement looks like a rather dreary prospect, it is probably less dreary than enjoying an eternal sabbath or singing endless hosannas.

Although the values of *paideia* were for the most part thought to be developed by literary and rhetorical training, the philosophical kind of training continued to exist throughout antiquity and remained a rival tradition of education until Justinian closed the philosophical schools. The modern student is likely to have far more sympathy with the philosophical curriculum of antiquity than the rhetorical one, and there are a number of reasons for this. The rhetorical conventions of antiquity grew more and more rigid and there is no doubt that some of the productions of this tradition led to a sterile, verbal virtuosity with elaborate ways of saying little. On the other hand, we moderns are hopelessly unsympathetic to the formalities of rhetorical tradition. It somehow seems to us to stifle "sincerity" (whatever we may mean by this apparently simple word). At its best, however, the traditions of rhetoric served as a set of indispensable conventions which serve to order and clarify thought and expression. The elaborate rules of the classical fugue in music may have seemed confining or artificial to a composer of the romantic period but Bach clearly found them "liberating," capable of guiding and shaping the fullness of his expression. In the hands of a master, rhetoric gave to prose the same sort of discipline and artistic order that verse forms give to poetry.

Classical art—and the same is true of the classical revival of Renaissance humanists and artists—is essentially conventional. Originality, except within the framework of clearly defined artistic convention, is not desirable, and such art is proudly imitative. The individual artist, to be sure, leaves the traces of his own personal diffraction of convention on his work, but he does so by subtle modulations of convention within a narrow spectrum of possibilities. The classical artist or thinker wants to be understood, above all, and "self-expression" has no place in the economy of his psyche. He writes, in a very specific way, for a public, and his adherence to the structures of convention, to familiar stories, techniques, allusions, and motifs, serves as the bridge between himself and his audience. Convention allows the artist to be intelligible to his own time and provides the vehicle on which his original note can quickly reach the apprehension of his audience. No classical artist of whatever time or place would have dreamed of himself, like Stendhal, writing for an audience which would come into existence one hundred years later. The ancient rhetorical training was thus the repository of convention in this broad sense, as that system of traditional meanings and allusions which makes experience intelligible and lightens the burden of communication.

Proponents of the rival training in philosophy had something of the distaste for rhetoric, in theory at least, which we moderns have, although in antiquity no educated Greek or Roman would have been nearly as unresponsive to formal rhetorical structures and values as most of our contemporaries. Indeed, in the course of time, the two rival curricula came to adopt much of each other's forms, methods, and goals.

Nevertheless, the two traditions remained distinct and their conflict, finally, was a reflection of the perennial conflict within the human soul itself. The ultimate goal of the philosophical curriculum was the making of the sage. Whether, as the Epicureans thought, the sage embodied *ataraxia,* inner tranquillity resulting from a measured indulgence in refined and civilized pleasures, or following the Stoics, he achieved *apathia,* controlled indifference to the perturbations of the soul, the ethical schools of antiquity agreed that the final product of the philosophical discipline would be the "wise man." On the other hand, the rhetorical tradition, which started in the attempt to mold skillful debaters and lawyers, came to have as its goal the making of the linguistic and, therefore, cultural virtuoso, the consummate artist in words capable of perceiving and expressing all the nuances of experience and of making discriminating responses to it.

Like many men of all times and places, the educated man in antiquity desired to be both a sage and an artist, and he sought this ideal union of apparent contraries more passionately, perhaps, than the men of any other time. Throughout the course of ancient education, this choice, once posed, became more difficult to avoid and more consequential after it was made. For the store of philosophical, historical, and scientific knowledge in antiquity continually increased—the Hellenistic era was a time of great scholarly and scientific achievement—and, as it did so, both of the rival curricula tended to become more crowded and encyclopedic. This was especially true of the philosophical curriculum; for ancient philosophy, by definition and tradition both, included all things knowable.

The classical educational conviction, universally shared, concerning the personal, gracious, and humane character of all learning whatsoever was thus threatened by the rapid growth of knowledge and the encyclopedic tendency to incorporate it into the curriculum almost as fast as it grew. The attempt to counter the danger of "professional deformation," which the weight of sheer erudition could bring, led to a corrective countermovement of fostering the amateur spirit in matters intellectual. This amateurism was no new tendency in classical thought, and from the beginning Greek moralists and thinkers had been very concerned with the effects of profession upon character.[20] Their horror of infinity, of the unlimited, was matched by their horror of the lop-sided and the deformed. The amateur spirit was their answer to the dangers of intellectual disproportion.

If the philosophical schools were sometimes carried away by the encyclopedic tendency, or the manufacture of sages, and produced those bizarre eccentrics that Lucian satirized so brilliantly, the rhetorical schools, in spite of their defects, remained in many respects closer to the spirit of Hellenism in the emphasis on form, proportion, and style. When the latter failed, they produced windbags and stuffed shirts, no doubt, but their alumni were at least social beings. No man could be as uncouth or boorish as a zealous Cynic. Even in decay, what remained of the ideal of high amateurism, of knowledge and skill informed by proportion and grace, was the possession of the rhetorical training and when, at the end of antiquity, these ideals were lost, they remained lost until the Renaissance. Castiglione's *Courtier* is the first work of modern times in which we discover them again as the goal of education.

The rhetorical training became the central educational tradition of imperial antiquity because ancient civilization, at that point, had less need of moral exemplars, heroes of virtue and wisdom, than of cultivated, resourceful men of the world. After all, if the professional and governing classes of society were to be educated to take their places in the world, the quasi-ascetic disciplines common in the philosophical schools were scarcely suitable for this purpose. The conviction was generally current that neither mathematics nor the more recondite branches of philosophy could do what rhetorical and literary study could to develop and refine moral sensitivity, express the particularities and complexities of human experience, or convey a discriminating sense of what human existence is like both in its possibilities and in its limitations. It would, in short, serve to keep intellectual and moral culture within the measure of the human.

Yet the embodiments of these ideals, although admired and emulated, came to have less and less of a functional role in the society of empire as it began to confront the economic and social problems which signaled the beginnings of its decline. The public intentions of the literary and rhetorical curriculum gradually became less and less realizable until solitary self-cultivation and overripe "connoisseurship" became its true ends. *Humanitas* had become a kind of *individualitas.*

The ancient education declined but the term *humanitas* persisted throughout the Middle Ages, even though Cicero would never have been able to recognize it with its new meaning. In classical antiquity, as we have seen, the term derived from *paideia* and referred to a cluster of ideas and ideals describing that kind of moral and intellectual culture which distinguishes the truly human man, *homo humanus,* not only from the animals but also from the barbarians and the unlettered masses. Only such a man has *arete* or *virtus,* the truly human kind of excellence. An educated Roman, for example, would have that particular kind of reverence and respect for moral obligations and intellectual culture which was called *pietas* and would manifest a sober and grand decorum in his bearing called *gravitas.* These were among the most important components of his *virtus* as a citizen and they were conferred by his participation in *humanitas.* Even his bravery in war, his military *virtus,* was distinguished from the kind of courage displayed by barbarians. The latter only had *furor,* as Livy tells us so often and so subtly. Even

Hannibal, who, the Romans had to agree, was as great a soldier as any in antiquity, fell outside the charmed circle of those possessing *virtus* simply because he was a Carthaginian.

All this was lost in the Middle Ages in spite of the fact that Virgil and Livy, the two master propagandists of the Roman ethos, were read all during the era by men who could read Latin at all. The content of *humanitas* became unintelligible, but the word survived to distinguish man and his lot from God. As classical forms in art were used in the medieval period to portray biblical figures, so the classical word was emptied of its classical content and used to describe the condition of mankind in the Christian scheme of things. It came to be used with adjectives like *fragilis,* "weak," or *caduca,* "fallen." [21] The word which in antiquity had trailed clouds of earthly glory came to connote the vanity of all things in this world.

In the Renaissance, the classical meaning comes to be reintegrated with the classical word without, however, losing all the connotations it had acquired during the Middle Ages. The secularization of culture, the rise of a middle class, the growth of cities as centers of political and cultural influence, created a kind of society for which the urbane ideals of classical education made a good deal more sense than the disciplines offered by the medieval church and court. Yet this society was still Christian at the same time that it was secularizing itself, and the effect of two diverse interpretations of *humanitas* can be felt in the "anthropology" of Renaissance thinkers. Thus Pico's definition of man as an epitome of the universe containing within himself all the orders of being is, in some respects, quite traditional, but he drew consequences from it which were, as we have seen, different from medieval and ancient views of man as a microcosm or epitome.

For Pico, man's dignity lies in his freedom to dwell on different levels of being, all of which not only make up the external world but are epitomized within him. Thus he can freely choose to live on the angelic level or descend to the grosser levels of existence, and his dignity lies precisely in his freedom to ascend the hierarchy of being, not in his possession of an immortal soul and his patrimony of eternal life, although Pico does not minimize this particular human prerogative. Moreover, Pico's conception of man is also a limit, ordering man in relation to the pure spirits above him as well as in respect to the lower orders of nature. The traditional medieval hierarchy of being and of psychic and organic functions with its elaborate conceptions of limiting order is the traditional frame in which Pico expresses a fresh conception of man's freedom and rationality. Man's glorious freedom is also finite, and the radical liberty he possesses to exalt or debase himself to various levels of being defines him, to be sure, as of the highest worth, but also as fallible and prone to error.

Neither Pico's humanism nor that of any other Renaissance thinker should be confused with the beliefs which prompted the French revolutionaries to enthrone the goddess of reason and to divinize humanity. Traditional Christian ideas still were important and they served a function very close to that of ancient religion in specifying the divine as the upper limit of the order of values and possibilities, as that in contrast to which man must define his own condition and his own possibilities. The revival of antique ideals led, with optimists like Pico, to a more buoyant view of those possibilities than any serious thinker of the Middle Ages would have been able to imagine. Nevertheless, Renaissance thought created its own variation in the immemorial paradoxical view of man as *ni ange ni brute,* a mode of looking at man which was both exalting and humbling, which simultaneously grasped that if man was well above the other animals and only a little lower than the angels, he was nevertheless a very long way from God. At its best, in Erasmus for example, the synthesis of ancient and medieval ideals of *humanitas* was conducive to a tolerant view of mankind faithful to all the contradictory aspects of the "glory, jest and riddle of the world."

The revival of ancient ideals rested on a wider knowledge of ancient civilization and on the existence of a society for which those ideals might have some immediate relevance. It is most important for us to remember that all the texts which the Renaissance humanists were searching for and on which they labored so assiduously had been preserved in at least one copy during the Middle Ages. Obviously there was sufficient interest in them for someone to make a copy for posterity. Indeed, it has been conjectured that more classical authors were lost in the second century with the transfer of authors from perishable papyrus scrolls to the more durable vellum codex than were lost during the Middle Ages. If someone failed to copy an author on parchment in time, he was likely to perish. In view of this fact, Renaissance humanism cannot be viewed as the result of a simple act of erudition, of a revival of learning. It is also a prodigious act of the historical imagination. The humanists, indeed, knew more about the classical past than their medieval predecessors, although the latter were not as benighted as they were once thought to be. What is more important than their greater erudition is that they brought to their study an utterly new sense of history and an utterly different approach to the uses of classical learning. The medieval scholar did not interpret the classics as works written at another time and place, for other people whose ideals had to be understood as temporally conditioned and which, if attractive, had to be deliberately restored. On the contrary, for the medieval scholar, the works of the past lived in an eternal present and, whenever a text seemed remote, the solution to difficulties of interpretation did not lie in historical or philological data but in an act of allegorical exegesis.

We might illustrate this difference in outlook by comparing the manner in which St. Thomas Aquinas read Aristotle's *Politics* and the way in which he was read by the scholars of the Renaissance. For St. Thomas, the *Politics* is really a collection of arguments, propositions which the reader attempts to understand and which he then elaborates upon and develops. Aristotle was read in much the same way as one might read Euclid, as a statement of essentially timeless propositions. The scholar of the Renaissance at work on the same text would bring to it a consciousness that a particular civilization and a particular kind of political experience lay behind the text. He brought to it an awareness of its historical context and the realization that classical antiquity was a discrete civilization. However valuable its thought and culture, however useful the models it presented, the ancient world was not a continuum extending into the present, as it was for the great medieval thinkers.

This kind of historical consciousness means that the humanists of the Renaissance saw themselves as detached from their immediate past in the Middle Ages and spiritually at home in a remote past more to their taste. It also means that they are aware of living in a new time. Historical categories like "Middle Ages" or "Renaissance" are, of course, inventions, and with all such categories there will be endless debates concerning just what they should or should not comprehend. With all the arguments over just when the Renaissance began and precisely what we mean by the term, there still remains the fact that in the fourteenth century in Italy we find the most thoughtful and articulate people defining themselves and their own times in terms of a restoration of classical ideas and values. The Renaissance was a revolution of consciousness which first took place in the minds of the cultural leaders of Europe before it transformed their institutions and culture.

The very word *antiquitas* came to be charged with a new meaning and the humanists used it in much the way we might use a phrase like "the classical world." Indeed, the classical ages even became the true *sacrosancta antiquitas* for them, and the first changes inspired by the new reverence for a pagan sacred past were, as we might have expected, in educational ideals, for the restoration of antiquity had to begin with the restoration of the educational system which molded classical men. As we have seen, the medieval curriculum, especially after the impact of the recovery and dissemination of the major works of Aristotle, was essentially a professional or preprofessional one. It emphasized logical training and the careful study of a small selection of classical texts and textbooks. By the thirteenth century, the major centers of higher learning were largely professional schools training men for the church, medicine, or the law. Preparatory education for the higher studies was centered about the famous *trivium* and *quadrivium,* the medieval scheme of the liberal arts, quite different in theory and practice from the *studia humanitatis* of Cicero. The medieval version of liberal education comprehended both humanistic and "scientific" subjects, rhetoric as well as logic, mathematics, and astronomy. There was, however, little room for poetry and virtually none for history. When the young bachelor of arts proceeded to higher studies, to philosophy, for example, he was largely concerned with metaphysics and cosmology, not with moral philosophy as enshrined in the essays, letters, and memorials of antiquity.

The humanistic curriculum included some of the old subjects such as grammar and rhetoric, but it emphasized literature, history, and moral philosophy instead of mathematics and the more technical and scientific branches of philosophy. The Renaissance humanist, in fact, was the first to voice in modern times the concept of a humanistic training as something distinct from and almost antithetical to a scientific or a professional one. This distinction, however well intentioned, proved to be a mixed blessing, at least to the extent that it fostered the notion that humane studies are somehow "useless" or that scientific and professional subjects are necessarily illiberal.

While the humanists were recovering the curriculum and thereby the cultural legacy of antiquity, that other group of "founders" of the Renaissance, creative artists and poets, were initiating that "rebirth" of the arts from which Renaissance historians dated the new era and which they pointed to as evidence for their new historiography. Indeed, this conviction of rebirth begins in the artists before we can find evidence of it among the historians. Dante himself, in spite of his loyalty to the institutions and modes of the medieval world, had much of this consciousness of bringing poetry again to a level it had not reached since antiquity. Petrarch is a more complete example of this new attitude in his rejection of scholasticism in the realm of the intellect, of the ideals of universal empire in the realm of history and politics, and in his choice of Latin as the vehicle for what he believed to be his major works. Moreover, with Petrarch, in spite of his religious interests and conflicts, we can see a major beginning in that process of the secularization of knowledge which is the most outstanding characteristic of Renaissance culture.

Humanism and the new movements in art and literature soon

changed the entire picture of the past and the historians' way of writing about it. The Renaissance historians of Italy scrapped the ideology of empire in all its forms and, by the time of Leonardo Bruni, had fully evolved a new scheme of periodization. For Bruni, both the creation of the empire and the barbarian invasions were, strikingly enough, events of the same general significance. They both mark the loss of liberty, in the first instance to an autocrat and, in the second, to uncivilized nations. His story is the story of the loss and gain of liberty, and the true political and historical unit is the city-state, in his case Florence. He divides history into five periods: first, the Roman republic in which a state of the right size enjoyed true political liberty; second, the empire which signaled the loss of liberty; third, the barbarian invasions; fourth, a Carolingian restoration of the empire; and fifth, the period of the rise of factions in the Italian cities, the beginning of the only period of Italian liberty after the Roman republic.[22]

Indeed, Bruni maintained that the collapse of the empire served to free many subordinated states from oppression and that, far from being a disaster, it was certainly an inevitability, and even a desirable event. The empire, whatever some medieval historians may have thought, was not a divinely ordained institution and, like all things in the order of nature, it had to die when its term of life was over to give way to the new and creative forms of political order emerging in history. Bruni brings to its culmination a long line of reflection on the history of Italy, and its relation to its classical past, which began in the generation of Petrarch; and his statement in its general outlines is typical of the views of leading Italian humanistic historians of the *quattrocento* like Machiavelli and Guicciardini.

It is clear that if the humanists venerated the ancient world, it was not a blind admiration of all of the historical experience of the classical past. There were many unsurpassable exemplars in the history of Greece and Rome, but very many warnings as well. The humanists' admiration of Rome, unlike that of their medieval predecessors, was not of a perennial state, a state which Christ himself had recognized and which had not only lasted into the present but would last until the end of the world. On the contrary, Rome had ceased to be, great as it was. Its history was that of a great human achievement, and like all such, it was uneven. Historians like Bruni were acutely aware of the differences between the ancient and the medieval empires, and valued the history of the republic well above that of the empire even at its most powerful. In short, history for the new historians, whatever their pieties or lack of them, was not the inexorable unfolding of a divine plan. Its pattern of change, when they offered to discern one, was cyclical. Such a vision of events as succeeding each other in a continual rise and fall did not arise from or induce in them a pessimistic view of the human condition. The cyclical theory was not for them what it was to be for Spengler in our own time, an intellectual instrument for diagnosing the imminent death of a civilization. On the contrary, the humanist historians generally felt themselves to be on the upswing of a new cycle and destined to witness great events. If the down-turn would inevitably come, that was the worry of more or less remote future generations.

The cyclical theory served to interpret the pattern of development in various spheres of human activity, cultural as well as political. When Vasari came to review the great achievements of the artists of every kind from Giotto to his own time, he thought of their work as irrefutable witness to a renewal of the arts, as evidence that the cycle of great creativity in art had turned up again after having been down all during the medieval period. Machiavelli sought, with less success, for evidence of such an upturn in the political cycle of Italy. In both cases, cyclical theories were meant to free men from the pessimistic determinism of theories of providentially ordered decay and to encourage optimism concerning possibilities for creative action in art or politics. Vasari was more buoyant about the qualities of modern achievements simply because he had a good deal more evidence to give of great examples in the realm of art than Machiavelli could match for politics, Italian politics at any rate.

Not all of antiquity, then, was worthy of imitation, and some of the best of the humanists were aware of the dangers of imitating even the chosen models. Still others wondered whether they would ever be able truly to appropriate the ancient legacy and at least equal if not rival it. The most distinguished minds among them, a Poliziano or an Erasmus, preferred to emulate rather than to imitate the ancients. *Aemulatio* meant to make a free use of antique models, adapting them to new needs, while *imitatio* at its worst resulted in servile copies of ancient masterpieces void of life and relevance.[23]

This conflict over the uses of the ancient culture contained a more profound one over modern man's capacity to equal ancient achievements. Opinion ranged from the affirmation of Vasari that the greatest of modern artists, a Michelangelo, had gone beyond the Greeks, to the conviction of a long line of classicists that no modern could hope to equal the ancients. Between the boast of Vasari and the pessimism of a sizable number of educated men was a range of opinion like that of Machiavelli who expressed the guarded hope that some modern country, if not Italy, would produce leaders capable of reviving the political and military *virtù* of the Romans.

In the seventeenth century, the work of Galileo, Descartes, and Bacon sharpened this debate over the respective abilities of classical versus modern man by offering incontrovertible evidence of the greater modern knowledge of the workings of nature and by defining methods of inquiry which would increase that advantage. With these contributions the foundation was laid for the modern idea of progress, and if we can mark the end of the Renaissance by a cultural change as momentous as the ones introduced in that period, the development and diffusion of the idea of progress is the one we would have to choose.

Yet the new science arose from the great currents of Renaissance thought even as it helped to put an end to them. The process of the assimilation of ancient culture was also a process of creating rival achievements or wholly new ones, first in art and literature, then in social and political life, and finally in the sphere of knowledge itself. The great scientific achievements of the late Renaissance and seventeenth century can be viewed as the culmination of the most creative and original elements in humanism, as the fruit of the full assimilation of the intellectual legacy of Greece, however much a Galileo or a Bacon may have criticized that legacy. As the so-called "vernacular" humanists validated the resources of the modern languages and literatures, emulating the classical models in their own tongues and making a free and, above all, critical use of them, so the critical use of ancient science, the urge to test the ancient legacy of scientific knowledge, served to validate modern man's power to rival and even to surpass the ancients. The great new works in the vernacular literatures, the voyages of discovery which revealed a whole new geography, the artistic and architectural monuments which were transforming the face of Europe, and the new scientific achievements, finally weakened modern man's conviction of being in an eternal state of total pupilage to classical culture. Not until the nineteenth century was the debate over ancients and moderns, emulation or imitation, finally stilled, and the way opened for a historical relativism which would affirm the distinct and finite character of every great period of human civilization. The result was not to diminish the splendor of the classics and their inexhaustible power to educate us, even if a classical training is no longer the universal possession of educated men. Rather, the canon of classics was widened to include the great moderns, those works which by universal agreement were felt to possess a comparable imaginative and intellectual splendor.

Classicism of the traditional variety served both to free the mind of Western man from the medieval past and, at times, to burden it with a new and weightier traditional authority. But the best examples of ancient art, literature, and thought, precisely because they are the remarkable works they are, served finally to renew men's faith in themselves, even if many were too dazzled by their greatness for a time. Once men could view the classical world from the standpoint of a greater equality, realize their kinship with it and the common humanity which binds ancient and modern together, they gained the confidence to emulate the past even to the extent of shaking its authority.

The controversy over the uses of the classical past which dominated the intellectual life of the Renaissance took many forms, and it was a fundamental if not always an explicit part of the long and tedious Renaissance debate over the respective merits of the contemplative and active lives. The controversy was actually one over the uses of knowledge, however remote the terminology in which it was expressed. Is knowledge primarily for personal or for public uses? Is the aim of learning wisdom or power? Is the antique legacy of culture a spur to action or to contemplative self-cultivation? We can see in the abundant literature which turned on the *vita activa* controversy a modern version of the dilemma which confronted Hellenistic educators. Does education, as many of the upholders of the philosophical curriculum thought, produce the more or less solitary sage, or does it, as some of the proponents of the rhetorical training thought, make a public man who has mastered language, the medium of all public life?

A peculiar feature of the sizable literature devoted to such questions is that the alternatives of contemplation or action are regarded as mutually exclusive. One ideal is "higher" than the other, more distinctively "human," more worthy of a wholehearted dedication, and it is hard not to feel that much of this quarrel is little more than the traditional sort of artificial rhetorical debate which schoolmasters used to set up for their students to sharpen their wits. From antiquity to rather recent times, generations of schoolboys would debate whether roses were better than lilies, water better than wine, medicine more noble than law, and subjects of a similar nature. However useful they may have been as exercise, the debates of this nature had about as much point as the controversy over whether men are better than women.

However, we must understand that the major proponents of the active life were those humanists who were interested in the development of an educational curriculum which would prepare men for active citizenship in a polity which rested on the decisions of its citizens. All during the Middle Ages and beyond, the only sort of political education available had been in the courts, and this was dominated by the ideals and practices of chivalry. It was, indeed, largely a military training and its feudal ideology was hardly suitable for the new cities such as Florence, whose wealth was commercial and whose power rested on that wealth.

Wherever humanism was the work of clerics we find, on the other hand, an exaltation of contemplative ideas. An interesting example of this is furnished by the humanistically oriented educational reforms of the Brethren of the Common Life, the Netherlandic originators of the famous *devotio moderna*. They taught the ancient language and literatures, emphasized moral philosophy, and scrapped the logical and metaphysical apparatus of Scholastic philosophy and theology as religiously and morally irrelevant or even dangerous. Erasmus himself, the prince of the northern humanists, had been trained in this tradition, and like his teachers, he too was interested in a simplification of religious life, in the effort to bring religion back to Gospel simplicities and amalgamate it with humane culture. The result of educational reforms in this tradition was, frequently enough, to foster the rather introspective, solitary piety so typically and powerfully expressed in Thomas a Kempis' *Imitation of Christ*.

Some scholars have with justice pointed out that the first period of Italian humanism was apparently as deeply concerned with religious reform as northern humanism. They point to Petrarch's attack on Scholastic philosophy in the name of the Gospel, his advocacy of the study of literature and moral philosophy as more consonant with sound religious life than the disputatious learning of the medieval universities, his interest in the works of the church Fathers. Nevertheless, all this is only one aspect of Petrarch's activity and has little to do with his passionate classicism and his intense desire for a revival of ancient pagan glories. The influence of Petrarch and his successors served largely to secularize culture, and it is difficult to think of a distinguished Italian humanist as genuinely pious and as concerned, on the intellectual level, with religious questions as Erasmus. The reading of Latin and Greek literature and devotion to the presumed simplicities of the Gospel do not, in themselves, make a Renaissance. Reading the classics with one's Christian blinkers firmly on can easily eliminate their challenge. The Italian humanists made an essentially different use of their study of the classics, for they responded to them on classical terms, they sought to revive classical values and ideals. The crucial difference between the contemplative-religious humanism of the north and the humanism of the south lay in the more active and immediate use that the utterly different society of Italy wanted to make of the ancient legacy which had, in a special sense, been a continuous possession of theirs all during the Middle Ages. Italian humanism had a strongly social and political orientation, directly and indirectly, and this remained true even after political liberty was largely dead in Italy. If Bruni or Machiavelli wanted the new education to make active free citizens, Castiglione wanted to use the humanistic legacy to make gentlemen and courtiers, men whose chief task in life would be to advise the princely autocrats then ruling the Italian states.[24]

One result of the polemic waged by humanist proponents of the *vita activa* was the development of a new psychology which not only recognized the role of the passions, of ambition and desire, in the pursuit of military and political excellence, but generally validated the emotional side of human nature against the Christian-Stoic ideals of repression so pervasive among the religiously oriented humanists. In spite of his commitment at times to ascetic values, and his conflict, so revealingly expressed in the *Secretum,* between Christian renunciation and the lure of worldly fame and glory, Petrarch felt an enthusiasm for the literary and political heroes of antiquity and for the values and energies motivating them which quite overcame his occasional impulses toward "sanctity." If "two souls struggled" within his breast such is not the case with the leading thinkers in Italy by the end of the fifteenth century. The political and psychological realism of Machiavelli and Guicciardini, their imaginative use of classical history and culture as the most intelligible record of what men have actually experienced and of how and why they have triumphed or failed in their battle for order against chance or fate, their use of the humanistic legacy as a guide to action, completes a long process of development. They accept and use the ancient values such as "fame" or "glory" as easily and familiarly as the ancient authors themselves. They talk of "fortune" and "virtue," of chance and the human ability to deal with its blind workings, as if they lived in the same secular and pagan cosmos of Thucydides or Polybius, as indeed they did.

The religious elements in Italian humanism lived on in the thought of the Neoplatonists such as Ficino, and it is perhaps no accident that Neoplatonism, with its contemplative and mystical ideals, began to flourish mightily in a Florence that had lost its political liberties. Lorenzo de' Medici may well have felt that the rarefied aesthetic and religious atmosphere of Neoplatonism was a far more satisfactory one for political purposes than the turbulent climate the libertarian ideals of the old civic humanism would probably generate. The last thing he wanted was for the Florentine people, inspired by the ideals of civic glory, to raise the old revolutionary cry of *popolo e libertà*.

Even the Neoplatonists, however, were not entirely unaffected by the developments of a politically oriented secular humanism. Ficino, for example, regarded history as teaching a practical wisdom usable in political and civic life, as inculcating *prudentia,* not the contemplative wisdom, the *sapientia,* which medieval thinkers were inclined to identify as the "message" of historical knowledge.

The contrast between the so-called civic humanists and the Neoplatonizing humanists in Florentine culture remained a wide one in spite of mutual influence, and the differences between them were fundamental. Indeed, the two movements may be viewed as special versions of the more general opposition between proponents of the *vita activa* and proponents of the *vita contemplativa*. In the last analysis this opposition, on the intellectual level, was rooted in contrasting definitions of wisdom, in irreconcilable views concerning the uses of learning and the ultimate goal of the educational process. Each side claimed the possession of "wisdom" and, implicitly or explicitly, each side claimed to define it. Over and over again in the history of thought and culture, a prestigious word, such as "God" or "liberty," has been the rallying cry for opposing sides in some great controversy. In the controversy over the active and contemplative ideals of life and the uses of knowledge, it turned on the word *sapientia*.

Sapientia was certainly not the same as knowledge pure and simple, as *scientia*. It had to do with that which was somehow most worth knowing, with the most valuable truths as distinguished from facts, with the most important experiences as distinguished from what transpires every day. The transformations and interpretations of the term provide us with a fascinating example of just how the thinkers of the Renaissance dealt with the medieval legacy as well as with the classical one which was being recovered, for no word in the medieval vocabulary was better to conjure with than *sapientia*.[25]

In general, Christian ideals of ultimate wisdom, whether ancient or medieval, were otherworldly. Yet we should not assume that otherworldliness was a monopoly of the Christian tradition. In antiquity the Neoplatonists were the great teachers of the doctrine that ultimate wisdom was literally out of this world. They saw man as alienated from his true existence in the One and they taught a doctrine of aspiration whereby man, through a special training of his mind and his capacities for love, might return to his source. In other variations of this Platonic theme, men could, by transcending the sensory world, return in spirit to Plato's disembodied world of forms or to the heavenly bodies which were the first causes and the continuing governors of terrestrial phenomena. Christianity shared with Platonism this conception of man as alienated and aspiring, as lost and finding wisdom by transcending human and earthly things in meditating on Scripture or on the dogmas of revelation. Renaissance Christian mysticism and Renaissance Neoplatonism could both find ample precedents for their otherworldly ideas of wisdom.

The medieval Christian conception of wisdom gradually changed during the course of the Renaissance to mean something quite different from anything the Christian Fathers and doctors had ever meant by the term. The word *sapientia* gradually recovered something of its antique meaning in a fascinating process which again parallels the reintegration, in the arts, of classical themes with the classical forms in which these themes were originally symbolized. Obviously, like all of these instances of reintegration we have been considering, the recovery of antique meaning involves a profound change of historical consciousness, a lively sense that the motifs of ancient culture are truly *other,* not contemporary or timeless, and is part of that more general process by which men came to think of the immediate past as a "dark" age separating them from ancient light and glory. Paradoxically, classical culture found its revolutionary uses when it was finally recognized as remote, as a legacy having to be possessed by active effort, by acts of the historical imagination informed by the hope that what begins in the imagination may direct the energies of men to its re-creation in actuality.

Verbally, the medieval definition of wisdom was identical with that of Cicero, who attributes to the classic philosophers the definition that wisdom, *sapientia,* was no more than the knowledge of both divine and human realities and the causes which govern them.[26] Christianity, however, distinguished sharply between divine and human wisdom, although some theologians were more extreme than others in separating them. For Tertullian the wisdom of philosophers was indeed foolishness, while for St. Thomas, it might serve as a stepping stone to faith. Nevertheless, true wisdom was furnished by revelation and the believer was wise beyond all the learning of the unilluminated thinker. Frequently in the history of thought one finds this interesting and creative process of pouring new wine into old bottles, however monitory a figure this may be in the moral sphere. Thus *arete,* the Greek conception of "excellence" or *virtus,* is for Homer the sort of ability possessed by an Achilles, for Plato it is that which Socrates defines, and by the time of Gregory of Nyssa, it has become the excellence of the true believer.[27]

The humanists begin the process of separating the idea of wisdom from the idea of divine revelation. Erasmus, although a sincere believer, identifies wisdom with ethical knowledge, and finds harmonies and identities between the ethical precepts of the New Testament and the teachings of Cicero and Seneca. In effect, he makes salvation hinge on the achievement of a limpid ethical purity and, although Erasmus would not have denied the necessity and value of revelation, he does not think of salvation as resting on the possession, through grace, of a firm faith in what is otherwise inapprehensible, on belief in a divine message which is a scandal and a stumbling block, if not utter foolishness, to reason. Although there was in Erasmus much of the Pauline type of the "Greek," of the seeker after wisdom to whom the Cross is a stumbling block, he was sensitive to the paradoxes of Christianity and gave them an interpretation consonant with his humanistic ideals. For him, there is indeed a wise folly which is specifically Christian, but it has little to do with theologically sophisticated attempts to explain the Incarnation or the Trinity. The folly of Christianity is not so much intellectual as moral, for the folly of Christianity lies in the heroic morality of its founder. Such conduct and such sacrifice will always appear as folly to selfish and evil men, just as it appeared such to the evil men of Athens when they encountered it in the person of Socrates. Indeed, Socrates is truly worthy of being called St. Socrates, in spite of his ignorance of Christianity, while the large majority of self-styled Christians are not worthy of the name.

In effect, Erasmus subsumes the Christian concept of wisdom into the concept of *humanitas,* for quiet charitableness and broad tolerance is the possession of truly rational men, men endowed with natural reason which is at the same time "right" reason, who have been ethically formed according to that "primary" wisdom or *prisca sapientia* which inheres in reason itself and which is perfected and strengthened through the complementary and compatible precepts of the Gospels.

During the course of the Renaissance, the idea of wisdom became secularized in various degrees and in various ways. As we have seen, Erasmus still thought of wisdom in religious terms, although he detached it from its traditional religious definition in terms of the data of revelation and precisely defined theories of grace. Rather, he attempted to redefine wisdom and make it the result of ethical insight and of a natural upright reason without entirely detaching it from its religious moorings. In so doing he conflated the best of ancient moral wisdom with what he took to be the essence of Christianity. The boldness of this move should not be underestimated, for the main tradition of Christian theology and philosophy during the Middle Ages was far more inclined to try to adapt classical metaphysics and science to the uses of Christianity than ancient morality. Even when Scholastics like St. Thomas read the *Nicomachean Ethics* with large approval, they sought rather to Christianize whatever Aristotelian concepts could be so treated than to conflate them with Christian teachings.

Erasmus' view is midway between orthodox Christian definitions of wisdom and a purely secular view of it which is typical of the thinking of the civic humanists and other proponents of the *vita activa* as early as Salutati and Bruni. They sought for that kind of knowledge and experience which develops wisdom concerning *res humanae,* "human realities," and in this quest the records of human experience as they are contained in the literary and historical writings of antiquity and in the reflections of the ancient moral philosophers on that experience were the guides.

The great debate over the active ideal of life in Italy, in the last analysis, marked the emergence of an ethic which expressed the aspirations of the new middle classes of the Italian city-states, especially of Florence, a code of values and conduct which was for them what chivalry was to the medieval society of the courts and castles. Courtly chivalry with its ideals of courtly love and military honor emerged with the growth of a cultured, secular society in a world in which the centers of learning and culture had been primarily monastic and ecclesiastical. As the ethic of chivalry meant that the quest for virtue or excellence was no longer the exclusive prerogative of a priestly class, nor exclusively definable in priestly terms, the secularization of the idea of wisdom in the Italian city-states gave to active men of the world a claim to the highest excellence of spirit which had successively been the claim of the pious churchman or the chivalric hero.

Other crucial ancient concepts besides *sapientia* came to be reintegrated with their classical meanings after having lost them during the Middle Ages, and one of the most interesting was the Roman term *virtus* which we have already encountered in connection with *humanitas*. *Virtus* is easier to describe than to define, and the reader who remembers Livy's stories of heroes like Cincinnatus who left his plow to govern Rome as dictator during a crisis and then modestly returned to his farm, or the tale of Mucius Scaevola thrusting his hand into a burning fire in defiance of the Carthaginians, will have an adequate idea of its connotation. It was less a concept than a symbol for a group of related ideals, that constellation of military and political abilities, executed with skill and courage, which was the possession of the great Roman civic and martial heroes.

The notion of *virtus,* originally a kind of "manliness," came finally to mean a supreme virtue which encompassed any lesser ones, the most perfect human achievement possible in this world. Indeed, Virtus became a Roman goddess of considerable importance in late antiquity, one whose prestige and authority were matched only by her companion Fortuna. St. Augustine rightly singled out these two divinities for the major part of his attack on pagan religion, Fortuna because chance denied God's beneficent government of the world, and Virtus because a supreme virtue could only be the gift of God. Men might try, indeed, to cultivate particular virtues of one kind or another, but supreme virtue was not a secular prize or a secular ideal; it was a supernatural gift.

Medieval thinkers, following the authority of St. Augustine, largely confined themselves to an analysis of virtues, *virtutes,* and left the singular *virtus* to the grace of God. A consequence of this is that medieval representations in art and literature of virtues and vices are always of a number of individual figures, while virtue and vice as singular, collective entities are never represented.

By the fifteenth century, however, the notion of supreme virtue referring to a secular state was again current. It had finally escaped the Augustinian veto and, like the idea of wisdom in the course of its secularization, found at times a semireligious justification. In the opinion of some, God himself had given men an innate capacity for this supreme virtue and the freedom to develop it. In a virtually Pelagian reversal of St. Augustine's position, man was re-endowed with freedom and given the goal of a supreme secular virtue for it. Supreme virtue was not only conceived in a secular way, in spite of its divine origin, but it was no longer, however conceived, a supernatural gift conferred on the chosen few but a universal gift of God to human nature.

Pico's oration is a high point in the process of rehabilitating the ancient ideal of virtue, particularly because he revived antique notions of human freedom without which the idea of *virtus* would make no sense whatever. He helped to complete, thereby, a process which was well under way in the time of Petrarch, who, for example, cited with enthusiasm a famous statement in Cicero's *Tusculan Disputations* (2, 18, 43) that *virtus* is the quality which makes a man into a human being in the most perfect degree. Although Petrarch was not sufficiently speculative to work out the implications of the idea and its intrinsic relation to particular ideas of freedom and human nature, he made the ancient concept of virtue his major category for the interpretation of history.

It is through *virtus* that men can overcome all obstacles, and the close of Petrarch's famous Canzone, *Italia,* which Machiavelli later cited in the final exhortation in *The Prince* to Italians to rise and throw out the barbarian invader, echoes the Livian contrast between Roman *virtus* and barbaric furor: "Virtue will take up arms against furor" and will conquer (*vertù contra furore prenderà l'arme* . . .).

We cannot underestimate the significance of the fact that Petrarch's major historical work, *De viris illustribus,* treats the military and political heroes of antiquity as incarnations of *virtus*. In a sharp break with the traditions of medieval historiography and biography, Dante's for example, the classic heroes are not conceived of as divine instruments, nor are they the passive tools of fortune. On the contrary, they possess *virtus,* their own ability, and are prompted by *gloria,* their driving desire for fame. While Petrarch does not expressly dismiss the possibility of a divine cause for the appearance of a Scipio on the stage of history, he scarcely calls divine agencies into play in his account of the past. "Glory" and "virtue" inspire each other and they are, for all practical purposes, the driving forces of historical change and achievement. We are not very far from Machiavelli in this belief, and all that was required to arrive at his view was a more thoroughgoing naturalistic framework for such ideas.

As we have seen, the reconstruction of the ancient idea of virtue is intrinsically related to the recovery of ancient conceptions of freedom. Since they were theologians, the medieval Scholastics discussed the idea of freedom largely in terms of its paradoxical relations to grace. Wherever else the analysis of freedom might begin, it had to end in the theological realm. However pessimistic the main line of orthodox thought on the question of man's freedom might be at times, it stayed clear of outright determinism. Man's ultimate freedom and his most crucial act of choice lay in the exercise of his ability freely to reject or accept God's freely given grace. His dignity lay less in the act of choice itself than in the fact that he was made in the image of God and stood in relation to God as a child does to his father. Pico, however religious his vocabulary from time to time, locates the dignity of man in man's radical freedom, in the very ability he has to choose between the variety of "drives" or desires generated at different levels of his being. The human situation as the drama of a choice had been expressed in the story of Adam with his loss of bliss through the erroneous exercise of freedom. With his fall, he lost a good deal of that freedom and much of the perfection of his true nature. The Fall was, in fact, the single greatest disaster which had befallen the human race and it all came about through mistaken choice. In the Renaissance, an analogous symbolic vision of the human situation in relation to freedom is expressed in terms of two great classic heroes, Prometheus the defiant rebel, the civilizer and fire-bringer, and Hercules, heroically poised at the crossroads of decision between pleasure and virtue.[28]

The choice of such figures shows that the re-creation of antique concepts of virtue and freedom carried with it a new and more heroic view of human nature and possibilities. And these heroic values were claimed not only by poets—and in this there was ancient precedent—but by artists who had not in antiquity ever been brought within the orbit of inspired, prophetic, and preternaturally wise beings. Dante revives for poets, and for the first time since antiquity, the notion of the poet as an inspired genius and teacher of mankind. At least he is the first convincing example of such a claim since the classical world. It is no accident that Dante when he meets Virgil finds his voice "hoarse with long silence." In the course of the Renaissance, Platonic and Neoplatonic theories of poetic inspiration as a kind of divine madness come to be extended to artists. They too claim a source for their creative powers from above, but even though supremely gifted, they nevertheless do not storm the heights of genius without paying a price. From the beginning of the sixteenth century the fully developed notion of inspiration and genius comes to be intertwined with the idea of melancholy, and the curious history of the interrelations between creative gifts, especially artistic ones, and mental and emotional instability begins.[29]

While many of the great changes which characterize the Renaissance went on quietly, quite unconsciously as it were, in the form I have described as pouring old wine into new bottles, others were quite conscious and deliberate. I have already referred to the explicit conviction of the humanists that they were living in a new age, and that they stood in a different relation to the immediate past of the Middle Ages and the remote past of the ancient world than the generations preceding them. This historical self-awareness was not simply a perception or a belief, but a conviction and a mission. The very term "dark ages," the rallying cry of the eighteenth-century apostles of enlightenment, came to birth with the humanists of the Italian Renaissance who used it in much the same derogatory way. Their sense of being apostles of enlightenment, of renewing the culture by fetching light from the classical past, led them to emphasize —indeed, overemphasize—the contrast between their generation and the preceding period which, in their view, lived in a virtually absolute ignorance of the meaning of classical culture. I have already indicated that the Middle Ages were not quite as ignorant of classical culture as the humanists thought, and that they approached what classics they possessed intelligently but with a completely different sense of the possible uses of classical culture. Nevertheless, the humanists made the distinction between themselves and their predecessors virtually absolute. They were renovators who were bringing old glories to a new birth. Moreover, they were—in another popular metaphor—rekindling the light of civilization after intervening ages of darkness.

This metaphor of light and darkness applied to history takes its origin in Christianity and the persistent scriptural symbolism, especially of the Gospel according to St. John, of the light of Christ and the darkness of the world. In his pious and "medieval" moments, Petrarch used the metaphor in quite this Christian way and, indeed, he mourned that Cicero died so short a time before the light of Christ entered the world. We might be forgiven for not being over-impressed by Petrarch's grief at Cicero's necessarily pagan death when we recall the widespread legend during the Middle Ages that St. Paul had mourned at Virgil's tomb for precisely the same reasons. Even as a Christian, Petrarch admired ancient precedents.[30]

Although Petrarch, as a Christian, held that the ancient pagan world was in general darkness, he nevertheless maintained that the eyes of his pagan heroes were keen and that their genius shone forth in the general gloom. He never actually used the term "dark ages" to apply to any period of history, but he appears to be among the very first men to shift the light-dark metaphor of historical periodization from a religious to a historico-cultural context. He was able to give to pagan antiquity, or at least to its great men, a kind of secular luminosity if not a religious one. In effect, the pagan world was "light" in respect to letters and politics although "dark" in respect to religion, while the intervening centuries after Christianity were bright with a divine light but became progressively gloomier in all those respects which interested a humanist.

This way of looking at the past was quickly adopted and developed by Petrarch's successors. Boccaccio, Villani, and Ghiberti, among many others, emphatically contrast the luminous rebirth of the various arts and branches of learning that occurred in the generation of Giotto and Dante with the cultural darkness that had preceded. Gradually, that same pagan antiquity which had been the "dark ages" of the church Fathers and doctors came to be, from the cultural point of view, the age of light for humanists. Not until the eighteenth century do historians explicitly refuse to exempt Christianity from the presumed general darkness of medieval culture. Indeed, with Gibbon, Christianity is itself the major cause of Roman decline. The historians of the Renaissance, even when they are skeptical about Christianity, like Machiavelli generally refrain from making a thoroughgoing contrast between ages of light and darkness, although that contrast, which began among artists and scholars, came to be the foundation of their own historiography.

Petrarch gradually came to possess an overwhelming conviction concerning the crucial and absolute character of Rome in the scheme of things. It became for him truly the city of light, and his love of Rome was as passionate and, in its own way, as mystical as Dante's. Yet there are profound differences in their respective views which mark the difference, not between a generation, but between the Middle Ages and the Renaissance. Dante, like his contemporaries, believed that Rome was continuous, that the empire still existed. There had been, with Charlemagne, a *translatio imperii,* a transfer of authority from the Greeks, that is, the Byzantines, to the Germans, and the long line of Roman princes stretched from antiquity to his own time. A Charlemagne or an Otto was as much Caesar as Augustus.

For Petrarch, on the other hand, the constructive and glorious part of Roman history was largely confined to the republic and extended no further than the early empire. He actually speaks with contempt of those emperors who were ethnically of non-Roman origin, and while he does not attack the concept of continuity in theoretical or legal terms, he scorns the ability of all the Roman rulers after Titus and thinks of them as barbarians. So narrowly did Petrarch come to view the era of Roman greatness that he changed the original plan of *De viris illustribus* from a study of all the greatest men of all times and places, to a study of all the great men of Rome from Romulus to Titus, the last "Italian" emperor.

By the time Petrarch was crowned with the poet's laurel in Rome on April 8, 1341, the splendid ruins of the ancient city had completed the work begun in Petrarch's imagination by his study of the Latin authors: he came to feel that the ancient glory was not

really dead but dormant, ready to rise again, and that the very cor-
onation of a poet in the eternal city was perhaps a sign of the coming resurrection. He may well have fancied himself another, but
Roman, Amphion whose lyrical skill might bring the very stones
together and rebuild the city. History, he tells us late in his life, is
nothing else than the praise of Rome and there is no doubt that
Petrarch saw his poetic powers, the powers to praise the deeds of
famous men, as his major instrument for reviving something of the
ancient glory.

In a more theoretical mood, Petrarch divided the course of history into two utterly distinct eras, antiquity and his own time. A
possible or even probable third era of rebirth lay in the future and
thus did not form part of history. Petrarch, most of the time at any
rate, felt himself to be living in what we would think of as a "middle ages," albeit at the end of it. His uncertainty about the definition of his own time contrasts with a lesser uncertainty concerning
when antiquity ended. His most elaborate theory, as we have seen,
dated the end with the last "Italian" emperor. At other times he
thought that a preferable date would be the adoption of Christianity as the official religion of the empire.

However his historiographical ideas may have varied, there is
implicit in Petrarch's view not only the utter rejection of medieval
theories of providentially ordered history, but the whole ecumeni-
cal and cosmopolitan structure which Roman lawyers and Stoic
philosophers worked out as the ideological basis of the empire.
There is, in fact, a germ of Italian nationalism in Petrarch's
thought, and an early stage of that peculiar conflation of Roman
and Italian nationalism which has been such a baleful influence on
the course of Italian political history until our own time. Petrarch's
nationalism is not to be confounded with Dante's Italianism. The
latter remains truly within the medieval scheme of things. Italy was
to be the garden of the empire, the queen of provinces, to be sure,
but only part of that divinely ordained universal political order
which would comprehend all of mankind. Within the medieval
scheme there was no room for nationalism of the sort we begin to
detect in Petrarch. The medieval historian wrote universal history,

so much so that even a local chronicle would customarily begin with an account of the creation. Their principles of periodization were twofold, one the scheme of six world-ages which was the legacy of St. Augustine, the other the scheme of four world-empires which came from St. Jerome. Both schemes were biblical, both treated mankind as a unity, and both placed mankind in an end-time. Jerome had maintained that Rome was the last of the world-empires, the other three, Babylon, Persia, and Greece having had their day, while St. Augustine maintained that we were now living in the sixth and final era, although he would not predict how long it would last.[31]

In both schemes the Incarnation was the central point of history, the great demarcation point in the history of the human race. Petrarch, without abandoning his Christian convictions, adopts a strictly secular viewpoint and makes the decline of Rome (whether early with the first foreign emperors or later with Constantine) the pivotal point of history. His thought contains the essential outline of the new humanist historiography which was fully developed by the middle of the next century when it clearly took the familiar modern pattern of ancient, medieval, and modern.

We can now return to our opening attempt to "define" the Renaissance and amplify some of our introductory remarks.

Perhaps the greatest single achievement of nineteenth-century historical scholarship was the reconstruction of the Middle Ages. Romanticism had generated a revival of interest in that period and helped to harness the energies of some of the best minds of Europe and America to the task of understanding medieval culture. One result of the great work was that the medievalists of the early twentieth century became the most acute critics of the concept of the Renaissance. New knowledge had revealed all kinds of great continuities between the Middle Ages and the Renaissance. Michelet's thesis that the culture of the earlier period forbade scientific inquiry and was dominated by a contempt for nature was revealed as too simplistic and tendentious. The thesis that medieval scholars and thinkers were well-nigh utterly ignorant of classical letters and culture was also shown to be much too inaccurate. Nor could the greater knowledge of the complexities and contrasts of Renaissance culture permit scholars to use the Renaissance as a club with which, following Symonds, they might belabor prudish Victorians or, following Nietzsche, attack Christians and the *bourgeoisie*. In its own way, the Renaissance was as creative in religion as the Middle Ages, and the earlier period produced its share of spectacular personalities, men and women like Eleanor of Aquitaine and Frederick of Sicily who were not supposed to be visible on the stage of history until a later act.

We can thus detect in Petrarch and his humanist successors the trait which distinguishes them from all kinds of medieval classicists and the standard-bearers of all earlier "Renaissances": the consciousness of living in a new time and a profound desire to break with the immediate past. They were, in fact, able to view the classical past in a historical perspective, as something distant, yet accessible, different, yet intelligible and eminently usable. As the natural landscape that the Renaissance artist painted existed in a mathematically intelligible space, so the ancient world existed for the humanists in a well-defined and structured historical space.[32]

New and more precise historical knowledge was, unfortunately, not the only factor influencing our interpretation of the Renaissance. Medieval and Renaissance scholarship in the last two generations has also been marked, frequently enough, by a covert political or religious apologetic in which "medieval" or "Renaissance" were rallying cries as often as they were historical categories.[33] Indeed, some of the sharpest criticisms of Burckhardt's book were motivated by such criteria, in spite of the fact that the progress of scholarship in the last two generations has led to a general confirmation of the main outlines of the thesis Burckhardt presented to the world in his classic study of the Renaissance in Italy. He was accused, with little justice, of being simplistic in his historiographical thought, of derogating the Middle Ages and, like Symonds, of harboring a semicovert admiration for some of the more unscrupulous and flamboyant figures of Renaissance history. Presumably, Burckhardt ignored a good deal of evidence and gave us an Italian Renaissance populated with vital but lecherous, brilliant but knavish heroes. In short, he is supposed to have invented a pagan Renaissance.

Such views are based on a peculiarly lopsided reading of Burckhardt's work and an equally peculiar ignorance of the context of his book and its avowed intention. His central thesis about the Italian Renaissance—and this now seems incontestable—was that the breakdown of the feudal hierarchical order and the growth of the city-states, gave rise to a new type of society which possessed those traits we can immediately recognize as modern. With this great social change, there was a corresponding change in the whole mode of operation of the individual, in his aspirations and ideals, in his way of experiencing himself and the world and, indeed, in the qualities and powers of his very organs of perception.[34]

Burckhardt was looking for the emergence in Western civilization of the first signs of the secular state, of secular society, secular culture, and even secular "psyches." It is no accident that one of his most important studies was on Constantine and the conversion of the empire, the final step in the theocratizing of Europe which marked, as much as any single date can mark, the beginning of the Middle Ages. On the other hand, his study of the Renaissance in Italy was not intended to be an exhaustive account of everything that was going on in Italy at that time, although a careful reading of his work will show that he gave attention to such medieval "antecedents" of Renaissance culture as the Franciscan revaluation of nature. He did not do more with "forerunners" because he selected his material to illustrate his thesis.

He rightly rejected, as a determinative causative influence in generating the Renaissance, renascent classicism and classical scholarship, simply because he was well informed about the classical elements in medieval culture. There were, as he well knew, important classical revivals at intervals during the Middle Ages, but he could not interpret the cultural history of Europe as a set of movements to and from classical revivals because he also knew that the city-states and princely courts of Renaissance Italy constituted new societies, societies which were making an utterly different use of classical exemplars than the classicists around Charlemagne in the ninth century, or Otto in the eleventh, or the humanists of Chartres and Orléans in the twelfth.

For the same reason—the awareness of a new society making a distinctively different and secular use of classical learning and classical precedent—he rejected the conflation of the cultural movements of the Italian Renaissance with apparently similar tendencies in the Middle Ages. The conflict between empire and Papacy, for example, had given rise on the imperial side to naturalistic political theories, of which the best known is perhaps that of Marsilius of Padua in the fourteenth century. But Burckhardt realized that whatever similarities there may have been between the thought of Marsilius and that of Machiavelli, the latter lived in a society which was *toto genere* different. So too with other movements put forward by medievalizers of the Renaissance—heterodox mysticism of the late Middle Ages, nominalism in philosophy, or Occamistic science. Burckhardt did not confuse resemblances with identities or possible antecedents with actual consequences.

He did not emphasize as much as modern scholars have, the important theory advanced by Adam Ferguson and Sismondi in the nineteenth century that the social basis of the Italian Renaissance lay in the revival in Europe of the forms of ancient *polis* life with its competitive ideals and its democratic institutions. In fact, Burckhardt found the most highly developed and typical specimens of Renaissance man in the cultivated courtiers who surrounded the tyrant princes of the Renaissance courts after free political institutions had decayed or been extirpated. Some have claimed that Burckhardt was influenced in this judgment by his distrust of the growing mass movements of his own time and the increasing frequency of mob political action. I think however that he had better reasons for his judgment than this.

I grant that it is tempting to agree with Sismondi and his modern followers that what has come to be called "civic humanism" marked the truly creative and original phase of humanistic activity, a fresh realization of the political and social values of the greatest of ancient classics and the attempt to implement them in contemporary life. There is doubtless a good deal of truth in this view. Yet it is difficult to see how the humanistic movement could have progressed without the princely forms of patronage which were essential to its development after the fifteenth century. It is equally difficult to envisage the history of Italian art and architecture in the Renaissance without the Medici, the Este, the Sforza, and other "tyrants" who commissioned great works, collected the great libraries, and housed the visible remains of antiquity. Above all, it is impossible to conceive of the Renaissance as somehow over by the beginning of the sixteenth century unless one adopts a more or less exclusively political criterion and measures the civilization of the Renaissance the way Bruni measured history, as the gain and loss of political liberty. So in this, as in many other respects, we have come full circle in our appraisal of Burckhardt, after having, to be sure, qualified some of the more encompassing generalizations. The category of the Renaissance seems to be quite valid. At least, it is indispensable, and Burckhardt's short work, which he thought of as an essay, remains the best single introduction to it.

Notes
*

1 See Tinsley Helton (ed.), *The Renaissance: A Reconsideration of the Theories and Interpretations of the Age* (Madison, Wis., 1964), Introduction.
2 See Wallace K. Ferguson, *The Renaissance* (New York, 1940) and the same author's *The Renaissance in Historical Thought* (Boston, 1948) for excellent accounts of the problems of Renaissance historiography.
3 Garrett Mattingly, "Some Revisions of the Political History of the Renaissance," in Helton (ed.), *The Renaissance,* pp. 3-25.
4 For a luminous example of the achievements of art historians in interpreting the Renaissance with excellent examples of their leading criteria see Erwin Panofsky, *Renaissance and Renascences in Western Art* (Stockholm, 1960). For a briefer treatment of some of the highlights of this work see the author's "Artist, Scientist, Genius: Notes on the 'Renaissance-Dämmerung'" *The Renaissance, Six Essays* (New York, 1962), pp. 121-182. This essay was originally published in *The Renaissance: A Symposium* (New York, 1953). My own brief comments on Renaissance Italian art owe a great deal to the work of Panofsky. For a

remarkable study of the evolution of the methods of representing reality see the work of E. H. Gombrich, *Art and Illusion: A Study in the Psychology of Pictorial Representation* (New York, 1961).

5 See Panofsky, *Renaissance and Renascences,* pp. 84-113, for a full treatment of this phenomenon, which he calls the "law of disjunction." The disjunction of classical form from classical motif did not effectively take place until about the twelfth century. Until that time both the visual and literary representations of ancient art and myth remained, however degenerate, recognizably "integrated." After that ancient motifs and techniques were used for Christian figures while ancient figures took on the contemporary medieval dress and outlook.

6 See the remarks and references in Earl Rosenthal, "Changing Interpretations of the Renaissance in the History of Art," in Helton (ed.), *The Renaissance,* p. 56.

7 See Edgar Wind, *Pagan Mysteries of the Renaissance* (New Haven, 1958) for an illuminating account of the allegorical significance of the Renaissance.

8 For a recent study of magic in the Renaissance see Frances A. Yates, *Giordano Bruno and the Hermetic Tradition* (Chicago, 1964).

9 For an excellent brief survey of the intellectual history of the Renaissance with ample suggestions for further reading see P. O. Kristeller, "Changing Views of the Intellectual History of the Renaissance since Jacob Burckhardt," in Helton (ed.), *The Renaissance,* pp. 27-52. See also Kristeller, *The Classics and Renaissance Thought* (Cambridge, Mass., 1955). An excellent anthology of philosophical writing of the major thinkers of the early Italian Renaissance is Ernst Cassirer, *et al., The Renaissance Philosophy of Man* (Chicago, 1948).

10 See the selections from Petrarch and the critical introductions in Cassirer, *et al., The Renaissance Philosophy of Man,* and also J. H. Randall, Jr., *The School of Padua and the Emergence of Modern Science* (Padua, 1961) and the opening chapters of Randall's *The Career of Philosophy* (New York, 1962), Vol. I.

11 On the origins of Italian humanism see Roberto Weiss, *The Dawn of Humanism in Italy* (London, 1947) and his *The Spread of Humanism* (London, 1964).

12 For a comprehensive survey of the history of the transmission of classical learning and culture see R. R. Bolgar, *The Classical Heritage and Its Beneficiaries* (Cambridge, Eng., 1954); also available as a Harper Torchbook.

13 Biondo seems to have been the first to refer to a "middle ages," a *media aetas* or *media antiquitas,* which he sees as beginning with Constantine's division of the empire.

14 Trans. by George Lamb (New York, 1956). My treatment of ancient education leans heavily on this classic study.

15 See Werner Jaeger, *Paideia: The Ideals of Greek Culture,* trans. Gilbert Highet (3 vols., New York, 1936), esp. the preface and the opening chapters.

16 Of course the Plato who wrote the *Symposium* and the *Phaedrus* furnished the traditional rationale for the view that the true poet was an inspired seer, possessed of a more than natural wisdom of ultimate reality. In the history of thought, Plato has had the great merit of furnishing the upholders of both sides of a question with their arguments.

17 See Alfred Zimmern, *The Greek Commonwealth* (5th ed., New York, 1956).

18 H.-I. Marrou, *History of Education in Antiquity* (New York, 1956), p. 161.

19 Marrou, pp. 98-99.

20 Zimmern, pp. 224-225.

21 Cf. Erwin Panofsky, "The History of Art as a Humanistic Discipline," in *Meaning in the Visual Arts* (New York, 1955), pp. 1-25, esp. pp. 1-5. This essay is also available in the author's *Studies in Iconology* (New York, 1929).

22 On the "revival" in literature see Roberto Weiss, *The Spread of Italian Humanism* (London, 1964), and on Bruni and humanistic historiography see "Leonardo Bruni and Humanist Historiography," in B. L. Ullmann, *Studies in the Italian Renaissance* (Rome, 1955). See also H. Weisinger, "Ideas of History during the Renaissance," *Journal of the History of Ideas,* VI (1945), 415-435.

23 The term "imitation" took on various meanings and in some of its uses it means the same thing as *aemulatio*. Obviously, the concept of imitation, however interpreted, was a vital one for those interested in the renewal of ancient civilization and the problem of appropriating it in an active way.

24 Hans Baron's important studies have stressed the crucial importance of Italian civic humanism for our understanding of the Renaissance and his analysis is centered on figures like Leonardo Bruni. Civic humanism, however, cannot be thought of as a comprehensive definition of humanism even though it points to what I think is the most distinctive and original aspect of the movement. The civic humanists were typically, although not without exception, upholders of the active life against the contemplative, and of free republican government against monarchy. Again typically, this was a Florentine phenomenon and a response to the particular political and social history of the city. For a time conditions were such in Florence that intellectual and political leaders were able to make a fresh and imaginative "active" use of the classical legacy, its values, exemplars, and historical experience. The movement exhausts itself with Machiavelli and Guicciardini at the very time when the political liberties of Florence had come to end. See Baron, *The Crisis of the Early Italian Renaissance* (2 vols., Princeton, 1955) and his contribution to *The New Cambridge Modern History,* Vol. I, *The Renaissance.*

25 For the ensuing discussion of the concept of wisdom, I am heavily indebted to the study of Eugene F. Rice, Jr., *The Renaissance Idea of Wisdom* (Cambridge, Mass., 1958).

26 Cicero, *De officiis* II, 2, 5: "Sapientia autem est, ut a veteribus philosophis definitum est, rerum divinarum et humanarum causarumque quibus eae res continentur. . . ."

27 Cf. Werner Jaeger, *Early Christianity and Greek Paideia* (Cambridge, Mass., 1962).

28 See O. Raggio, "The Myth of Prometheus: Its Survival and Metamorphoses up to the Eighteenth Century," *Journal of the Warburg and Courtauld Institutes,* XXI (1958), 44 ff., and T. E. Mommsen, "Petrarch and the Story of Hercules," in *idem.,* XVI (1953), 78 ff. The medieval thinkers could not make much sense of the story of Hercules because they could not grasp the notion of a single "virtue" definable as a self-conquered human perfection. The model of perfection was Christ, and he alone, the divine man, contained any virtue which might conceivably be referred to by the singular.

29 The relations between the influence of the planet Saturn and the interrelations of melancholy and genius were first explored in the pioneering study of Erwin Panofsky and Fritz Saxl, *Dürer's "Melancholia I," Eine quellen-und typengeschichtliche Untersuchung* (Studien der Bibliothek Warburg, II; Leipzig und Berlin, 1923). See also Panofsky's book *Life and Art of Albrecht Dürer* (4th ed., Princeton, 1954). It was in northern Europe that the notion of genius and of true creation as within the artist's power first came to be applied to the visual arts. On the difference between the medieval and Renaissance doctrine of creation see my *Medieval Cultural Tradition in Dante's Comedy* (Ithaca, N.Y., 1960), the chapter on Dante's analogy of creation.

Bruno, late in the sixteenth century, completes the process of attributing all poetic and creative powers to a superrational *furor poetico*. See his influential dialogue *Degli Eroici Furori* and, for the subsequent fortunes of some notions of the superrational in art, the article by S. H. Monk, "A Grace Beyond the Reach of Art," *Journal of the History of Ideas,* V (1944), 131 ff.

30 See the important studies on Petrarch in T. E. Mommsen's *Medieval and Renaissance Studies,* ed. E. F. Rice, Jr. (Ithaca, N.Y., 1959).

31 Jerome's scheme was based on the imagery in Daniel 2:31 and 7:1 concerning a statue of four different metals and also the allusion to four symbolic beasts. St. Augustine's is based on the biblical scheme as a whole. The six ages are measured as follows: (1) From Adam to the deluge, (2) from the deluge to Abraham, (3) from Abraham to David, (4) from David to the Captivity, (5) from the Captivity to the Incarnation, (6) the sixth which is now passing and cannot be numbered in generations.

32 The remarks of Panofsky in "Artist, Scientist, Genius," in *The Renaissance, Six Essays,* p. 129.

33 See the remarks of Harry Levin, "English Literature of the Renaissance," in Helton (ed.), *The Renaissance,* pp. 125-151, on this problem.

34 Burckhardt's pioneering work into what is now beginning to be called historical psychology was remarkable. He gave greater attention to col-

lective psychological changes, in taste, perception, and sensibility than any other historian of his era. He seems to have been the first to understand that the history of art and literature is the historian's index for understanding the transformation of sentiment, those ill-understood processes by which men come to feel about the world in new ways and see it differently. For recent observations on the development of perception see Zevedei Barbu, *Problems of Historical Psychology* (New York, 1960).

II

MACHIAVELLI:

The New Ethics and Politics

Niccolò di Bernardo dei Machiavelli was born in Florence in 1469 and died there in 1527. He held high office during the restored Florentine republic under Piero Soderini and was sent on important missions not only within Italy but also to France and Germany. The reports which he sent back to his government from these diplomatic journeys are a significant fraction of Machiavelli's literary work and, although he did not then think of them in this light, they became the indispensable preparation for the great works of his later life. The restoration of the Medici terminated his active political career and he was even briefly imprisoned and tortured as a suspected anti-Medicean. He was, however, soon released and exiled to his estate near Florence. During this long period of enforced inactivity he wrote his most important works, *The Prince* in 1513 and the *Discourses on the First Decade of Livy,* probably between 1513 and 1517. He was a prolific writer and late in his life, after he had been restored in some small measure to the good graces of the Medici, he wrote his *Florentine History* at the request of Cosimo. His works include, in addition to diplomatic, historical, and political writings, several literary works, among them the brilliant comedy *Mandragola,* perhaps the greatest comedy of the Italian Renaissance.[1]

Oddly enough, although it was widely read, *The Prince* did not provoke any great cry of moral indignation at first. The Pope authorized its publication on August 23, 1531, and the first two editions appeared in 1532. These first editions were followed by another twenty-five in the next twenty years alone. With its diffusion, however, the revolutionary character of the work was perceived and in 1559 the Inquisition condemned it along with all of Machiavelli's works, a decision which was upheld by the Council of Trent in 1564.

Thus within thirty-three years the black reputation of the author was established, with the help of violent attacks by Cardinal Pole, Ambrogio Caterino, Paulus Jovius, and prominent spokesmen of the Jesuit order among others. In part these men were guilty of misrepresenting Machiavelli's thought, but not entirely, for Machiavelli certainly offended orthodox sensibility and those consciences molded entirely by traditional ethical principles. Very few of his critics were prepared to consider Moses simply as a secular figure or to accept the unflattering comparison in the *Discourses* (II, 2) between Christianity and paganism.

However, the most extreme and truly gross misrepresentation of Machiavelli's thought came from the pen of a French Huguenot, Innocent Gentillet who, in 1576, wrote his *Discours sur les Moyens de bien gouverner et maintenir en bonne paix un Royaume . . . contre Nicolas Machivel, Florentin* in which, among other things, Machiavelli was accused of atheism and of being responsible for the St. Bartholomew's day massacre. An English version of this work was published in 1602 by Simon Patericke, and it has generally been assumed, probably correctly, that the numerous explicit defamatory references to Machiavelli in Elizabethan drama must have been derived from Gentillet in the original or in translation.

Nevertheless, a more authentic Machiavelli seems to have had a serious influence on men of affairs such as William Thomas, author of the *Historie of Italie* and *Disquisition on Affairs of State,* and on statesmen like Thomas Cromwell, Leicester, and Cecil. Although *The Prince* was not printed in English until 1640, it was available in printed form for the serious reader in, of course, Italian but also in Latin and three French translations by 1571.[2]

Machiavelli's thought, whether in its true accents or in one or another of its caricatures, was bound to disturb his contemporaries. The "Satanic" interpretation of Machiavellian ideas, crude as it may have been, was nevertheless in some crucial respects more accurate than that impassioned glorification of him as a patriot so characteristic of Italian nationalists of the romantic era. He did in fact shatter the great images of moral and cosmological order which still dominated the imaginations of his contemporaries and which had served to organize human experience. Dante's great ordering of life, his classic celebration of the central myths and intellectual models of understanding of his age, whose synthesis had been the slow work of time, remained the type if not the model of order and meaning. This was true for most men in spite of all the political, social, religious, and cultural upheavals of the Renaissance.

Indeed, Machiavelli might at first glance seem to stand looking out into chaos from the circumference of a circle in which Dante occupies the center, the perspective of perfect order. Where Dante finds symmetry and coherence, Machiavelli would appear to find only fragmentary and tenuous relations. Dante was able finally to time all of his encounters and experiences so as to lead to one another, to be exhaustively usable, while Machiavelli often found his ambiguous even if he never failed to learn something from each of them. For Dante all experience was finally mediation while, for Machiavelli, each experience could only, with certainty, illuminate its own immediate context and not point very far beyond itself.

Perhaps another way of stating this is that Dante can imagine a *Purgatory* or a *Paradise* but Machiavelli can only imagine a *Hell*. This would seem to place them at opposite ends of the spectrum of moral and imaginative possibilities, but the category of hell in fact unites the two great Florentines, for Machiavelli's analysis of experience is made entirely in terms of incontinence, force, and fraud, Dante's three categories of sin. In Machiavelli we find them not as three great stages in a descent to the abyss but as the three terms of a dynamic system in terms of which life is lived, a system which is not a pure Dantesque hell but which includes some purgatorial possibilities and perhaps even a few momentary paradisiacal ones. Machiavelli, like Dante, sees men as driven by infinite desire, but the infinite goal and the ladder to it has, for all practical purposes, disappeared. The enormous energies which Dante had seen as focused on the infinite, Machiavelli sees as unleashed in the world, in a world which has no object that can bind them. In Machiavelli, man appears in fundamental contradiction with his universe, for he is hopelessly incontinent, infinitely desirous, endlessly ambitious, yet his survival depends on some degree of renunciation and restraint. Because of this situation, Machiavelli tells us, force, whether as violence or as the power of law, must come into operation to check incontinence and, if force is not available in sufficient quantity, then fraud must make up the difference. Fraud, in Machiavelli's context, is by no means always deliberate deception but includes a good many of the conventions, fictions, and illusions that society requires for its self-regulation. Biological survival as well as culture rest on this system of thrust and counterthrust.

The Breakdown of Hierarchy and the Emergence of Fortune and Virtue

Dante lived in a hierarchical order, cosmologically as well as morally, and his universe contained a fundamental distinction between a perfect "higher" world of circular motion and incorruptible quintessential bodies, and an imperfect "lower" world of changing elements and linear motion. Machiavelli's statecraft, like Galileo's natural science, starts from the principle of the uniformity and homogeneity of nature, the obedience of all events to invariable laws which are everywhere the same. All periods of history, like all segments of nature, possess the same fundamental structure, so that a contemporary event will find its analogue in the past. Machiavelli utterly rejected the medieval concept of correspondence between political, moral, cosmological, ecclesiastical, and celestial orders; the notion of the divine source of power; indeed, the whole metaphysical rationalization of feudalism.[3]

The universe for Machiavelli no longer possessed the extraordinary degree of symmetrical and rational order that the Scholastics had conferred upon it. Its outlines had become indefinite, its consistency uniform. It had become in one respect much simpler and in another more complex and ambiguous, for chance had replaced providence as the ruling principle. *Fortuna* again received her due in her old pagan form, wily, capricious, and unpredictable. The old, highly specified, supernatural had become irrelevant and had been replaced with an indefinite natural world, imperfectly knowable, but certainly knowable in some sufficient degree to permit successful action, at least at times. Indeed, the problem of action is at the heart of Machiavelli's thought, and it would be an error to dwell too much on the relation of his thought to scientific and cultural changes. Machiavelli is first and foremost a political thinker and man of letters, and his vague cosmology is not an end in itself but the most appropriate frame for containing a universe of discourse about action which will be true to all the ambiguities inherent in it. He is concerned with those questions about human action which involve consideration of what can be deliberately planned as an end and what cannot, what goals of desire disappear precisely because they are desired, what goals of planning disappear precisely because they are planned. He knows that action with chaotic and ruinous consequences can first appear as rationality and morality. So he, along with his contemporaries and Renaissance predecessors, revived the old deities of *fortuna* and *virtus* because their very indefiniteness permitted greater fidelity to the problematic character of both personal and political affairs.

The revival of the old concepts in the Renaissance was not unique to Machiavelli. The problem of fortune and virtue, chance and ability, was much discussed from Petrarch to Bruno and beyond. Before Machiavelli, however, the emphasis had been placed on personal fortune or the role of chance in private affairs.[4] Machiavelli, however, applied the concept, like Polybius, to public rather than private life. It seemed to him the best expression of what he had learned from long experience of public life, that the whole problem of politics could be summed up in one platitude: The best advice and the most exact implementation of it cannot always succeed. Therefore all attempts at rational prediction must take account of what we might call an irreducible element of chaos,

fatality, necessity, or ignorance, a realm of darkness whose bound-
ary, however, can never be clearly defined. It may appear as chance
or fate, only apparently opposites, and it can only be discovered in
action itself. When action succeeds we have experienced freedom
and created order; when it fails we have experienced fate or malevolent chance. Historical experience teaches us, according to Machiavelli, that it is possible for will to overcome fate or chance
about half the time and, unlike many fatalists in the Renaissance
who toyed with similar ideas, Machiavelli strikes a new note in
giving man a fifty-fifty chance against the malice of the inanimate
as well as against the malice and irrationality of the animate.

Machiavelli follows Polybius in using two concepts of historical
explanation, one in terms of chance or fortune, the other in terms
of cause and ability. Thus Polybius says that the Romans, to be
sure, gained their empire by ability, caused it to come into being,
but that they should have been able to do this at a time and place
when their abilities, their causal power, could succeed must be attributed to fortune. Similarly, Cesare Borgia succeeded by his ability, his *virtù,* and only failed at the end because of the sudden death
of his father and his own simultaneous illness. This outcome was
the work of a truly malignant fortune, since, great as his abilities
were, they did not come into play at the right time.[5]

As we examine the use of the concept of fortune in Machiavelli
or Polybius we gradually become aware that it simultaneously refers to a cluster of related ideas of causality and limit from which
we might, for example, abstract three categories among others
which, singly or in combination, enter into a description of action:
determinism or fatality, chance, and intentionality. To describe all
of the real world of action in terms of any single one of these categories would result in a drastic simplification of the character of
experience, and the gain in consistency would be more than offset
by the loss of a genuine grasp of reality. The ambiguities of *fortuna*
do not stem from confusion of thought. Rather, the term contains
within itself the necessary categories for grasping the conditions of
action and the nature of events, in spite of the fact that these categories logically exclude one another when we abstract them from

their position as nuances of a symbol. In fact, these categories may all be applied at once to the same event, depending on who is viewing it.

To use the term *fortuna* permits us to see that action is always ironic, that it may be fate to a victim, freedom for a victor, chance to a bystander, that a man's ability may be his fortune, that his intentions may be necessitated. Machiavelli's *fortuna* is indeed the old, powerful pagan goddess come alive again in all her richness and power. We have only to turn to Dante's image of fortune in the seventh canto of the *Inferno* to grasp what a tremendous act of the historical imagination Machiavelli's *fortuna* represents, how she restores to human action in time and space all the ironies that Dante confines to the dynamic of sin when it ends in eternal damnation.

For Dante, fortune is purely an arm of providence, of divine intentionality, and the poet's possession of a highly specified hierarchical and supernatural order permits him finally to transcend all antinomies and all conflict. His is a world in which chance is merely an appearance, after all, and ability of any kind may finally be only a charismatic event, generated or negated by grace. It is, I think, irrelevant to talk, as T. S. Eliot has done, of Machiavelli's honest, realistic but "graceless" view of the world, if only because Machiavelli does not define himself in terms of the Christian anthropology of grace whether negatively or positively.[6] Grace after all is a very personal matter and involves a single individual's relation to his God. At least St. Augustine, among Christian thinkers, to whose pessimism Machiavelli would appear to be most nearly related, did not believe that the Holy Spirit was a God of Battles and indeed affirmed that God gave empire to the good and bad alike. With this judgment Machiavelli would have heartily agreed, and yet St. Augustine thought the same thing in a "graceful" world that Machiavelli thought in a "graceless" one. Both in effect agreed that grace is politically irrelevant.

While Machiavelli does not define human nature in terms of sin and grace he does define it in terms of an anthropology of desire which has much in common with both Christian and pre-Christian thought. His great figures—in a different context, to be sure—strive after their goals as hard as Plato's wakened lovers, are as infatuated by great hopes and endless desires as the actors in Thucydides' great narrative. They live in a universe in which human desire is infinite but in which all human acts are finite and, since Machiavelli's universe is neither Christian nor Platonic, there exists no act, natural or supernatural, which encompasses an infinite object.

I wish first to cite a brief passage from the *Discourses* on the nature of man which is the underlying principle of all of Machiavelli's thinking. Early in the *Discourses* (I, 3) he tells us:

All those who have written upon civil institutions demonstrate (and history is full of examples to support them) that whosoever desires to found a state and give it laws, must start by assuming that all men are bad and ever ready to display their vicious nature, whenever they may find an occasion for it. If their evil disposition remains concealed for a time, it must be attributed to some unknown reason; and we must assume that it lacked occasion to show itself; but time, which has been said to be the father of all truth, does not fail to bring it to light.[7]

It would seem that Machiavelli's pessimism about human nature is the flat assertion of a historian who, surveying the wreckage of history, simply points to the abundant evidence which the records of the past provide for this stern conclusion. But Machiavelli also passes from history to psychology and deepens this assertion later on in the *Discourses* (I, 37). There we find the analysis of human nature which our first statement seemed to require.

It was a saying of ancient writers, that men afflict themselves in evil, and become weary of the good, and that both these dispositions produce the same effects. For when men are no longer obliged to fight from necessity, they fight from ambition, which passion is so powerful in the hearts of men that it never leaves them, no matter to what height they may rise. The reason of this is that nature has created men so that they desire everything, but are unable to attain it; desire being thus always greater than the faculty of acquiring, discontent with what they have and dissatisfaction with themselves result from it. This causes the changes in their fortunes; for as some men desire to have more, whilst others fear to lose what they may have, enmities and war are the consequences; and this brings about the ruin of one province and the elevation of another.

The central thought of this passage is that human desire is infinite but lacks an infinite object. Man stands in a state of continual striving, continual tension and frustration. Each conquest of desire is accompanied by a dissatisfaction so great that it demands a new and fresh object. This dissatisfaction of fruition is both with the self and with the object which that self has just possessed or enjoyed.

As a starting point, this view of man can lead in various directions. As in Plato's *Phaedrus* and Dante's *Divine Comedy* it leads along a hierarchy of all value and being to an infinite object placed outside of space and time. In St. Augustine's *City of God* insatiable cupidity explains why states pass from external wars to internal ones and why there can really be no true justice in a temporal condition. Death will release the elect from this bondage and we can perhaps assume that the damned will go on living a kind of intensified earthly life. In Goethe's *Faust* the striving, itself of infinite desire, seems, to some interpreters at least, to be posited as a form of ultimate value. Machiavelli's view is different from all of these. Desire, for him, is not intrinsically valuable nor does it point to a realm outside of space and time. It is simply and fully there. Life *is* incontinence. Church and state are not pedagogical institutions but restrictive ones, using force or myth, which serve to protect men, at best, from the most extreme consequences of their own nature.

Let us now consider what great devices can be used against incontinence. Two passages are most germane to our discussion at this point, one from the *Discourses* and one from *The Prince*. In chapter 13 of Book II of the *Discourses* Machiavelli maintains that cunning and deceit will serve a man better than force to rise from a base condition to great fortune:

I believe it to be most true that it seldom happens that men rise from low condition to high rank without employing either force or fraud, unless that rank should be attained either by gift or by inheritance. Nor do I believe that force alone will ever be found to suffice, whilst it will often be the case that cunning alone serves the purpose; as is clearly seen by whoever reads the life of Philip of Macedon, or that of Agathocles the Sicilian, and many others, who from the lowest or most moderate condition have achieved thrones and great empires. Xenophon shows in his life of Cyrus the necessity of deception to success: the first expedition of Cyrus against the king of Armenia is replete with fraud, and it was deceit alone, and not force, that enabled him to seize that kingdom. And Xenophon draws no other conclusion from it than that a prince who wishes to achieve great things must learn to deceive. . . . Nor do I believe that there was ever a man who from obscure condition arrived at great power by merely employing open force; but there are many who have succeeded by fraud alone. . . . And that which princes are obliged to do in the beginning of their rise, republics are equally obliged to practice until they have become powerful enough so that force suffices them.

Let us note here that Machiavelli devalues brute force as an instrument for the acquisition of political power or for the aggrandizement of the state. Force is indispensable, of course, and almost every page of Machiavelli calls our attention to that fact. But fraud is often better, and it is the indispensable supplement to force until such an internal equilibrium obtains that force alone will suffice for perpetuating and increasing the power and safety of the state.

The Symbol of the Man-Beast

Machiavelli usually provides us with the best commentaries on his own work and we will now gloss this text with a very famous one from *The Prince*, from the eighteenth chapter, on how rulers must keep faith. There he tells us, in virtually the identical words of Cicero, that there are only two methods of fighting, one by means of law and the other by means of force. The first is proper to men, the other to beasts. However, he continues, the method of law is not always effective and then one must have recourse to force. It is therefore necessary that rulers know how to use both the beast and the man. Machiavelli then tells us that this doctrine was the secret meaning of the ancient story of Chiron, the semihuman and semi-animal tutor of princes such as Achilles.[8]

Machiavelli then subdivides the beast element into two separate qualities, symbolized respectively by the lion and the fox, again adapting some remarks of Cicero (*De officiis,* I, 13, 41) to his own purpose. The lion cannot protect himself from traps and the fox cannot defend himself from wolves. The ruler therefore has to be a fox in order to recognize traps and a lion to frighten the wolves. Princes who wish to be nothing but lions do not understand the necessity of also being foxes, that is, the necessity of breaking faith when it is no longer to their interest.

It is most important to observe here that Machiavelli first described the beast nature of the prince entirely with the category of force but then metaphorically subdivided this category into that of the lion, "force" in some more restricted sense, and into that of the fox or fraud. As his Ciceronian source tells us, the qualities of the fox are precisely those of fraud (*fraus*) while the qualities of the lion are those of violence (*vis*). Thus Machiavelli first used the word *forza* to mean power in its widest sense and then, implicitly and through symbol, subdivided it into *forza* meaning the exercise of violence or brute force and—that which he usually explicitly calls *frode*—other means of exercising power which involve dissimulation. Let us note that this defense of dissimulation as an art of government is simultaneously an attack on those princes who place all their trust in being lions, in the use of violence. This chapter is therefore also an acute critique of the simple-minded militarist who simplifies the complex structure of power into that of brute force.

Princes are urged to break faith because all men are not good. If all men were good this precept would not be a good one and it is precisely those princes who have behaved most like foxes who have succeeded best. To act like a fox, however, requires great powers of simulation and dissimulation, requires a great capacity to be one thing and to seem another. Machiavelli gives us only one example, a contemporary one, of the ruler as a fox, the example of Pope Alexander VI Borgia, and what a perfect example it is! All of his seeming, his appearances, were those of the Vicar of Christ on earth, but no man was a greater master of the arts of deception. Machiavelli does not draw from this the conclusion that Alexander was a hypocrite or that traditional moral values are not good. He simply says that the ruler, although he should display all the moral virtues and act on them whenever it is possible, must also be able to do evil if constrained. Indeed, to possess the traditional moral virtues and always act on them is dangerous, while to appear to possess them and know when to break them is useful. The tension between appearance and reality, "ought" and "must," which, in the private citizen, at peace, is small enough to be ignored is immeasurably intensified in the ruler. Let us not forget also that Machiavelli does not say that the ruler is all beast. The human half of the symbol of Chiron is the law but, as Machiavelli never tires of telling us, the law depends on good custom or the willingness of the ruled to respect it.

In Machiavelli the composite figure stands for two discontinuous but not unrelated moral realms or scenes of action. In an ironic way Sir Thomas Browne's definition of man can be applied to Machiavelli's ruler. He is a great Amphibium who lives in divided and distinguished worlds. But each world relates to the other. The threat of the beast can help to preserve the rule of law, and the action of the beast may create the condition for its institution if it does not exist. Behind all forms of the legitimation of power lies power itself whether as the naked power of coercion, the ideologically and publicly constituted power of authority, or the unscrupulous secret manipulation by rulers of the ruled. It is precisely because new rulers have so little claim to legitimacy that they must be fully aware of their "chironic" nature.

Machiavelli, in fact, uses the man-beast to symbolize his opposition in political life to an ethic of principles so rigidly held that it would lead to destruction. The statesman who acts unconditionally by moral maxims, who justifies his actions, whatever the consequences, simply by congratulating himself for his good intentions, who as it were trusts in God for the outcome of his action—such a man is really immoral. There is no doubt that the ethic of concern for consequences can be so formulated that it is subject to distorted, capricious, and grossly immoral use. Nevertheless with all its risks, this must be the statesman's ethic. His unpardonable sin is to deploy himself so that he is a prey to wickedness of others, and his fault is even more serious if he does so out of rigid adherence to an ethical maxim no matter how valid that maxim might be in its own sphere of operation. The statesman who does not recognize the existence of a plurality of ethical spheres, of levels of validity for ethical precepts, dooms himself to failure.

The Meaning of Fraud

We might at this point ask ourselves what, more exactly, does Machiavelli mean by fraud? Certainly one of the meanings is just plain and simple trickery. Cesare Borgia invites his enemies to a parlay and kills them. A ruler promises peace and makes war. And so on *ad nauseam*. All these are certainly instances of fraud. But Machiavelli gives a much wider meaning to fraud, as any careful reader of his work will grasp. I will call in the authority of the most careful reader he ever possessed, Francesco Guicciardini, his contemporary, whose comment on the very passage of the *Discourses* I quoted will be illuminating. Guicciardini says that he agrees in general with Machiavelli that pure force seldom raises political figures from low to high estate, although with his customary distrust of too universal a principle Guicciardini will not go so far as to say that pure force never can do so or that pure fraud can. It all depends, he continues, on what Machiavelli means by fraud. Guicciardini is prepared to agree with Machiavelli if the latter means to extend the word fraud to include all kinds of shrewd actions (*ogni astuzia*) or dissimulation. However, if Machiavelli means to confine the meaning of fraud to that which really is fraud, such as breaking faith, then many can be found who achieved great realms without fraud in his narrower and more immoral sense.[9]

When Machiavelli talks of force he means coercion, the explicit and ultimate form of power. When he talks of fraud he is also talking of power but in its covert forms, the forms it takes when it is either insufficient to reveal itself nakedly or when it can afford to dissimulate its appearance because of a voluntary obedience of its subjects. Fraud includes the power and genuine authority Numa gained when he fraudulently founded a religion which the Romans believed in and which justified in their eyes the power he claimed but did not safely possess until he gained it in this fraudulent way. Fraud also includes the secret, gross forms of connivance, deception, treachery, and manipulation in which the people are not even presented with a pious fraud or fiction but where they are the ignorant and unknowing objects of the power operations of the apparatus of state. Power thus can wear many faces and Machiavelli saw them all. This is what some of his students have meant when they refer to his creation of a "grammar of power," a "physics of politics" or to his isolation of politics as an autonomous activity. Machiavelli's important words and concepts have to be studied in terms of what we can grasp as the total intention of his thought if we are not to restrict their meaning or misunderstand what varied meanings they are intended to carry.

We should also bear in mind one other thing when Machiavelli talks of fraud, that he esteems other values besides success. For example, in chapter 40 of Book III of the *Discourses* he tells us that we must not confuse the employment of deceit and stratagems in war with perfidy. The latter is dishonorable and should be avoided. This is only one example of many. Again and again Machiavelli talks of the ideal of liberty under law, praises the value of glory which is, or should be, some sort of limit on the agent of action. Nevertheless, Machiavelli has no sooner condemned perfidy in war than he says—in the words of the title of his next chapter— "One's country must be defended, whether with glory or with shame; it must be defended anyhow." I cite this not as an example of inconsistency, for it is not. It is, rather, an example of the way in which Machiavelli refuses all absolutes as guides to action and how his acute awareness of the problematic conditions of action leads him not only to give some words like "fraud" a wider extension than we would give it but also leads him to restrict the meaning of perfidy to a considerably narrower range than we would give it.

The relative fluidity of the meanings of such key words in his writing reflects the shifting which stern necessity commands that we adopt in different circumstances. If no one principle of political action is always good then, under some tragic circumstances, we may be forced to acknowledge that no one principle of political action is always necessarily bad.

Machiavelli, in fact, was the first modern author to think of statecraft as an art or a craft, not in the sense in which Plato might have used that term, as knowledge of universal theoretical principles of politics, or as a theory of the legal and ethical state, but statecraft as a body of general principles and maxims concerning particular courses of action in characteristic political situations. His vision of the state was attractive, whatever its limitations, in an age of growing centralized monarchies in which the main political problems involved the consolidation of power. If Machiavelli saw the state as a dynamic unit with no particular internal goal, a quantity of power awaiting a ruler to achieve direction, so did the great statesmen of the rising sixteenth-century national states. Aristotle's injunction to educate the citizenry because that is the best preservative of the state seemed far less important than subduing the Irish or weakening the Spaniards.

The Interpretation and Uses of History: The Problem of Action

Classical and medieval political theory was not really very useful to such men, for it had been subordinated to traditional ethics. I wish here to stress the word "theory," for power politics obviously existed before Machiavelli and continues after him. Although the amoral character of at least some necessary political action did not escape the attention of political theorists before him, they could not help analyzing such behavior and judging it from the traditional ethical point of view. This ambivalence was even stronger in men of affairs, who frequently offered and may even still offer dubious ethical generalizations for their own behavior. While traditional legal theory before Machiavelli had recognized instances where the force of facts dictated courses of action not entirely justifiable from the ethical perspective, political theory continued to keep itself subordinated to ethics in the hierarchy of knowledge.

This cultural situation changed with the writing of *The Prince*. In that book Machiavelli studied politics as an activity with an autonomous aspect and attempted to arrive at the principles of statecraft by inference from actual instances of political success drawn from contemporary and ancient history. Not that *The Prince* is entirely a technical and descriptive work. It is certainly true that Machiavelli sometimes could not help making covert ethical judgments and that he had ideals and goals which he wished realized. Nevertheless, it is certainly the first great work in which divine moral injunctions and traditional ethical authority are in irreconcilable collision with secular human concerns, and this is true precisely to the extent that *The Prince* is in great part a technical treatise. In it the state appears in its simplest and most basic form, essentially although not entirely isolated from all the conditions which Machiavelli considered extraneous, including religious, social, and cultural ones.[10]

Machiavelli's political examples are types of experience and models of behavior and, if his theoretical temper made him attribute too great a share in controlling political events to political astuteness, diplomacy, or military strength, still he was useful where others were not. In addition, he offered a theory of the rights of nations as such without reference to the various notions of legitimacy tied up with hereditary monarchy, an attractive conception in a Europe in which many revolutionary movements began by raising the question of the legitimacy of the ruler to rule.

A revolutionary departure in thought and feeling is generally associated with profound historical and cultural changes, and *The Prince* is no exception. By 1513, the date of the writing of *The Prince,* political affairs in Italy had reached a point where moral persuasion and ideological abstractions were no longer effective in maintaining order. The French invasion had destroyed the balance of power so carefully maintained by Lorenzo the Magnificent up to his death in 1492, and had turned Italy into a European battleground, for French success had encouraged the Spaniards and the empire. This situation had been preceded by internal troubles in the major city-states of Italy which, by Machiavelli's time, had led to the surrender of all power to despots, the only authorities, it would seem, able to curb class war and political factionalism. Government had become not only despotic but personal, and affairs were more and more subject to the whims and judgment of single individuals.

Italy had come to such a pass that, to Machiavelli, men seemed even more what they had always seemed—essentially evil, and history looked more and more like the work of a largely incomprehensible and uncontrollable power, a power which, nevertheless, Machiavelli attempted to understand by trying to learn how much human foresight and prudence could do to mitigate the operations of chance or fortune.

Thus Machiavelli boldly rejected all providential and theological interpretations of the course of history, but his pessimistic view of human nature is traditional and allies him with the Augustinian tradition within Christianity. Both St. Augustine and Machiavelli would have agreed that men are born bad and generally do not do good unless they are forced to do so. Machiavelli was convinced that few men had mastered the art of self-restraint and that coercion and forceful repression were the only means through which the destructive impulses in man could be kept in check and civilization endure. We emphatically should not conclude from this that Machiavelli was a proponent of dictatorship or tyranny. The rule of law and good custom is the best government, but where the political will is corrupt, force must be brought into play. It is precisely because men are inordinately self-seeking and rapacious that Machiavelli advocates the mixed constitution of the *Discourses*. In that work he tells us that by distributing power and authority, and giving to each group in the commonwealth something of what it wants, people will check their desires if only to enjoy the fruits of their own cupidity.[11]

Machiavelli and St. Augustine would also have agreed that power seeks more power, that the nature of the state is essentially expansive, and that from its origin to its apogee, the story of the state is the quest for power, first over internal enemies and next over neighboring states.

While this point of view concerning the nature of man and the state underlies all of Machiavelli's work, it is most dramatically expressed in *The Prince*. Unlike the *Discourses,* in which Machiavelli also studied the state as a going concern, one in which laws and good customs are at least operative to some degree, *The Prince* is written with one special kind of situation in view, a situation of "necessity" (*necessità*) in which the general corruption has become so great that laws and custom cannot halt the dissolution of the political structure, a situation in which only a forceful monarch (*mano regia*) can reverse the trend to anarchy or establish a new state out of chaos.[12]

We might add that by "monarch," Machiavelli does not mean "tyrant," nor does he claim that a true civil society is less stable than absolute rule. Quite the contrary: tyranny and other degenerate forms of true civil governments are the least stable forms.[13] Machiavelli, in fact, is almost obsessed by the problem of political stability. *The Prince* is finally concerned with the problem of how to free Italy from internal anarchy severely aggravated by external interference, but Machiavelli spends the major part of the treatise discussing how states can be formed and made to endure. The verbs "to maintain" (*mantenere*), "to endure" (*durare*), appear insistently in his political writing in connection with the state,[14] and he everywhere attempts to offer advice on how man, through the exercise of prudence, can achieve the maximum stability in the political order. If no state is eternal, it can at least endure as long as Sparta or Rome, the two longest-lived states Machiavelli knew about.[15]

Stability, longevity are, in fact, the primary task of each and every state, and survival is something that ethically good or bad governments can achieve. If over the long term a strong civil society of some form has an advantage over degenerate forms such as tyranny or oligarchy, the latter, if they are strong, may have the advantage over divided, vacillating, inconsistent states of any kind.

As we have seen, Italy's political stability had formerly relied on a delicate balance of power, but the French invasion in 1494 had rapidly diminished constructive diplomatic alternatives within the peninsula. New quantities and variables had entered the Italian political equation, and the only possibility for Italian stability and freedom lay in the creation of larger units of power. The inability or unwillingness of the Italian states to achieve greater strength through a permanent coalition left only one alternative, a unification by force. External weakness was matched in many cases by internal instability, so that wherever he looked Machiavelli found little comfort. The situation in every respect had become one of *necessità* and the only recourse was "strong medicine." The patient was in a desperate condition, and the cure, if any, had to be a nasty one.

In addition to this pessimistic view of human nature and of the life cycle of the state, we find two other broad principles which govern Machiavelli's thought, and they are so closely interrelated in his mind that they are best discussed together: the doctrine of imitation, so important to the whole of Renaissance culture, and the view of history as a perpetual repetition of a finite number of virtually interconvertible events. In Machiavelli's view, the past afforded models of political behavior which could be imitated in the closest detail, and the finest repository of such models was to be found in the history of Rome. In this respect, Machiavelli works in a humanistic version of the medieval literary tradition of *exempla,* of types of virtuous behavior to be imitated. But his *exempla* are not examples of static virtues or of conquering vices, but specimen instances of men coping with typical political situations in circumstances which are particular and, because they will repeat themselves, also general and useful to know about.[16]

Rome was the great state with the longest history and had therefore traversed more of the historical possibilities than any other. Since those possibilities are finite and the essential character of history is to repeat the same events and situations, it is possible to deduce general principles of political behavior from historical evidence, especially Roman evidence. It was because history was potentially so useful that Machiavelli applied to the interpretation of history the same outlook and techniques that he applied to contemporary events, in many of which he had been involved during his active career as a diplomat.

In spite of this contemporary and utilitarian outlook on the past, Machiavelli nevertheless felt that the experience of the more remote ancient world was superior as a guide for action to the experience of the recent past. For this I think we can find two reasons. History, in Machiavelli's view, tends to repeat itself in progressively degenerate form so that Roman experience was better simply by virtue of being ancient. On the other hand, human passions remain the same, causing in every age the same actions, and the Romans, in their long, full political cycle, could be assumed to have very nearly exhausted the possibilities of human behavior. The men of Machiavelli's own time were in another cycle, which had not yet gone far enough to run through the gamut of types of action.

In a somewhat obscure manner Machiavelli thus blends two views of history, the cyclical and the degenerative. The image for his view of history would therefore be a descending cyclical series. The constancy of human nature and the natural tendency of men to imitate ensure that the same limited number of constant factors will repeat themselves and that there can be no historical evolution. However, the repetition of history will always be retrograde, for all things are equally subject to the law of decay. Any hope of reform lies, analogically, in a retrograde movement to the more vigorous starting point. For example, any state that wishes to renew itself must return to its old ethos, a return which, Machiavelli says, can only be the work of one powerful man. To an even greater degree must the creation of a new state or institution be the work of a single individual, for it is only a single unusual person who can arrest the natural processes of decay. Machiavelli thus pins all his hopes on one man even though, inconsistently enough, he also believes that *vox populi vox Dei*.[17]

Nevertheless, the possibility of reform is distinctly limited, and even the most remarkable leadership cannot overcome the fact that everything human, men and their institutions, contains the seeds of its own destruction. The life of states or institutions, like human life, can be prolonged or even renewed, but only for a time. When the acme has been reached, the descent inevitably begins. We can recognize in this doctrine an interesting adaptation of Aristotle's theory of generation and corruption applied to historical phenomena. Both Machiavelli and Aristotle hold that decay is indispensable to further growth and all growth feeds on decay. Applied to the moral and political sphere, this physical and biological doctrine means that evil can give rise to good and good to evil, a bold conclusion which Machiavelli does not fail to draw. For him, good and evil not only succeed each other but create each other. The relative proportions of growth or decay, good or evil, are constant and only their relations change. While one society is decaying another is coming to birth. Thus political vigor and ability originally belonged to the Assyrians, from whom it passed to the Medes, Persians, and finally to the Romans, the quantity of it remaining constant.[18]

While Machiavelli's mixture of a theory of historical decay with one of cyclical returns has little theoretical vigor, its intent is clearly to indicate the limits of human mastery of historical events while at the same time allowing to human prudence, knowledge, and foresight some measure of control over the longevity and vitality of the state. It is true that the destructive and anarchic side of human nature makes it inevitable that a state shall go from political virtue and peace to idleness, disorder, and finally ruin. Yet even if no state is eternal, strong laws and good customs can help to modify and control the process.

It is clear that Machiavelli reserves areas of freedom, of the possibility for successful action, within a total framework which anticipates a far more pessimistic eventual outcome to political efforts. Yet had the great founders and perpetuators of Rome and Sparta been obsessed with the inevitability of the dissolution of all their achievements, their states would either not have come into existence or would soon have perished. Human freedom and creativity operate precisely within limits set by the span of the longest- and shortest-lived states. The knowledge of men is limited and the unknown is immense, but ability counts and may be in your favor as well as against you. You must not try to plot your exact point on the curve of the life of the state.

Machiavelli views political and social events from this complex perspective, in which the fundamental human passions remain the only constants, while all action and thought have become problematic and discontinuous. The heroes of many of the dramas which unfold themselves in his universe are endowed with great courage and agitated, restless wills. Although they have, like all men, finite intellects and limited powers of foresight, they are nevertheless driven by boundless desires, desires which outstrip whatever goals and checks their thought can posit. Superficially, this looks like the beginning of certain ruin, of nemesis, and Machiavelli's moral cosmology might, up to this point, suggest the kind of pattern we are familiar with in Boccaccio's *De casibus* or Lydgate's *Fall of Princes*. However, the last acts of Machiavelli's little dramas are seldom so edifying. The good and bad succeed and fail alike; the bad in their success may bring about good consequences, the good may succeed only in bringing about disasters. Like any great artist Machiavelli does not simplify our moral judgments while he helps us to clarify them. On the contrary he complicates our moral vision, making it almost impossible for us to use the various simple categories we often keep ready to receive even some of the more complex characters we come to know.

Machiavelli's hopes for creative political action rested on the courage and ability of the single individual. Hence, again and again in his works, historical as well as political and diplomatic, we encounter powerful and fascinating personalities, rapidly drawn and highly individuated through some characteristic act or bold decision which reveals their temper. Although they are presented to us as historical figures, they really belong as much or more to literature than to history. If, for example, the historian were to try to reconstruct the actual life of Castruccio Castracane of Lucca, of whom Machiavelli wrote a short biography, he would discover that Machiavelli chose and suppressed details with the freedom of a novelist. The same would be true, although in lesser degree, of his version of the characters of some of his own contemporaries such as Julius II and Cesare Borgia. Rather than actual portraits, such figures are really types of men whose advent Machiavelli desired, creations of the wishes of an unarmed prophet disposed to attribute to his heroes even more of the same abilities that he detected in them.

The extent to which man can control the inherent tendency to decay in all things human was, as we have seen, the central concern of Machiavelli, and it was a problem with which he struggled all of his life. His favorite way of stating it was through the use of two polar concepts, or rather symbols, that of the goddess Fortuna and that of Virtue, also an ancient goddess. Judging from St. Augustine's attack on these two deities in the *City of God,* they must have still retained a strong hold on the imagination of his contemporaries. And we can well understand this, for, in a poetic way, they stood for two complementary and polar aspects of human experience. The human power to effect change and control events was subsumed in the image of *virtù,* not the plural *virtutes* of Christian tradition but a single quality, which, to the pagan mind, manifested itself as civic and martial ability. Around the image of *fortuna* there clustered a host of related concepts—all the impersonal agencies active in the lives, collective or individual, of men, the force or logic of history, the frequently mysterious concatenation of events which can neither be predicted nor understood after they have come to pass, blind chance or, at times, an equally blind fate. It is in this essentially pagan form that Machiavelli revived the goddesses of antiquity whom St. Augustine had banished, for they seemed to describe the actual course of history more accurately than Christian theology. The uncertainty of the concepts only reflects the uncertainty of prediction in the world, especially one in which the decision of a single powerful individual may make the best advice and the most complete knowledge useless.

These terms as terms are indeed rather ambiguous, but they are really poetic, allegorical symbols pointing to a variety of related concepts, which taken together are not necessarily logically coherent. Thus from one point of view, *fortuna* would seem to signify the inevitable character of processes of nature, of growth and decay, while *virtù* is the human power which, guided by an understanding of the nature of things, can do what is possible to arrest decline. But it is clear that "fortune" is also the unknown, and that man cannot completely know or conquer her. Machiavelli tells us that he can only operate with and minimize her bad effects or, if he is very lucky, turn them to advantage. In any case Machiavelli maintains that *fortuna* and *virtù* divide the world between them half and half, so that human effort ought to succeed in about half of the events which occur.

Machiavelli derived these polar deities, like most of his conception of historical causation and recurrence, from Polybius and, like him, used the concepts with the skill and flexibility of a poet rather than the abstract rigor of a philosopher.[19] Thus *fortuna,* or *tyche,* appears in both authors as a half-personalized and semidivine power that bends events to her will. In this respect fortune is simply that which the agent of action could not reasonably foresee, including even natural events and events with unknown causes, such as floods, storms, and plagues. Both would consider it illegitimate to attribute to fortune whatever can be understood by humans and concerning which humans can exercise foresight and control, whether actively, by taking measures, or passively, by avoiding action.

The external circumstances, the particular conditions for action which fortune may give, Machiavelli calls the *occasione* or "occasion," and the degree to which a man is aware of and able to take advantage of the occasion is a function of his *virtù.* Yet personal fortune may be said to coincide with or overlap *virtù* in the sense that the mysterious ability to find quickly the successful course of action in a complex situation can sometimes hardly be distinguished from some impetus, internal or external, which virtually impels the agent to act successfully among many imponderables. The terms *virtù* and *fortuna,* while primarily antithetical, sometimes shade into one another. Machiavelli even virtually identifies the two when he says that good laws make good fortune, and it is obvious that the excellence of one individual may play a leading role in the fate of another.[20] The rhetorical flourishes which Machiavelli makes—fortune as a turning wheel, as unpredictable as shifting winds, as one who disregards all human feeling and justice, as a capricious woman, as a personified power that wants to raise everything that's down and lower everything that's up—all these are best interpreted as metaphors expressive of how men *feel* about chance and its unfathomable mystery, not of how men ought to *think* about it.

Virtù, the corollary of *fortuna,* is certainly a simpler concept, although at times equally amorphous. Its primary sense is classical and means what Livy might have meant by it, military skill and valor and the kind of civic integrity associated with the old Roman republican heroes like Cincinnatus, Horatius, or Mucius Scaevola. Such *virtù* is the possession of peoples as well as individuals, although primarily of the latter.

But in the meaning which interests us most and which is the most singular use of the term, it quite clearly has no conventional ethical connotation and means sheer ability, prudence in the sense of practical insight and the power to act on it, without any ethical meaning attached. It involves an acute understanding of the real nature of things and circumstances as well as the ability to act on that understanding. It points to the obscure and complex realm which the general principle must traverse before it can effectively govern a unique and particular instance. Aristotle's ethical man knows what good to do to the right person, to the right extent, at the right time, with the right motive, and in the right way, something which Aristotle tells us is not for everyone, nor easy. If we transpose all of these skills into Machiavelli's world, stripping the term "right" of its customary ethical values, we will have something very close to what Machiavelli means by *virtù.* It is the power of constant adaptability to circumstances, the power to operate in conditions which men are not responsible for and on realities which they did not bring into being. The exercise of *virtù* requires constant flexibility, knowledge of how circumstances alter cases and, above all, the knack of always avoiding rigidity. Only by such behavior can man minimize the effects of fortune.

It is clear from this analysis of some of Machiavelli's leading

ideas and presuppositions that he is not a political scientist in the
sense that he possesses a system of politics. On the contrary, his is
essentially a literary intelligence, aware that life escapes all the abstract schemes we may construct to control it. He would have said
that a systematic approach to experience would have disastrous
practical consequences, for no single principle is always, in every
instance, good. It is the prime necessity for flexibility in statecraft
as well as other spheres of action that leads Machiavelli to organize
his thinking around mythic, poetic, and indefinite concepts like
fortuna and *virtù* in a way that precludes any logically coherent
result. Yet the indefiniteness is, in this case, part of the precision,
for, like all effective poetic symbols, the realities they capture are
themselves indefinite and problematic. Fidelity to the element of
risk and chance in all action whatever, actually compels Machiavelli to be unsystematic. Avoiding large abstractions, he teaches
like an artist, by concrete examples to be applied to specific and
typical situations, and by subtle repetitions.

His great words and images—*fortuna, virtù, necessità, occasione*
—appear and reappear like expanding figures running through the
texture of his work, each new appearance subtly modifying the
meaning of the last and all enriching each other. In this sense, Machiavelli's thought is his style and we can no more preserve its variety and subtlety through paraphrase and summary than we can the
meaning of a poem.

Machiavelli on the Origin of the State

Machiavelli's realism and utility rested on a naturalistic conception
of the state. In his view, the state began when primitive population
increased and men came together to form larger communities. In
order to stabilize these new communities they agreed in their own
interest to be ruled by the most powerful and courageous men
among them. There was thus a surrender and transfer of power at
the beginning of political society and this original "contract" marks
the first step in the growth of man's awareness of good and evil.
Universal convictions concerning right and wrong grew out of the

system of rewards and punishments the newly constituted rulers instituted to govern and organize society. The fact that our ideas of good and evil have such an origin means that right and wrong are not absolute but must be judged in reference to man's original and continuing effort to control forms of activity which he recognizes as inimical to his own well-being.

Machiavelli, in effect, denies the validity of any *lex aeterna* and therefore of natural law itself. Men's intuitions of goodness are not glimpses into a divinely constituted order even though men have come to think so. What is good is that which protects the life, property, and honor of the majority of individuals over the longest period of time. In this denial of natural law Machiavelli is simply following a long Italian tradition of political realism which goes back at least as far as the *Defensor pacis* and whose roots lie, politically, in the conflict between empire and Papacy and, intellectually, in the nominalism of the late Middle Ages.[21]

Machiavelli's conception of good as self-interest points to a characteristic tension between the one and the many which we shall find repeated in his conception of the will, and which is formally echoed in those polarities, such as virtue and fortune, in terms of which he organizes his thought. The member of a state, in his own self-interest, wishes his fellow citizens to behave in a way that he will call good. But he and his fellows will in their own individual self-interest be all too ready to behave in ways which contradict their standard of goodness for others. Self-interest, however, is not only society's disease but also its remedy. It certainly marks man as being in some permanent aspect of his nature anarchic or, at least, unsocial. However, as we recall from Machiavelli's myth of the origin of the state, we would not be here at all if man did not have the capacity to be ruled and accept limitations, at least when he becomes aware of the lethal dangers ensuing from rapacious and unlimited pursuit of self-interest. Machiavelli places his conception of self-interest at the very heart of all his political thinking and of his analysis of the main problems of governing and being governed. It accounts for the abiding elements of divisiveness in any society and also explains the conditions necessary for social cohesion.

Machiavelli would have agreed with Hobbes that man is bad and society restrains him, but he is far more dialectical than Hobbes, whose theory of man's radical selfishness leads him to a defense of absolutism simply because he could find little possibility of self-limitation in the very dialectic of self-interest itself. Machiavelli's admiration for the mixed constitution is based on the conviction that areas of freedom and reason can be preserved in a society and interstices created between the one and the many if all conflicting wills in the society are allowed to limit one another through the partial indulgence of each. Men will limit their essentially limitless rapacity if they are allowed to enjoy the fruits of a partially indulged cupidity. Any democratic theory of government which also rests on a pessimistic view of human nature must accept this possibility. In addition, Machiavelli never uses his theory either of the origin of the state or of the nature of man to legitimate society or any particular form of government. Some kinds of order are preferable to others but more than one kind is possible and workable. His myth of a primitive "contract" is simply in the service of finding an origin for society and for explaining the sources of social order and of morality.

Laws, justice, good customs, institutions—all evolve from the system of rewards and punishments which the strong instituted after the weak agreed to be governed by them. This evolution rests on the fact that the wills of the governed learn to conform to the will of the governors at least to the degree that obedience becomes habitual. It is the growth of habitual obedience that curbs original corruption and lawlessness, lessens the need for the ruler's exercise of incessant coercion, and thereby permits a genuine civil society to exist. While morality may ultimately be derived from fear of force, a state cannot function or endure long by coercion alone. Law and good customs must obtain if a genuine civil society is to exist. Right is the true interest of the majority but they must will and recognize that right.[22]

In the last analysis, Machiavelli's myth of the origin of the state is the presupposition for an analysis of the concept of the state into two categories of coercion: forceful, external coercion, and that form of self-coercion which leads to obedience. The one element grows as the other diminishes, and that society is truly civil in which coercion is reduced to its minimum. As we shall see, myth, convention, religion, pious or even impious frauds, may all be instrumental in reducing the role of force.

The first observation we should make of Machiavelli's discussion of the origin of the state is that it does not constitute an argument for any particular form of government. His political preferences do not follow ineluctably from his assumptions, which could lead in various directions and justify various kinds of political order, as indeed the history of his influence shows they have.

This absence of systematic rigor is a characteristic of all of his thought and it must be understood as deliberate and not as a failure. Machiavelli concerned himself with the effective reality of things, with things as they are. While the phrase may be ambiguous the locus of knowledge concerning the effective reality of things was not. It lay in the history of actual states, judged in the light of his own political experience. That history taught Machiavelli many particular lessons and one big one: the ruler's employment of too rigid or theoretical a system of politics as a guide to action would have disastrous practical consequences. The ambiguity of Machiavelli's thought is deliberate, and his universe of discourse precludes theoretical consistency simply because the prime requisite of effective political action is flexibility.

Thus he sometimes reads like a collector of maxims and examples, some of which recur frequently in his writings. Both examples and maxims are generally concrete and vivid, drawn from specific situations and applicable to equally specific ones which appear often enough in the course of history to allow for the general utility of what Machiavelli learned from the past.

To the extent that Machiavelli is interested in generalizing from the political records of the past he demonstrates, of course, a theoretical side. He did attempt to introduce some theory and some degree of systematic organization into the art of statecraft and even on occasion was rigid in trying to formulate general principles of action on a rather slender basis. He certainly does not confine himself to describing the practices of statesmen but tries to set forth principles of action for his own contemporaries. Nevertheless, we must firmly grasp that his passion for historical analysis was not of an abstract or truly theoretical character. Machiavelli was not interested in understanding the growth and structure of various kinds of states or, despite his preferences, in classifying them. His great effort and achievement is focused on the clarification of the manner in which historical conditions may affect political action.

Machiavelli's Relation to His Predecessors

We can perhaps best deepen our understanding of the nature of Machiavelli's thought if we compare him to his predecessors, medieval and humanistic.

The prevailing medieval concept of the ruler was based on the Pauline analogy between the state and the human organism, a convincing image for the feudal ideal of organization. In this view, the ruler's relation to his subjects was understood by analogy with the governing organ of a living body. With the recovery of the Aristotelian corpus, writers of the medieval literature on princes extended their range from more or less exclusive concern with the relationship between ruler and ruled to include the whole field of political institutions, especially military and judicial ones. On the whole, however, this new and rich material was incorporated in the old framework and its interpretation was still governed by the conception of the ruler as the head of a bodily organism.

This conservative tendency in medieval political theory accounts for the fact that the first secular state since antiquity, Frederick II's realm in thirteenth-century Sicily, remained outside the consideration of political theorists. Even those who recognized his greatness, like Dante, had to condemn him on moral grounds, and they did not recognize the originality of his political achievement. Even less would the general run of medieval theorists have tried to justify it as an attempt to create a truly secular state.

Machiavelli, of course, owed some things to both the medieval and the humanistic writers on the art of ruling. However, as we shall see, even where Machiavelli resembles his predecessors the resemblance is frequently formal or verbal. Thus, in the framework of the natural-rights theory of the state, both state and sovereign had been described as "free from laws" (*legibus solutus*). This might, at first glance, seem to imply some sort of doctrine of reason of state. However, all that the phrase meant was that the state and sovereign could not be legally coerced, not that they were free from accepting moral responsibility for their actions in the sense in which an ordinary citizen holding traditional ethical values might have understood the word "moral."

In regard to his humanist predecessors Machiavelli adopted or developed some of their innovations, such as a more secular orientation, the use of historical example, and the positing of worldly fame rather than eternal salvation as the reward for a good ruler. Nevertheless, even a superficial examination of his predecessors will demonstrate how much more abstract they were and how strong was their tendency merely to reproduce classical ideas and modes of thought.

Far more important than Machiavelli's indebtedness to his predecessors was the fact that he was the aware observer of new political phenomena. The contemporary states of Italy were really new, revealed new elements previously unrecognized and old ones in a new light. The new secular states, founded and maintained by the virtually naked use of force, could not be satisfactorily described in terms of classical, medieval, or humanistic theories. Their rulers were frequently "new men," men of power who could claim no divine authority and whose rule was unhallowed by tradition, genealogy or, indeed, any of the traditional mythological or ideological apparatus of government. It might seem paradoxical to claim that Machiavelli was the witness of new events when all he claimed was to have rediscovered the timeless effective reality of things, the way things have always been done. Nevertheless, we can claim that never before in history had the mechanics of political power been so starkly disclosed as in Renaissance Italy. There the difference between civil and external wars had been virtually annihilated, there he saw the simultaneous successful existence of a number of theoretically incompatible systems and modes of governing, there new men with no sanction but their own power carved out their realms.

Italy was thus a laboratory of political life. When religious and political mythologies began to lose the important role they once had in shaping political life, even if only temporarily and in some places, new ground had to be found for political thought; Machiavelli attempted to meet that need. Traditional political theory also was so tied to the concept of a single natural, theologically or philosophically sanctioned, political order that it could not account for the diversity of viable order that Machiavelli saw before his eyes. Hence his analysis of political life was forced to go below the level of its formal organization or ideological validation, below to the effective reality of things.

Machiavelli's predecessors, for example, tried to express the norm for the perfect ruler in what was at best a very unrealistic way, one especially so in the sixteenth century. For them, the ruler administered justice and preserved the peace—and, if he was a good man, would be quite successful in accomplishing these two tasks. They assumed his legitimacy, acceptance of the authority of his person and office and, above all, they assumed that the ideal man, ethically speaking, and the ideal ruler were one.[23]

Machiavelli agreed with the great tradition of political thought that a state governed by evil means or evil men is rarely well governed (*Discourses* I, 18). Like his humanistic predecessors he too raised the question concerning what catalogue of virtues applied to the ruler and whether they were the same as those which applied to the ideal ethical agent. Unlike them, however, he grasped the full significance of the problems this question raised and shattered the identity which had been assumed to exist between the ideal ruler and the ideal human being. In his thinking on the role of the prince, Machiavelli conserved the emphasis which his predecessors had laid on the personality and character of the ruler, on his power to manipulate events, but he saw that power as exercised in a completely realistic political universe.[24]

Having seen new and varied political phenomena and having

raised new questions, Machiavelli had to find new ground for his inquiry, and he found it in the study of historical examples. For him the great majority of such examples have virtually universal applicability. In this he is perhaps more rigid and abstract than his great contemporary Francesco Guicciardini. The latter emphasized rational reflection on personal experience rather than imitation of the past—although he also accepted the doctrine of historical recurrence—and was more inclined to note the difference rather than the similarity between past and present, the unique element in every historical event. Guicciardini was convinced that although general principles of statecraft could be derived from the study of history, such principles always had to be applied with full awareness of the differences, sometimes minute but crucial, between events of the past and the present. While I do not wish to suggest that Machiavelli was usually hasty about drawing general principles of action from past events, he certainly was more sanguine than Guicciardini about doing so.[25]

In the last analysis Machiavelli's use of history is a moral and psychological one. He is interested in the conditions under which men have acted politically in success and failure, the motives that have moved them, their awareness of the conditions of action. His history is not, like Dante's or Hegel's the story of the emergence of great public, universal values and institutions but a collection of finite *exempla* of human action determined by a constant psychological human nature. History is not the process in which the intentions and irrationalities of men are subsumed by grace or a world spirit into great rational structures somehow drawn from that chaos of individual conflicting wills. Machiavelli offers none of the specious consolations of historicism or providentialism, only insight into the nature of human action and the chance of using that insight constructively in the advancement of liberty.

This approach to history was related to a characteristic development in humanist historiography. If the medieval historian wrote universal history, the Renaissance historian wrote civic history. The one was convinced that history was moving toward the creation of a universal community, toward the fulfillment of an eschatology. The other, truly aware of the existence of the new polities which had emerged from the fall of the empire, classical and medieval, wrote the story of civil liberty, of its gain and its loss, of the conditions under which it might be reachieved.[26]

Machiavelli's emphasis on the history rather than on the theoretical political treatises of antiquity marks him as a humanist. Just as the artists, lawyers, physicians had all turned to the great achievements of the classical world for guidance so, Machiavelli tells us, the time had come for the statesmen to do the same. Indeed, Machiavelli felt that his great contribution to his time lay in calling the attention of his contemporaries to the political lessons to be imitated and learned from antiquity.[27]

His intense classicism, however, made him sneer at the use of firearms, an error for which the more flexible Guicciardini criticized him. As we shall see, a certain rigidity born of his intense admiration of Rome, occasionally led him into other errors of judgment, in spite of his firm conviction that there are cases for which it is impossible to formulate general rules from historical precedent.[28]

Machiavelli's humanism was in one way or another a constant in his thought. His belief that he was discovering the laws of political behavior, which the Romans knew and which had been forgotten, was a characteristic humanistic approach to the past and is especially conspicuous in the *Discourses*. Indeed, *The Prince* is the only one of his great works which draws heavily on modern examples and precedent.

In some respects, Machiavelli becomes even more humanistic in the later works. From the *Discourses,* he Latinizes his style, is more "idealistic," and his last major work, the *Florentine History,* is written in the characteristic humanistic mode, using selected historical events and persons as types or *exempla.* Yet he never gets so "humanistic" as to make historical writing simply the writing of an eloquent narrative. His humanism always remained of the general type of the vernacular humanists, that of an active man who was not a scholar purely for the sake of scholarship.

In the matter of a revival of Roman greatness, an almost obsessive theme among the humanists, Machiavelli was never optimistic.

In a letter to his friend Vettori of August 26, 1513, written while he was at work on *The Prince,* he felt that a little of the old *virtù* of the Romans might still be dormant in the Italian people. Somewhat later, in the *Discourses,* he has completely given up hope in the Italians and other "Latins," maintaining that only the northern races have any *virtù* in his world.[29] In respect to the revival of Roman glory, at least, Machiavelli became less of a humanist as he grew older.

It is probable that Machiavelli's growing concern with antiquity, his adoption of a Latinizing style and the forms of humanistic historiography, were in part the result of his prolonged association with a remarkable group of scholarly men of affairs who met in the famous *Orti Oricellari,* or Rucellai Gardens. Under the sponsorship of Bernardo Rucellai, early in the sixteenth century, the gardens became a place for the discussion of political and humanistic problems. These discussions were continued under Cosimo Rucellai to whom, among others, Machiavelli expounded the *Discourses.*

The particular kind of scholar-statesman or politician-humanist that frequented these meetings undoubtedly influenced Machiavelli in the development of the method we have come to see was his, the emphasis on experience as a guide to the solution of political problems and the study of Roman history in particular as the most extensive and useful record of past political experience.[30]

The flexibility—perhaps inconclusiveness—of this new political "history" developed in the garden meetings is demonstrated by the fact that, using the same methodology, Bernardo Rucellai came to favor an aristocratic government with an exclusive base of power while Machiavelli came to favor a democratic regime with an inclusive one. Each felt that his choice was best suited to solve the problem of stability and to help man control the inherent tendency of all things to decay. Lest we absorb Machiavelli too much into the traditional connotations of humanism it is necessary to make the observation that Machiavelli also belongs to what has been called the "Counter-Renaissance," the pessimistic current of Renaissance thought. Categories such as "humanism" or "Counter-Renaissance" are pretty slippery intellectual coin, but they will serve if we apply them to Machiavelli to mean that he shared an enthusiasm for antiquity and a belief in its contemporary utility with the humanists but tempered his enthusiasm with a pessimistic view of human nature.

Machiavelli on the Will

The darker, more profound, and perhaps more characteristic aspect of Machiavelli's thought grows out of his consideration of the nature of the human will. First and foremost, Machiavelli insists, that will is selfish and limitless and man is, above all possible definitions, the creature that cares only for himself. A man will reconcile himself sooner to the murderer of his own father than to the thief of his property, and gratitude is but the mask a man wears when he is still in hope of benefits to come. Men will break the bond of love, of obligation, at the first opportunity if it comes into conflict with their own self-interest.[31]

This black view of human nature, however, need not lead us to despair, for the selfishness and greed of men demands at least sufficient order and security so that they may enjoy the demands of their own selfishness. To the extent that he must have order a man must also demand it for others and, therefore, recognize some degree of coincidence between the general interest and his own. Nor does man's selfishness generally conduce to rebellion. On the contrary, as we know from the myth of the origin of the state, man finds it much more safe and comfortable to conform to the will of authority than to expose himself to the savage hardships of anarchic rebellion. Man is, in fact, not eager for change and, granted a sufficient indulgence of his selfishness, generally finds it easier and less dangerous to support the *status quo* than to change it very radically.

On the other hand few men can learn to disregard their personal interest and truly labor for the common good. As he tells us in the preface to the *Discourses* he is one of the few that can. What Machiavelli is in effect telling us is that because the infinite will of man is a selfish one it is therefore in contradiction with itself. This contradiction acts as a self-limiting element in the dynamics of the will. Because the infinite will is a selfish one it must curb its own infinite drive in order to gratify its own cupidity. Men can forgo their unlimited greedy aspirations in order to enjoy limited but actual gratifications. Machiavelli's belief in the genuine possibility of developing public spirit rests on this characteristic of the will.

The nature of man's will never changes. It is the constant which underlies all historical and political events, such as the cyclic changes of the forms of the state from monarchy to tyranny through transitional good and bad forms, aristocracy or oligarchy, "republicanism" or "democracy." All the large public monuments of history and politics may be seen as resulting from the achievement or disturbance of the uneasy equilibrium between infinite desire and actual gratification. The will is constantly the same, but conditions change and the nature of events is given by the interaction of the fixed nature of the will with changing circumstances. The contradictory nature of the will provides the possibility of political order but it also points to that quality in men and their institutions—the instruments of collective acts of self-interested will—which will destroy them. The universe after all offers only partial gratifications, finite goals, and therefore men are always unsatisfied. A society may be satisfied enough not to destroy itself for a time, but no society is ever completely satisfied with its equilibrium. Sooner or later, it seems, men will tire of their current indulgences and demand greater ones, they will forget the terrible conditions which led them to form the state, they will grow soft and "corrupt," they will indulge their selfishness too far and become decadent. In their decadence they become too pleasure-loving to meet the stern demands of war and the austerity which changing conditions may demand, or they become too rigid, too inflexible in meeting the demands of chance or fortune. Man's fundamentally changeless will must adapt itself to the continually altering circumstances of life but, all too often, it fails to do this. As Machiavelli in effect tells us in the famous chapter on fortune in *The Prince,* men can meet the caprices of fortune about half the time if they are flexible, but half the time they are not flexible enough. The central tragic contradiction of mankind is the possession of a more or less unalterable volitional nature in a world which demands constant flexibility.

Machiavelli's conception of the will thus accounts for the possibility of political stability and limits its duration; it accounts for the existence of the eternal political problem and points to a more or less temporary solution. The frequent complaints that Machiavelli has no theory of the state are all beside the point. He is serving notice to mankind that all political arrangements are provisional. Some are better than others, no doubt, but all are more or less inadequate. All are equally adequate to the extent that they secure life, property, honor, and rule by law. Political life is *essentially* conflict. A Utopia is not only not possible, it would not even contain life at all, because life itself is contradiction and conflict.

Machiavelli thus defines man as the desiring animal, the special quality of whose will leads to a fundamentally self-contradictory mode of existence, the self-contradictory mode of being manifests itself in the dialectical character of the relation between the infinity of his selfishness and its need for gratification, a relation which both creates and destroys political equilibrium. It further manifests itself in the irony that human desire may be so rapacious in its quest for gratification and security that it loses the very flexibility needed to manipulate reality. A final manifestation of this self-contradictory mode of being reveals itself in the fact that man simultaneously wills obedience and anarchy. Prompted by selfishness and actual gratification, he wills to obey; prompted by the infinity of his selfishness and blind greed for more possessions, he wills anarchy. As we shall see, a ruler exploits fraud, pious or impious, to capture obedience and force to curb anarchy.

This psychology of Machiavelli's is in the service of the clarification of the central problem of politics, that of the stability of the state. Throughout the *Discourses,* he refers again and again to the dependence of political stability on the creation of what we would call "public spirit." By this, Machiavelli means nothing more than the recognition on the part of a citizenry that the common welfare and their own selfish interests do in fact overlap sufficiently to justify the restraint and co-operation that society demands. Its growth, of course, depends on the existence of a government which secures life, honor, and property, and which administers the law impartially. This is what Machiavelli means by liberty, not a form of government, and its opposite is the arbitrary action of tyranny and that fearful egocentric state of society which he calls "corruption." Religion, especially a good civic religion like that of ancient Rome, fosters public spirit as does strong military force based on the service of the citizenry itself.

The highest form of public spirit, which includes patriotic sentiments such as those which carried Rome on its great career of conquest and glory depends, from the rational point of view, on "liberty" and the willing, grateful acceptance of restraint. Since relatively few men are as self-disciplined and rational as this, religion performs a great role in capturing willing obedience, thereby providing a ground for patriotic love of authority and a consequent readiness for self-sacrifice in the larger number of mankind. Religion helps the believer to reconcile himself to authority, to love what he would normally be tempted to rebel against, to accept present palpable restraints for intangible but psychologically significant rewards. Machiavelli's thought is often misrepresented as a simple analysis of force and fraud, but it is clear that his conception of the will introduces into his political cosmos all the perplexing problems of obedience and rebellion, the complex interrelations between the loves and hates of mankind under political and moral authority. How modulated and subtle his thought can be on such questions will be clear if we examine his views on religion.

Machiavelli on Religion

In chapter 11 of Book I of the *Discourses,* Machiavelli discusses the Roman religion. Numa, he tells us, found the Romans a very savage people and wished to reduce them to civil obedience. This he sought to do, not by the use of naked violence or coercion, but by the arts of peace. He therefore had recourse to religion, for he realized that it was the most necessary and reliable support of a civil society, and the religion he founded was of such a character that it facilitated the great Roman enterprises of conquest. By introducing discipline, religion served to create good armies, something difficult to do where religion does not exist. But Numa had to convince the Roman people of his authority to give them a religion and to assume this authority he had recourse to a fiction, what we would call a pious fraud. He pretended that he received it from a nymph. In this deception he was successful, and Numa was able to employ the new religion not only to create good armies but also to create good laws. This is an even more important achievement for a ruler than governing well in his own lifetime, for good laws perpetuate the safety of the state beyond the lifetime of any single ruler. Such good laws bring good fortune and good fortune results in happy success in all undertakings.

In this last remark we seem to catch Machiavelli in one of his more sanguine moments, for he virtually claims that good laws, a disciplined people, can reduce the element of chance in political action to the vanishing point. Let us remember, however, that the meaning of fortune varies for Machiavelli from context to context and that he is discussing an actual instance of what he considered such a reduction. As we know from other instances of the use of the term "fortune," especially in *The Prince,* chance will on the average allow us a fifty-fifty possibility of success.

Machiavelli then turns from Numa to Savonarola and, with a fine irony and some circumspection and indirection, indicates to the reader that his contemporaries have not outgrown this susceptibility to pious frauds.

And although untutored and ignorant men are more easily persuaded to adopt new laws or new opinions, yet that does not make it impossible to persuade civilized men who claim to be enlightened. The people of Florence are far from considering themselves ignorant and benighted, and yet Brother Girolamo Savonarola succeeded in persuading them that he held converse with God. I will not pretend to judge whether it was true or not, for we must speak with all respect of so great a man; but I may well say that an immense number believed it, without having seen any extraordinary manifestations that should have made them believe it; but it was the purity of his life, the doctrines he preached, and the subjects he selected for his discourses, that sufficed to make the people have faith in him. Let no one, then, fear not to be able to accomplish what others have done, for all men (as we have said in our Preface) are born and live and die in the same way, and therefore resemble each other.

We know from *The Prince* that Savonarola is a perfect example of the unarmed prophet who always fails. Whether his claims were fraudulent or not, he did not use the authority derived from supernatural claims to establish stable power through belief, and use that power to create a good army and good laws.

Was Savonarola one of those who, in a sense, was used by his religion through too much conviction instead of being able to use it? Was he one of those who destroyed the political efficacy he tried to exercise through his religion by not realizing the irreducible political claims of force and fraud? This possibility suggests itself when we turn to chapter 14 of Book I of the *Discourses*. There we learn that the Romans knew how to use their religion flexibly. They were able to interpret the auspices they took before any important action "by necessity," by the claims of the occasion itself, and did not rigidly follow the omens given in whether the sacred fowls ate or not. Nevertheless, they always at least pretended to observe the precepts of their religion even when necessity obliged them to disregard those precepts. Indeed, no careless disparagement of their religion went unpunished.

The Romans thus realized that religion has an important instrumental value as a system of fictions which can create and consolidate power through the belief of the ruled in the fictions offered to them by those who exercise power. While this is true of all religions, different religions vary in the degree of their political utility. In a famous chapter (Book II, chap. 12) of the *Discourses* Machiavelli draws a comparison between Christianity and paganism from the point of view of political and civic utility unfavorable to the former. Christianity teaches humility and submission, an otherworldly goal, and contempt for worldly ones; whereas paganism taught men to cultivate greatness of soul, the classical *magnanimitas,* and strength of body, values which served to make men formidable. The result of belief in Christianity has been to make men feeble, a prey to evil-minded men who can through its use more easily control the kind of people who believe they gain heaven by enduring injustices.

An interesting gloss on this comparison is provided in chapter 1 of Book III of the *Discourses* where Machiavelli discusses how it is necessary, in order to ensure a long existence to religious sects or republics, to bring them back to their original principles. His example of this return in the case of religion is provided by St. Francis and St. Dominic (Dante's two great *exempla* of reformers, by the way) who by their voluntary poverty and their example of following the life of Christ, revived the sentiment of religion in the hearts of men when it had almost been extinguished. At this point we might expect Machiavelli to conclude that the exalted morality of one or two men can regenerate the moral life of the state and so improve it. His conclusion, however, is quite different. The profound and honest goodness of these men gave them great influence over the people, to be sure. But this influence was used to persuade the people that it was evil even to speak ill of bad rulers, that it was right to render bad rulers obedience, leaving their punishment in the hands of God.

The result, according to Machiavelli, of the moral stature of these two great men is that evil rulers do as much wickedness as they please, especially since, unlike Francis and Dominic, they do not fear a supernatural kind of punishment, the kind which they cannot see and therefore do not believe in. Nevertheless, if the political effects of these two great saints were bad, their incorruptible goodness did in fact preserve the Christian religion into Machiavelli's own time.

With perfect consistency in his estimate of Christianity, Machiavelli shows how the moral goodness of its exemplary figures revived a corrupt religion, but he also shows how that some goodness had been in the service of subverting the civic values of magnanimity and strength. The humility of the saints had allowed the wicked to prosper.

Like our own near contemporary, George Santayana, Machiavelli felt that traditional Christianity was a religion of great disillusionments about this world and minute illusions about the other, and he was further aware of just what such a teaching might do to classic political values through the very austerity of its morality, in the form we have just described, when taken seriously. Among the many ironies of history those involved with moral reform are not the least paradoxical.

The general focus for these passing comments on religion and indeed for the whole of Machiavelli's thought can be found in chapter 5 of Book II of the *Discourses,* close to the center of the work as it is close to the center of his thought. There he maintains that changes of religion and language, together with the periodic occurrence of deluges and plagues destroy the record of things. Religions and linguistic changes are the work of men, while deluges and pestilences are the work of heaven by which, as we shall see, Machiavelli does not mean providence but the agencies of cyclical, natural change as manifested in the powers of the celestial bodies. Each new religion that men create attempts to destroy the records and symbols of the preceding one, just as the Christians tried to destroy every vestige of paganism. Machiavelli does not attribute the Christian failure to destroy entirely "the glorious deeds of the illustrious men of the ancient creed" to any change of heart on their part or to any kind of genuine respect for pagan achievement. In his eyes it was the unsought result of the fact that they were forced to keep up the Latin language as the instrument for formulating their own new laws. Indeed, he tells us, if we bear in mind their other persecutions, nothing would have been left of antiquity had the Christians been able to employ a different language for the formulation of their new creed.

Whoever reads the proceedings of St. Gregory, and of the other heads of the Christian religion, will see with what obstinacy they persecuted all ancient memorials, burning the works of the historians and poets, destroying the statues and images and despoiling everything else that gave but an indication of antiquity. So that, if they had added a new language to this persecution, everything related to previous events would in a very short time have been sunk in oblivion.

The destruction produced by heaven, which periodically reduces the inhabitants in some parts of the world to a very small number, is pestilence, famine, and flood. Famine and flood are the most important of the three, partly because they are most generally destructive and also because the few that escape their ravages are chiefly barbarous mountaineers, too ignorant to have knowledge to transmit or who, if they have it, pervert it in the process of transmitting it. This they do because such people can only use knowledge to gain influence and reputation, a use of knowledge characteristic of the semicivilized who are unable to distinguish between truthfulness and self-interest.

Machiavelli conceives of this periodic destruction as a natural process which corresponds in the cosmic or social order to the spontaneous and health-preserving purgation of the individual, or so-called "simple" body.

And so it is with that compound body, the human race; when countries become over-populated and there is no longer any room for all the inhabitants to live, nor any other place for them to go to, these being likewise all fully occupied,—and when human cunning and wickedness have gone as far as they can go,—then of necessity the world must relieve itself of this excess population by one of these three causes; so that mankind, having been chastised and reduced in numbers, may become better and live with more convenience.

Language and religion, that is the world of culture, are man-made. They come into being and pass away as men make and unmake them. Dante, we may recall, when he meets Adam in Paradise, learns that language is an ever changing creation. It is one measure of the distance we traverse between the two great Florentines that Machiavelli extends convention to include religion.

For Machiavelli, men act out the process of creating language and religion on the universal stage of nature, a nature which purges —by necessity—overpopulation and, be it noted, excessive cunning and wickedness. This it does through periodic catastrophes in which cycles of cultural change are counterpointed, so to speak, against cycles of natural change. At times these cycles, as it were, will coincide when the trough of one meets the trough of the other.

Some such pattern would seem to account for Machiavelli's claim that overpopulation and corruption of a moral sort are one and the same or, at least, prerequisites of one another. Nature or heaven—the celestial instruments of the natural process of generation and corruption—brings the human race and its cultural potential back to a new beginning in one and the same process. Nature's destructive processes are periodically the necessary prerequisite of new points of departure for mankind.

It is most important that we recognize the way in which Machiavelli both distinguished the biological from the cultural and related them. The race and its cultural artifacts, like the organism, like nature itself, of which they are all finally parts, are governed by the eternal cyclical rhythm of destruction-purgation on the one hand, generation-health on the other. That languages and religions are man-made and continually changing or decaying, being reborn and growing, means that there is no utopianism in Machiavelli, if that obvious truth really needs to be mentioned. It is clear that, for Machiavelli, culture is necessary if men are to survive in the world, but it is also clear that culture is inevitably the realm of the operation of force and fraud as well as the realm of freedom, glory, and reason. Man is a part of nature, a biological organism, but he is an organism whose health and vitality depend on culture with its illusions and opportunities as the necessary condition for his biological survival. But when men have become too numerous and culture has become so much the arena for cunning and wickedness that life becomes too corrupt and too uncomfortable, then nature itself in its catastrophic and destructive upheavals prepares the conditions simultaneously for a new biological and cultural beginning.

Machiavelli offers no eschatology which would permit us to transcend this eternal situation, nor does he try to celebrate it by elevating it into an exact, comprehensive, rigid system of thought. He rejects both of these tendencies and does so, I believe, because he would have thought them finally dishonest. Life, for him, is neither rational enough nor irrational enough for either possibility. The system of political and social appearances of any society is a form of fraud precisely to the extent that those appearances obscure the true nature of decision and status. The claims of the great human institutions are, in a sense, always partly true and partly false. The cause of freedom and reason is always embedded, so to speak, in the struggle for power within the state and also between states. Furthermore, power and forceful leadership are the indispensable prerequisites for freedom and the exercise of reason. This truth leads us to the paradox that, although reason and freedom are intrinsically realized by individuals and not by institutions, special collective structures of power are necessary for the exercise of freedom and reason. They therefore exist in a continual dialogue with force and fraud and this is the eternal condition of their existence.

The purpose of historical or philosophical studies for Machiavelli is not that we may learn about objects or facts. Rather, such studies should alter consciousness in such a way that we will be better able to cognize situations, should transform our attitude to experience so that we can grasp it as the scene of action. It is clear that effective action or the decision which leads to such action is never derivable from some universally valid abstract principle but by an original act, so to speak, grounded in the history and awareness of the agent of action. Moreover this agent acts in a temporal hell, a community in which none can do without the other and where each cannot really accept the other. It is a world in which men may make their plans but in which half the time, at least, something emerges which no one willed. It is a world in which new situations demand incessant adjustments of thought and perception and in which the process of interpretation as preparation for action can really reach no end. It is a world unified only partially, and usually by danger, a world in which leaders must be understood but can only be understood by all to the extent that they deal in some form of fraud, benign or not. His intellectual posture is his greatest achievement and a difficult one it is to maintain: incessant flexibility with incessant decisiveness, acute awareness with readiness for action, a cautious attitude with a readiness to take risks. This I think is his legacy as artist and statesman and this is the way in which, I believe, he would want posterity to follow him.

Machiavelli orients thought toward a world which is indefinite, various, a world which cannot be made completely or consistently luminous. There is no transcendence in reality, that is to say, reality is not hierarchical. If Machiavelli has any possibility for transcendence in his universe it is given in the work of reason as it continually penetrates reality and in the act of reason when it recognizes the fact that force and fraud, power and illusion, in one form or another, in one degree or another, will always be there. They are in fact the precondition for existence in the world of culture and they are precisely what calls forth the work of reason. To worship force and fraud is just as simple-minded as to abdicate from them altogether. A naïve trust in coercion, ideology, or trickery can be just as catastrophic and irresponsible as a naïve belief that conflict can be entirely avoided.

Freedom, reason, glory, law, ability, are embedded in force, fraud, desire, change, natural and cultural necessity. While these polarities may at times overcome one another we must also grasp the fact that they create each other. Life presents us with the opportunities for the realization of order and value, what Machiavelli calls "occasions," and we must learn to grasp them before they lapse back into the chaos from which they emerged.

The Character of Machiavelli's Nationalism

It is perhaps time to point out that Machiavelli's brilliant inquiries into history and political action, the profundity of his basic perspectives, the great courage and realism of his conclusions, are not unmixed with some remarkable errors.

First of all the method of historical analogy itself is risky. For example, Rome, which Machiavelli frequently compares with his time, was in many respects a misleading analogy for him to use. The peculiar combination of agrarian and military greatness in ancient Rome was hardly comparable to the commercially based power of the states of Renaissance Europe.

Also his disparagement of Italian mercenary armies and his attribution of the disasters of Italy primarily to them is by no means correct and derives from his tendency to overgeneralize and, sometimes, to oversimplify. There is no doubt that the economic growth of Florence had greatly separated civil and military life. Machiavelli mourned the loss of the old citizen soldiery. They had been the mainstay of Roman power during its most creative period, the republic, and the same institution, he thought, would have served Florence equally well. He did not grasp that the art of warfare had changed so much that no state of his time could have dispensed with mercenary soldiers. All needed to hire outside professionals if they were to have a balanced army and get the proper combination of the various arms, infantry, cavalry, and artillery needed to fight contemporary wars. Thus England hired its cavalry in Burgundy while the Germans and the Swiss provided Europe with infantry.

Certainly, the Italian wars were not as bloodless as Machiavelli implied, nor were the *condottieri,* the paid captains of hired troops, necessarily overcautious or treacherous. The *condottieri* bands frequently settled on their conquests, and thus they fought for more than a stipend, indeed for new homes. Their commanders were not always adventurers but were often related to the princely families which they served and whose dynastic interests were thus of intimate concern to them. Italian military difficulties came not from such causes but from divided commands, national disunity, and from too much reliance on political action.[32]

Nevertheless, although some of Machiavelli's methods and attitudes resulted in certain weakness of judgment, others permit us to understand political action with greater clarity. He is, for example, free of the confusions which romantic nationalism introduced into political thinking. He worked and thought before the nation state had come into being and before wars had become mass conflicts fought in the name of symbols and ideologies of romantic nationalism. His analysis, based on a situation when the old city-state was giving way to the modern nation state, has recovered a great deal of its original relevance in a time in which the traditional classic nation state is no longer a viable unit of political power.

We must not forget in regard to Machiavelli's freedom from nationalistic bias that his great exhortation to free Italy from the barbarian has nothing to do with a nationalistic mystique but is simply the recognition on the part of a passionate Florentine of the need for a large unit of power on the Italian peninsula in order to preserve the freedom of its peoples. These Italian peoples indeed share a common cultural tradition in their Roman past which the course of history has turned into an Italian present. They are not, however, in any sense a "folk," and Machiavelli is never very precise about just how many of the various peoples of the peninsula or adjacent islands would constitute this larger unit of power.

For Machiavelli the nation is not the instrument of progress, much less a divine instrument, for he did not believe in progress at all. It is a mechanism for achieving security, a quantity of power which unified, or reunified, a group of people who ought to be one. The Italians were simply the descendants of the Romans, whether or not the ancient *virtù* was latent in them, and they ought for their own well-being to be together. Indeed, whenever Machiavelli wants to express something close to what we might mean by "nation" he uses the word *provincia*.[33]

The true *patria,* "fatherland," or *nazione,* "place of birth," is the city-state such as Florence, and most of the deepest patriotic sentiment of the time was directed to this political unit, a phenomenon still persistent in modern Italy with its strong regional loyalties. Yet Machiavelli grasped that the city-state was doomed to instability in his changing world and that the strong regional loyalties were as destructive to peace and order as the ultranationalism of the modern nation state has been.

Yet Machiavelli had no illusions concerning the then emerging nation state, for the state, large or small, is by nature an expansive, aggressive, and energetically active organization. He never lost sight of the fact that Rome itself had grown by absorbing smaller nation states as well as city-states. Whatever the state may be for him, it is certainly not necessarily benevolent or a custodian of popular rights. The same rules of power apply, in his view, to its external as well as its internal operations so that he never conceived of an internally ethical state which operates by an entirely different and amoral set of rules externally. The inner logic of power politics—and it is in the essence a logic of unlimited power—operates in all the activities of the ruler.

Part of the difficulty in assessing the exact nature of Machiavelli's nationalism lies in the fact that he frequently uses the same word to express different ideas, or expresses the same idea with different words. In addition, changes were taking place in the very meanings of the words he used. This is particularly true of the word *stato,* or state. *Status, lo stato, l'état*—none of these words meant the modern state prior to the seventeenth century. Nor does Machiavelli generally use *stato* to mean the fundamental condition of the realm, the rights and duties of the ruler or his prerogative, both legitimate medieval uses of the term. Rather, he uses it in a restricted political sense to refer to that which the ruler acquires, holds, maintains, loses, or has taken from him, and the term is frequently used with these verbs (i.e., *acquistare, tenere, mantenere, togliere, perdere*). He is no more consistent with this term in its denotations than he is with *fortuna* or *virtù,* but its fundamental connotation is that of *imperium,* command over men. That is why there can be degrees of it, and one can have too little or enough.

Stato is thus not the *patria* or *nazione* or *città,* not the fatherland or the body politic. For the body politic Machiavelli uses terms such as *il vivere libero, il vivere civile* or *il vivere politico.* Thus his statecraft does not involve a theory of right such as "reason of state," for there is, as we have seen, no mystique of the state which rationalizes placing it beyond ethical judgments, no sense of an overriding obligation to the future which positively enjoins on the ruler repugnant actions, no sense of the body politic as transcending its constituent members, and no well-developed theory of the common good.[34]

Power and Legitimacy: Ethics and Politics

For Machiavelli, the state is essentially effective control over men and thereby the instrument of acts of power. These may be ordering or exploitative, politically creative or destructive, but their existence testifies to the existence of the state itself. The charges of immorality leveled against *The Prince* finally derive from the fact that there Machiavelli's focus is on the substratum of power any state needs in order to exist. He thus largely prescinds from questions concerning the common welfare, and even where he refers to such values he does not justify the behavior of a ruler on that ground but on the ground of pure self-interest.

He does not identify the nation as a group of people autonomously organized in a specified territory with the state as the authoritative structure over them which monopolizes the legitimate use of force. He is free of the confusions concerning the legitimate use of force because he does not identify the state with a particular government or with the bearers of a particular cultural tradition. He faces the problem of the legitimation of power in its starkest terms. Force is legitimate when the people consent to the state's monopoly of it for reasons which to them seem good ones, whether out of religious piety, respect for law, reverence for tradition or some combination of these. But force may also be legitimate when the alternative is wholesale slavery, destruction, or chaos, any one or any combination of these.

Such claims concerning force must be taken seriously not because they may justify ruthlessly effective ways of guiding political conduct but because it is precisely the state that claims a monopoly of the legitimate use of force over the community and territory which comprises it. Whatever right men may assume they have to use violence either on their co-nationals or on foreign countries in war, they derive from the state, and even internal politics is concerned with the sharing or distribution of the legitimate right to use force. The very skeleton of the state is force, and Machiavelli is inordinately aware of it for very good reasons. Most important perhaps is that almost none of the major Italian states of his time— with the possible exception of the Papacy—possessed any of the usual means through which the rulers could legitimate their rule. They were new men, like the Medici or the Sforza, without long tradition, who ruled populaces which did not have the habit of conforming. No ruler in Italy had the kind of charismatic domination exercised by prophets and demagogues, nor could anyone claim the kind of absolute devotion derived from personal confidence in the leader's ability, his possession of a revelation, or his heroism. Nor, finally, was the principle of legality always operative, since the new rulers were often dictators who had usurped the old democratic communes or traditional monarchies after the latter had torn themselves apart through class warfare.

As we have seen Italy furnished examples of states which lacked all of the customary modes of the legitimation of power. The enormous building programs of Renaissance despots and their handsome subsidies to artists and scholars can be seen as an attempt to achieve the external appurtenances of grandeur which history had not bequeathed them, and to create new symbols for the old ones, no longer operative but which had served in the past to legitimate enforced obedience.[35]

Like artists, the new princes were often men of talent, not of birth, and they strongly identified themselves with men of artistic ability, so much so that Burckhardt was virtually forced by the evidence to evolve his brilliant concept of the Renaissance artist-prince who considers the state as a work of art, molding and shaping the inchoate mass of people under his rule into citizens.

Machiavelli was thus able to observe states in, so to speak, their elementary conditions, those conditions in which all the elements entering into political action were simplified and reduced to the absolute essentials—power and the dynamics of power. He simply could not avoid the question of whether or not the traditional ethic —or indeed, any ethic—could establish principles of similar content for erotic, familial, commercial, military, and political relations.

He was compelled to recognize that the absolute ethic could be disastrous in politics. The statesman must know how to resist evil by force, must operate in terms of an ethic of responsibility for the actual consequences of his actions. I don't think, in spite of Machiavelli's bitter irony, that he ever advocated raw opportunism and he certainly did not maintain that an ethic of ultimate ends is *identical* with complete irresponsibility. In his own life and aspirations the two supplement each other, for he sought peace and order for Italy, the ultimate end of all his effort. He simply felt that the statesman is responsible for the disasters that befall his country and its allies no matter how pure his intentions may have been. He must take account of the average morality of the people whom he governs and with whom he deals, and must never presuppose any too sanguine idea of their goodness. He must not dodge the fact that he may be compelled, as ruler, to commit acts which would be culpable in a private person. He must operate in terms of the principle that good may come from evil or evil may come from good.

It would probably be an error to refer to Machiavelli's answer to this whole question of the relation between politics and ethics as an absolute separation of the two. Even where Machiavelli appears to advocate the most unethical courses of action he is guided, implicitly or explicitly, by the welfare or the interest of the individuals in the political community. What is good is what promotes that welfare and what is bad is what destroys the welfare of the whole. Those general principles of conduct which govern the relations between the individuals in a community cannot be applied without great difficulty to politics, simply because the ruler must act for all while the individual is more or less free to pursue his own self-interest. If homicide or deception on the part of a ruler can promote the welfare of the collective then it can be called good even though they are injurious of the common good when practiced by private individuals. The important point to grasp here is that the same criterion of good or evil will lead to a different judgment of the same act depending on whether it is in the private or the political sphere. It is not the intention which validates an act but its result. Sentiments, intuitions concerning right and wrong, appeals to an objective absolute moral order—all these are irrelevant.

Machiavelli's view of war must be taken with reference to his thinking on the question of political ethics. Certainly, he was convinced that wars may act as regenerators of the state insofar as they unify it and dispose the people to obedience to the ruler, the fundamental precondition for political order. If war is necessary to make the state cohere then like all measures which contribute to the common welfare, war is good. This is certainly the case when the alternative to order—any viable order—would be chaos. There is however no trace in Machiavelli's thought of the romantic glorification of war. It has a strictly political function and even when Machiavelli thought of war as the health of the state and condemned the Latin races for being overcivilized he simply meant that any nation must be ready to wage war to protect its own liberty.[36] Both militarism and pacifism would be pathological extremes, both would be unrealistic alternatives and negate the prudential considerations indispensable to successful political action. In a sense, neither the conscience-burdened nor the conscienceless belong in politics. Political authority reaches its greatest crisis at the point where it may fail to create, or maintain, the individual's necessity for order, and it may fail in this essential task precisely on the grounds of the exercise of too little or too much conscience. There is a moral pathology of goodness as well as evil, and one can be as perilous as the other.

It is perhaps the greatest strength of Machiavelli that, while he is acutely aware of the limitations of an ethic of good intention or of absolute ends, he is also aware of the limitations of an ethic of results or responsibility. The ethic of result has its own dilemma in that it introduces the dimension of time into the act of ethical judgment so that judgment becomes ambiguous simply because we cannot always determine the farther consequences of any particular result. Which of the many results, predictable or unforeseen of any action of Alexander Borgia, for example, should be the criterion for judging it? Machiavelli symbolizes this whole area of ambiguity concerning the results of action in that aspect of *fortuna* which defeats or ironically alters the desired results of action. In effect he tells us that we must have our good intentions but that we must understand that they cannot be always agreeably or painlessly implemented and that, even if we appear to have succeeded, the further consequences of apparent success may be failure.

If Machiavelli is not a political scientist, or a heroic patriot and prophet of the *Risorgimento,* he has his own kind of greatness. In the first place he is a great writer, a matchless ironist, and a master of narrative. The more one reads him the more one is inclined to agree with Foscolo that Machiavelli's is the finest Italian prose. At his best, he writes the flexible, direct language of the so-called vernacular humanists such as Leonardo, close to the rhythms of Tuscan speech and of immediate thought, free from the misunderstood classicism which was to dominate so many writers of the Italian cinquecento and leave the writing of some of the most significant literature to amateurs like Michelangelo or Cellini. The virtual incorruptibility of true genius aside, we might say that Machiavelli was free to be bold in his thinking because he escaped the growing Ciceronianism of the scholarly academies.

Yet he is also of great intellectual interest to us now because his work, especially *The Prince,* is still a powerful statement of the problem of the relationship of conscious intention of the agent of action to the actual effects achieved in society. On the level of personal interaction this problem is at the heart of literature, and one of the central concerns of both the tragic and the comic vision of life. Machiavelli applied this great literary vision to society and, like the artist he was, did not merely study the intention by itself or the result by itself, but focused his awareness on the complex relations between them.

Machiavelli's universe, like that of Montaigne, Shakespeare, and Cervantes, is open at the farther end. It is finally beyond ideology, political or otherwise. Questions are brilliantly illuminated from various points of view and the differing conclusions afforded by various perspectives may all be validated and, as it were, left in suspension. Experience transcends system, and it is for this reason that Machiavelli can maintain that there is something bad about so-called good intentions which produce catastrophes, and that the agent of such results is responsible for them no matter what his intention may have been. Men, especially statesmen, must learn some bitter lessons. Even the best of intentions, and even when coupled with accurate insights into how to bring about a good result, cannot always be effectively realized entirely through the agency of apparently good actions. What appears to be a good means and what, indeed, may be good in itself is frequently so interwoven with other elements that the total result which would flow from using it may not be desirable. The ultimate context in which the affairs of men take place is one with disproportions and incommensurabilities between guilt and retribution, intention and result, known causes and perceived results. Where Machiavelli is truly original is not in his awareness of the difficulty at times in knowing what is a good or a bad thing to do, but in the fact that his whole analysis of politics and history is made from a new perspective, that of the ethical irrationality of human experience taken as a whole. Unlike any of his predecessors, he works from the conviction that no set of moral principles of identical content can govern all areas of life, public, private, professional, and personal. In addition he fully grasped the fact that force is not simply a means that the state uses but is a means specific to the state, a part of its very nature.

Why does Machiavelli emphasize this aspect of politics so? There is more to it than force, essential as that may be. We have suggested some answers, but the final answer, I think, lies in the conditions of Italy in his time, in the ruthless and suspicious character of the diplomacy of his era, riddled with treason and betrayal, in which money and threats seemed the only effective instruments. Hence his despair, his irony, and his bitter injunction to be either wholly good or wholly evil.

Machiavelli's final vision is the tragic one, for he places us in a paradoxical realm where chance and ability meet and overlap, where culpability and self-awareness are in an obscure relationship to one another, a world whose "justice" is not our justice. It is a world in which men must frequently choose between bad alternatives and where even the best choices entail losses. Only in an imaginary world of perfect knaves and fools, such as we find in his *Mandragola,* can everyone come off happily, and then only to the extent that the fools are delusively pleased by the success of the knaves.

The first scene of this great comedy finds Callimaco hopelessly in love with Lucrezia, the beautiful young wife of the aged Messer

Nicia, a foolish, pompous know-it-all. Callimaco opens the play with an analysis of his erotic situation which sounds like the syllogistic and disjunctive analyses of *The Prince*. Succinctly and powerfully he sets forth his attitudes and his possible courses of action. Hopeful, although not sanguine, about his chances of success, he realizes that his best course of action lies in exploiting the foolishness of Messer Nicia, foolishness reinforced by Nicia's inordinate desire for a child. In addition he plans to exploit the corrupt character of Nicia's mother-in-law, Sostrata. Later in the play, with the aid of his parasite, Ligurio, Callimaco is also able to use the avarice of Fra Timoteo, a corrupt monk, to his advantage. By deftly playing on the corrupt and restless desires of assorted knaves and fools, Callimaco succeeds in corrupting Lucrezia, who, to her own surprise, discovers that corruption is delightful. This play could, of course, have been a tragedy, but the exact mixture and relation of gullibility and knavery leads to the felicity of all.

Indeed, the laws that govern the world of this great comedy are the same as those that govern the tragic universe of actuality. *Mandragola* is the model of what a perfect diplomatic solution would be, a solution which would be painfully realistic, yet one in which all sides would get what they want. Since this is impossible in the great political world, a world little tolerant of the deluded, the model must have a different setting. In the microcosm of that play, and in terms of a successful erotic chase, all appearances and realities, intentions and results, are harmonized, all losses and gains canceled, not in reality, but through the power of illusion and deception, the power of seeming rather than of being.

Machiavelli's famous maxim that it is sometimes really better to seem good than to be good has struck some observers as the most cynical of his principles. Perhaps it is, but it is also true that the life of effective action is never merely the immediate expression of a mysterious inner essence but the adoption of means, consciously or unconsciously, for the achievement of particular intentions, and this must be so precisely because the distance between an intention and result may be great and filled with antinomies. Life goes on not only in a system of cause and effect but in a system of action and counteraction simply because the object of personal and political action is not passive but reactive.

Whether in the imaginary world of comedy or the tragic world of political action, the felicitous solution may rest more on appearances than on realities. In the last analysis Machiavelli gives to appearances, conventions, fictions, and manners their proper status as necessary realities. Action demands that we be oblique as well as direct, and right action demands a high degree of awareness of both kinds of discourse. But what is the right course of action in any specific context depends on concrete particulars and they cannot be known before they appear. The agent of action must know very well what seems and what really is if he is to grasp the true particular features of a situation as it emerges from the unknown. Only then, if necessity demands deception, can he hope to make it right.

Perhaps Machiavelli's greatest gift is his ability to clarify the nature of the scene of political action without simplifying it. As against what Burckhardt would have called the "terrible simplifiers," Machiavelli is aware of the complexity of that scene. Moreover, his sense of complexity does not derive from any inadequacy of thought, nor does it paralyze action. Certainly, given enough time, men can identify causes and predict effects. But the scene of action does not always afford enough time for that, and men must therefore act in partial ignorance, an ignorance which can be reduced but never eliminated, and which must be accepted if men are to act at all. The agent of action has already reduced the risks of action when he grasps that he is one among many more or less cloudy centers of consciousness acting in finite intervals of time on concrete situations. He further reduces those risks when, paradoxically, he is prepared to take them armed with a full awareness of "the effective reality of things."

If Machiavelli is acutely aware of the ambiguities of action, he is surely equally aware of the necessity of intelligent planning for action. If he is acutely aware of the fact that a grim necessity can drive men to immoral action, he is also aware that an equally grim necessity can save men from taking action which would have catastrophic consequences. Unlike the "terrible simplifiers," he does not substitute abstract attitudinizing for concrete thought, nor does he confuse taking risks with being rash. He not only knows what can be gained through bold action but also, and equally important, what can be lost.

Notes

*

1 The dating and order of composition of Machiavelli's major works presents some problems. For a review of the question see Federico Chabod, *Machiavelli and the Renaissance,* trans. David Moore (London, 1958), 30 ff. This collection of Chabod's most important studies contains a very useful bibliography. It is probable that *The Prince* was composed in installments as Meinecke thought. See the section on Machiavelli in his *Die Idee der Staatsaison in der neuren Geschichte* (3rd ed., München, 1929) and the introduction to his edition of *The Prince, Der Fuerst,* in *Klassiker der Politick,* VIII (Berlin, 1923). See also the important article of Felix Gilbert, "The Humanist Concept of the Prince and *The Prince* of Machiavelli," *Journal of Modern History,* XI (1939), 481 ff. For a more ample and more thoroughy documented presentation of my own interpretation of Machiavelli I refer the reader to the appropriate chapters of my book, *Renaissance and Seventeenth Century Studies* (London and New York, 1964). All references to the works of Machiavelli are to the edition of Mario Casella and Guido Mazzoni, *Tutte le opere storiche e letterarie di Niccolò Machiavelli* (Florence, 1929).

2 Three different Elizabethan translations in manuscript have come to light, one of which has been published in our time by Hardin Craig (ed.), *Machiavelli's The Prince: An Elizabethan Translation* (Chapel Hill, N.C., 1944). For a delightful survey of English interest in the history and art of Renaissance Italy with numerous indications of the influence of "politick authors" such as Machiavelli and Guicciardini see J. R. Hale, *England and the Italian Renaissance: The Growth of Interest in Its History and Art* (London and New York, 1954), especially chaps. 1 and 2.

3 See Ernst Cassirer's penetrating chapters on Machiavelli in his *The Myth of the State* (New York, 1955). For a study of the medieval concept of hierarchy see the first chapter of my *Medieval Cultural Tradition in Dante's Comedy* (Ithaca, N.Y., 1960).

4 Felix Gilbert, "Bernardo Rucellai and the Orti Oricellari: A Study on the Origin of Modern Political Thought," *Journal of the Warburg and Courtauld Institutes,* XII (1949), 101-131, 103; Ernst Cassirer, *Individuum*

and Kosmos in der Renaissance (Leipzig, 1927), pp. 77-129, for the history of the concept; Giovanni Gentile, *Il pensiero italiano del Rinascimento* (3rd ed., Florence, 1940), chap. 3, "Il concetto dell'uomo nel Rinascimento," pp. 47-114.

5 It might here be well to consider briefly some of the peripheral meanings of *fortuna* and *virtù*. In the Livian connotation *virtù* is the opposite of barbaric *furor*, the savagery of the semicivilized which can hardly be called courage or ability but which is rather like animal instinct. Such *virtù* is the possession of peoples as well as individuals, although primarily of the latter. Machiavelli, however, sometimes uses the term *virtù* in quite its conventional ethical sense, meaning a good disposition toward correct ethical behavior, or a good moral quality in a person.

6 T. S. Eliot, "Niccolo Machiavelli," in *For Lancelot Andrewes* (New York, 1929).

7 C. E. Detmold's translation is the one cited for all quotations from the *Discourses* (New York, 1940). The most elaborate edition of the *Discourses* in a fresh translation and with an indispensable apparatus of notes and tables is that of L. J. Walker (2 vols., London, 1950).

8 Cf. Cicero, *De officiis*, I, 9, 34.

9 Francesco Guicciardini, *Considerazioni sopra i Discorsi del Machiavelli*, Book III, chap. 40, in *Scritti politici e Ricordi*, ed. R. Palmarocchi (Bari, 1933).

10 L. A. Burd, "Florence (II): Machiavelli," *The Cambridge Modern History*, Vol. I, *The Renaissance*, pp. 190-218, especially 213-214.

11 *The Prince*, chap. 18; *Discourses*, I, 3.

12 *Discourses*, I, 45, for *mano regia*. The word *necessità* occurs 76 times in *The Prince* and its derivatives would increase the number substantially. See J. H. Whitfield, *Machiavelli* (London, 1947), pp. 67-68.

13 Cf. *The Prince*, chap. 9, and *Discourses*, I, 10.

14 Whitfield, p. 76, and F. Colotti, *Machiavelli-Lo Stato* (Messina, 1939), p. 25.

15 Cf. *Discourses*, I, 48; Whitfield, pp. 144, 157.

16 See *The Prince*, chap. 6, and *Discourses*, III, 5, on imitation. Cf. also Herbert Butterfield, *The Statecraft of Machiavelli* (London, 1940), pp. 28 ff., and Leonardo Olschki, *Machiavelli the Scientist* (Berkeley, 1945), pp. 43-44.

17 *Discourses*, I, 58, 44; Burd, pp. 203-205; Cassirer, *The Myth of the State*, 183.

18 *Discourses*, Introduction to II; cf. Burd, p. 204.

19 Kurt Von Fritz, *The Theory of the Mixed Constitution in Antiquity: A Critical Analysis of Polybius' Political Ideas* (New York, 1954), Appendix II, "Polybius' Concept of Tyche and the Problem of the Development of His Thought," pp. 388-397, especially 389-390. Machiavelli also followed Polybius in his utilitarian view of religion as an instrument for obtaining political order and, more important, he adopted Polybius' theory of the mixed constitution as the most stable form of govern-

ment. Aristotle has described the stable constitution as a mixture of oligarchy or aristocracy with democracy, all under legal definition. For Polybius the mixed constitution was made up of monarchy, aristocracy, and democracy as these were represented in the Consuls, Senate, and people of the Roman constitution. In fact, Aristotle's mixed constitution is not really such at all but the description of a state with mixed principles. Polybius advanced a theory of checks and balances in which all units needed to co-operate to govern and according to which any unit may obstruct the rest. See Von Fritz, pp. 76-95, 396; and C. H. McIlwain, *The Growth of Political Thought in the West* (New York, 1932), pp. 100-101. On the problem of how Machiavelli may have come to know Polybius' doctrine of the mixed constitution, when that part of the latter's work was unknown to him, see J. H. Hexter, "Seyssel, Machiavelli and Polybius VI: The Mystery of the Missing Translation," *Studies in the Renaissance,* III (1956), 75-96.

20 *Discourses,* I, 2.

21 J. W. Allen, *A History of Political Thought in the Sixteenth Century,* ed. with revised bibliography (London, 1957), p. 452. "Machiavelli's realistic mode of thought was only an extreme illustration of a tendency visible in Italian thought since the days of the last Hohenstaufen Emperor."

22 *Discourses,* II, 2.

23 Felix Gilbert, "The Humanist Concept of the Prince," pp. 449-483, especially 459, 462-464.

24 *Ibid.,* 464-471.

25 *Discourses,* X, 39; III, 43; Butterfield, p. 39; Cassirer, pp. 155-157; Felix Gilbert, "Machiavelli and Guicciardini," *Journal of the Warburg Institute,* II (1938), 263-266.

26 On this question of humanist historiography see B. L. Ullman, "Leonardo Bruni and Humanistic Historiography," in *Studies in the Italian Renaissance* (Rome, 1955), pp. 321-344; T. E. Mommsen, "Petrarch's Conception of the 'Dark Ages,'" *Speculum,* XVII (1942), 226-242; Claudio Varese, "Aspetti e limiti quattrocenteschi della 'fiorentina' libertas,'" *La rassegna della letteratura italiana,* Anno 64-Serie VII (1960), 196-206; Hans Baron, "Secularization of Wisdom and Political Humanism in the Renaissance," *Journal of the History of Ideas,* XXI (1960), 131-150; Hans Baron, "The *Querelle* of the Ancients and Moderns as a Problem for Renaissance Scholarship," *Journal of the History of Ideas,* XX (1959), 3-22; Hans Baron, *The Crisis of the Early Italian Renaissance* (Princeton, 1955), especially pp. 300-312, 422-429.

27 *Discourses,* Introduction, and III, 5; *The Prince,* chap. 6.

28 *The Prince,* chaps. 9, 20; *Discourses,* I, 18.

29 *Discourses,* I, 55.

30 Felix Gilbert, "Bernardo Rucellai and the Orti Oricellari: A Study on the Origin of Modern Political Thought," *Journal of the Warburg and Courtauld Institutes,* XII (1949), 101-131. Bernardo Rucellai introduced the term "balance of power" to the political vocabulary in his history of

the French invasion of Italy led by Charles VIII, *De bello Italico.* See E. W. Nelson, "The Origins of Modern Balance-of-Power Politics," *Medievalia et Humanistica,* I (1943), 129.

31 *The Prince,* chap. 17.

32 *The New Cambridge Modern History,* Vol. I, *The Renaissance,* pp. 273, 277-280, 285. Machiavelli had also overestimated the invulnerability of the Swiss when he claimed that they could not be defeated by the French. The battle of Marignano proved him wrong (*ibid.,* p. 364). Cf. Chabod, pp. 85 ff.

33 Felix Gilbert, "The Concept of Nationalism in Machiavelli's *Prince,*" *Studies in the Renaissance,* I (1954), 38-48; Machiavelli, *The Prince,* trans. Luigi Ricci, rev. E. R. P. Vincent with an introduction by Christian Gauss (New York, 1952), pp. 19, 25, 28. Whitfield, p. 65. On these terms see especially Vincent Ilardi, " 'Italianita among Some Italian Intellectuals in the Early Sixteenth Century," *Traditio,* XII (1956), 339-367, especially pp. 343, 357-369.

34 For Machiavelli on the state see the acute analysis by J. H. Hexter, *"Il Principe* and *lo stato," Studies in the Renaissance,* IV (1957), 113-138.

35 See Max Weber's classic essay, "Politics as a Vocation," in *From Max Weber: Essays in Sociology,* ed. with an introduction by H. H. Gerth and C. Wright Mills (New York, 1946), pp. 77-128, especially p. 78.

36 On war in the Renaissance with particular reference to Machiavelli's view of it see the excellent remarks of J. R. Hale, "War and Public Opinion in Renaissance Italy," in *Italian Renaissance Studies,* ed. E. F. Jacob (London, 1960), pp. 94-122, especially pp. 116 ff.

III

CASTIGLIONE'S *COURTIER:*

The Self as a Work of Art

It is said that Charles V kept three books by his bedside: Machiavelli's *Prince,* Castiglione's *Courtier,* and the Bible. Whether
Charles ever saw any difficulty in relating these three disparate uni-
verses is unknown, but the pomp and splendor of his court, the
realism of his politics and his final retirement to a monastery,
whatever disappointments drove him there, would seem to indicate
that he did not. Like other great figures of the Renaissance he was
quite able to be a Machiavellian Centaur, the man of power who
lives in divided and distinguished worlds of humanity and animality, and who, indeed, must live there if he is to retain both his
power and his humanity. He has Machiavelli for his guide when he
must employ force or fraud, the arts of the lion and the fox, Castiglione when he moves in the social world, the world of "small morals" or manners, and the Bible for the times when even Caesar
becomes burdened by those things which are his.

I need hardly mention how much commentary and scholarship
surrounds the Bible, and Machiavelli has attracted, I suppose, as
much scholarly and critical attention as any secular author of
equivalent stature. It is a little surprising to discover that Castiglione (1478-1529) has been relatively neglected. Most of the literature about him is of a philological or biographical character.
Works of interpretation are few but surprisingly diverse for what
appears to be a relatively simple text even if one of the most widely
read books in the history of our culture.

The enormous popularity of the *Courtier* began to wane at the
end of the nineteenth century. Leonard E. Opdyke who published

his translation in 1901 listed the following editions and translations of the *Courtier* up to that year: 78 editions of the Italian text, 18 Spanish editions, 16 French, 17 Latin, 11 English, and 3 German. The relative scarcity of German editions would doubtless have drawn some amusing comment from that great German Italiano-phile, Friedrich Nietzsche! The greatest number of these editions and translations appeared in the sixteenth century, following the first publication of the *Courtier* in 1528, and everywhere Casti-glione's book evoked unreserved admiration. Even such a savage critic of court life as Tasso praised Castiglione in *Il Mapiglio ov-vero della Corte*. The only dissenting voice to this chorus of praise came in 1583 when the *Courtier* was expurgated in the interest of Tridentine orthodoxy by Giacomo Ciccarelli. It must be said that the ecclesiastical revisions were in relatively good taste and simply involved the elimination of references to *fortuna* on the grounds that it was a pagan concept, and the excision of some of the jokes told at the expense of ecclesiastical figures.

Castiglione also enjoyed a great reputation as a poet in his own time. Scaliger ranked his Latin elegies above those of Propertius, and Gravina gave him a place among Latin poets next to that of Catullus. While the contemporary reader would not give his poetry quite this high a rank, there is no doubt that his Latin verse is one of the finer achievements of neo-Latin poetry, comparable in qual-ity to the best of Poliziano or Milton. His Italian style was equally admired, so much so that the Accademia della Crusca adopted the *Courtier* as one of the approved models of Italianity in spite of Castiglione's attack on classical Tuscan as the only true standard for the Italian language. Neither the Accademia nor Castiglione took this attack too seriously, for we know that Castiglione submitted his manuscript to Cardinal Bembo, the great Tuscanizer and authority on the language, for corrections. These were, how-ever, entirely of a linguistic character, and the style and structure of the book remained Castiglione's own. If this procedure seems odd and inconsistent, we must recall that Italy had no political instru-ment for standardizing the language, and the *problema della lingua* has pursued Italian writers down to our own time. Historically, Italian standards of correctness have been based on an ever ex-panding canon of classics, and the *Courtier*'s literary distinction forced its acceptance in spite of its violations of those rules of lin-guistic correctness based on the writings of Dante, Petrarch, and Boccaccio as classical standards.

It was largely in Italy and in his own times that Castiglione en-joyed the reputation of a major writer, in the narrower sense of that word, that is, as a master of the language and a revealer of its resources. His great influence outside his own country and in sub-sequent generations, both in and out of Italy, was cultural. In the past, and even now, the most widespread reading of Castiglione's work was as a normative book on education. This is certainly the view that all of his English scholars and critics have taken, from Hoby, to Dr. Johnson, who called it "the best book ever written on good breeding," to Sir Walter Raleigh in more recent times. For most of its readers, the *Courtier* has been a breviary of *savoir-faire* or *savoir-vivre,* a code of good society, a book concerned with manners in the most exalted sense of that word, with manners as "minor morals" dealing with that range of conduct which must be both ethical and beautiful at the same time, the kind of behavior which eases and graces the conduct of life. Another way of stating this interpretation of the *Courtier* is to say that, while it is in part a continuation and adaptation of the best elements of the chivalric tradition, it incorporates the revived ideals of ancient Greek *kalo-kagathia,* the conception of the gentleman as both an ethical agent and an artistically structured self, the man in whose actions there is no separation of what is good from what is beautiful.

Another reading of the *Courtier,* which overlaps this one, is as a "moral" work, in the French sense of the word: a work concerned with *mores,* with the customs and habits of man. On the whole, and with significant exceptions including Vittorio Cian, the leading Ca-stiglione scholar of recent times, this is an Italian view of the book, and Italians like Leopardi have read Castiglione in much the same way some Frenchmen have read Montaigne: for his reflections and maxims, for his observations on the various manifestations of the individual's character in society, and for suggestions as to the proper way of manipulating the self in society.

These two have been what we might call the "serious" readings of the *Courtier,* the way people read the book when it was felt to be of vital social, intellectual, or moral use, and both of them more or less correspond with Castiglione's intention *di formar con parole un perfetto Cortegiano.* It is only in relatively modern times, when both the world and ideals of Castiglione have come to seem distant, that the utility of the work has been largely reduced to that of a faithful portrait of the conversations and diversions of the Court of Urbino, to a valuable but remote historical document.

Given the expressed political intention of Castiglione—the task of the perfect courtier is in the last analysis that of giving political advice to his ruler—some readers have pointed to the fact that Castiglione is remarkably unrealistic or unconcerned about the way affairs of state are actually conducted. After all, he lived in the same chaotic Italy that Machiavelli inhabited and he too was a diplomat with ample opportunity to see the same truths. This sort of objection can really have no force once we understand that Castiglione's task is that of delineating a *perfect* Courtier, an ideal type, and not that of drafting a program of action to be implemented at every point. His book is a kind of Utopia, or better, an Arcadia, for it begins with a lament for the deaths of so many of the beautiful and charming people who graced the court of Urbino and created that perfect moment, now gone forever, of which the *Courtier* is an imaginative representation. Whether the events and people of the book ever existed as Castiglione gives them to us is less important than it is for us to understand that they were able to inspire a nostalgic vision of a perfect small society vitally concerned with perfection of the self.

The intention of delineating the perfect courtier links Castiglione to one of the important cultural impulses of his time. The Renaissance abounds with books on ideal commonwealths and ideal modes of personal, social, and professional existence. Books like More's *Utopia,* Alberti's *Della Famiglia,* Palmieri's *Della vita civile,* and Pontano's *De principe* are some among many of the books delineating one ideal or another of perfection. And human perfection, if I understand Castiglione's book correctly, is realizable in the life of the courtier and is the result of the harmonious relation of normally opposed impulses, the binding in a balanced unity of what, in a state of nature, are warring tendencies within the person. In other words, perfection lies in the development and mastery of the major capacities of human nature, a mastery which can only be achieved by the discipline, not by the suppression, of any important human potentiality, and by developing no single human function at an excessive charge against another one. This requires specially endowed people and a receptive society so that Castiglione does not posit his ideal of perfection as an easily obtainable one. In this he agrees with other Renaissance delineators of ideal types or roles. Such portraits really express Platonic forms, "ideas" which may serve as final causes, as the goals toward which men and societies may strive. Like all things in Aristotle's sublunary world, man may strive to reach perfection, as does the rest of nature, but he can never quite reach it even when he draws very near.[1]

Castiglione's conception of human perfection is stated explicitly in the form of instruction and precept, but it is perhaps best disclosed in the very character of the conversations which comprise the book. They never lose their social, indeed playful, tone. All the speakers carefully shy away from every occasion for pedantry, although they possess ample erudition, and time after time they delicately and gracefully refuse to elaborate and define certain ideas thoroughly. Their statements tend, rather, to supplement each other even when some of the ironies of their dialectical interchanges remain unresolved. This tone does not suggest, however, any frivolity or irresponsibility about whatever it is they think or believe, even when the disagreements that crop up are plainly contrived by the protagonists for comic effect, as in the protracted discussion over women in Book III. On the contrary, Castiglione manages to convey the underlying cultural, social, and human harmonies which support their debates, the identity of context in which their discourse takes place, the similarity of their assumptions and allusions. In other words, the perfection they reveal is of a "prudential" rather than an absolute character. For them, dialogue does not end in salvation or damnation but is the primary mode of self-realization. They reveal themselves as people possessing the highest capacity for making modulated choices and capable of the highest degree of flexible rationality. No one is driven or drives himself to absolute identification with the views of another.

The perfection that Castiglione presents is of the active life. Earlier, the active life had found very able defenders among the so-called "civic humanists," who contributed to a whole body of debate literature which has since come to be referred to as the *vita activa* controversy. The vigorous political life of the free citizens of the city-state republics in fifteenth-century Italy called forth equally vigorous defenders of the active life of the citizen against those who still maintained a philosophico-religious contemplative ideal of human perfection. Some defenders of the active life practically identified it with economic activity in the classical sense of the word, that sense which includes family and related social concerns as well as strictly economic ones.

With the rise of the tyrannical princedoms of the later Renaissance there was a subsequent shift from civic humanism—the last great voices of it are heard in the writings of Machiavelli and Guicciardini—to a courtly culture ideologically structured by Neoplatonism. The terms, then, of the *vita activa* controversy shifted, and although Castiglione finds some place for consideration of the contemplative ideal in his thought, he does not regard it as antithetical to the active life, nor does he use it in its classical meaning—the undisturbed pursuit of understanding. In fact, what Castiglione means by the contemplative ideal is theoretical knowledge of how to rule, of what good commands are, and the ability to see that they are executed (Book IV, 24-26). These abilities belong to the ruler and not to his courtiers, so that it is only the ruler who shares in Castiglione's version of the contemplative ideal, although, to be sure, he is also more deeply engaged in the active life. This conception of the contemplative ideal is really the active life colored by a weak version of the Platonic conception of the philosopher-king.

The old sharp antithesis between active and contemplative ideals of life survives in Castiglione as the contrast between the one man who rules and possesses the art of commanding, and all the rest of the people who are ruled, possess the art of obeying and, if they are courtiers, of advising the ruler. The love theory which Bembo presents in Book IV of the *Courtier* offers a contemplative ideal for all men, or at least all gentlemen, but it scarcely affects the political and social realities, the status of the ruler's subjects. It is by no means insignificant that Castiglione left the knowledge of government to one man and offered harmless erotic ecstasies to the rest. On the other hand, insofar as Neoplatonic love theory offered a theoretical base for the humanistic cult of friendship, Bembo's speech may be seen as a plea for those intimate and personal values which are the true subject of this apparently political book.[2]

We need not, then, be astonished by Castiglione's slender interest in the problems of political action, even if it was a major concern of some of the greatest thinkers of his era. The reader of Machiavelli or Guicciardini will recall that they framed their considerations of the problems of action in terms of fortune and virtue, the relations between man's ability to act with some knowledge of the probable outcome of his actions, and the irreducible element of chance and irony he always confronts in the scene of his action. Castiglione uses the *fortuna-virtù* concept so sparingly and unimaginatively, whether in the political or the personal context, that it is surprising that his censor found himself obliged to delete the term *fortuna*. Perhaps he did so because Castiglione used it about as sparingly and vaguely as he used the term "God."

Again, we find little reference in Castiglione's book to the idea of liberty but, after all, political decision had fled from Italy to France and Spain where it had passed into the hands of powerful monarchs. One wonders if Castiglione is saying that the only free society now is something much like the picture he gives us of the court of Urbino, a place, like Rabelais' Abbey of Thélème, where the most civilized customs were joined to the greatest freedom (*quivi onestissimi costumi erano con grandissima libertà congiunti*).[3]

The vision of a life "we happy few" lived for a time, Castiglione's grand aesthetic idealism and his apparent unconcern for the hard facts of the political life, is the first example of what later decayed into an aesthetic egotism which, according to self-critical Italians, is one of the besetting sins of their culture. Yet, as Burckhardt pointed out long ago, it was precisely the great political and moral losses suffered by Italy in the late Renaissance which turned men to those ideals of self-cultivation that we still admire.

One of the most interesting ironies of Italian cultural history is that the development of a courtly culture in Italy turned Italian writers back to a tradition of medieval chivalric, feudal, and aristocratic ideas of love and war which had not ever really been rooted in Italian soil. The values of courtly and erotic chivalry came to Italy from Provence and were almost immediately transformed into expressions of spiritual nobility. This, of course, was the work of Dante and his forerunners, especially Guido Guinicelli. Nobility and gentility were moralized and virtually made into synonyms of goodness. Like a good bourgeois, Dante insists that nobility is not really hereditary. In contrast, there is a protracted and almost inconclusive debate in Book I of Castiglione's *Courtier* on whether or not nobility is inherited nobility, but he did not toss off the weight of tradition descending from Dante through the humanists which attacked the notion that gentlemen are ever born and which offered instead a conception of the gentlemen as the creation of a particular kind of moral education and discipline. Castiglione settles the problem by suggesting that gentle birth confers certain advantages even if it is not indispensable: certainly, universal regard and the probable inheritance of those good qualities and aptitudes which will enable the born nobleman to become the ideal courtier with maximum ease.[4]

Castiglione's chivalric ideals are really of a nostalgic character— a nostalgia, by the way, which had become traditional and can be found in Boccaccio and Sacchetti decades earlier—not only for a romantic feudal past but for the values of that more recent past which had added connotations of self-culture and self-conquest to the medieval ideals of nobility. While Boiardo, Ariosto, and Tasso lament the virtual absence of chivalry and nobility in the courts of their time, Castiglione was able to find it completely incarnated in one court of his own time, at least for a while, and to create the most complete and imaginative ideal portrait of courtly perfection. Castiglione's nostalgia would seem to indicate that he had little hope for the reflowering of true chivalry and courtliness, but the existence of his book would show that he nourished some expectation that a beautiful model of courtliness might lure men back to the lost ideals or arrest their decay.

The curiously arcadian and pastoral atmosphere of the *Courtier* can be illuminated if we consider the fortunes of the chivalric poem from its origins in France to its final destiny in Italy. From the *Chanson de Roland* to Tasso the poem underwent changes which virtually eliminated its original epic character, its celebration of a more or less credible story about the deeds of heroes embodying national ideals of universal importance. Shared national and religious values came to occupy less and less of a role in the epic, which gradually became a tissue of *ambages pulcherrimae*.[5]

The social, historical, and even the religious basis of the Italian epics was more vague, more nostalgic. The representation of reality "according to the necessary or the probable" gave way to the "marvelous," to the play of fantasy over reality. The works were destined not so much for subjects or citizens but for the new courtiers who were to draw inspiration from the ideals of medieval chivalry. As in Castiglione, love, of a more or less Platonic variety, replaced politics.

Aldo Scaglione has in fact suggested that these works should perhaps be called idylls rather than epics: "In those works the poets create a pure world of the imagination, coherent only with itself and its laws, which do not necessarily obey the laws of common reality, but must be accepted by the audience as the rule of the game and in the name of beauty." [6] The events of the poems are structured, he further suggests, in an "oneiric" time, the time and space of dream, of pastoral and arcadian fantasy, rather than the space and time of reality. We might here draw on Johan Huizinga's concept of play, of those suprabiological cultural activities, whether actions or representations, which have the function of adorning real life with the spirit of poetry, with fantasies of the heroic or the pastoral life played out in an ideal realm of values such as honor, innocence, virtue, or beauty. It is no accident that when Don Quixote tired of the chivalric life he turned in his imagination to the possibility of leading a pastoral one.[7]

In a sense both the chivalric impulse and the pastoral one have as a primary intention the aesthetic transformation of the brutality of conflict, either through subsuming raw conflict into noble strife or avoiding it altogether by withdrawing to a simpler world of "natural" and primal innocence. The martial rituals and ceremonies of medieval chivalry or Japanese *bushido* are manifestations of this universal human impulse, and such codes of behavior are in fact styles of life, for they are governed by the same principles which govern style—rhythms, harmonies, regular movements and repetitions, modulated stresses and cadences.[8] Perhaps Plato's injunction in the *Laws* (VII, 796) to live life as play is simply an injunction to live life as poetry with style and imagination. It is by playing certain games, making certain sacrifices, singing and dancing, that man propitiates the gods, defends himself against his enemies, and wins in the contests. Plato finds a modern echo in another great student of the erotic life, Havelock Ellis, who wrote in the preface to his remarkable book *The Dance of Life:*

> . . . it is necessary to insist upon life as a dance. This is not a mere metaphor. The Dance is the rule of number and of rhythm and of measure and of order, of the controlling influence of form, of the subordination of the parts to the whole. That is what the dance is. . . . We are strictly correct when we regard not only life but the universe as a dance. For the universe is made up of a certain number of elements, less than a hundred, and the "periodic law" of these elements is metrical. . . . Thus our world is, even fundamentally, a dance, a single metrical stanza in a poem which will be for ever hidden from us.

If feudal chivalry and arcadian fantasies are human responses to the brutality of war, man has also aestheticized the blunt physiological facts of sex with ideal imaginative structures. Courtly and romantic love are surely such "fictions," and Renaissance writers revived the ancient Platonic ideas on love and beauty as a new conceptual framework for their transformation of the erotic values descended from the Middle Ages.

In fact, courtly society in Castiglione's time developed an essentially aesthetic world-view even though there was little or no conscious separation from the dogmas and teachings of the church. Beauty and love, whether in the macrocosm of the universe or in the microcosm of man, became the central cultural values. This development was the work, in great part, of the Florentine Neoplatonists who flourished in the court of the Medici after the loss of republican liberty in Florence and the subsequent decline of civic humanism. The same Bembo who appears as the great exponent of Platonism in the *Courtier* popularized this current of thought through his own writings, while Castiglione furthered its popularity by placing it in a social and truly general context.

The basic principle of the Florentine Platonists was an ancient one: Beauty comes from God and love returns man to Him. But for them, beauty was primarily the attribute of women, and in this we see the continuity of that Italian tradition which moralized and conceptualized the idiom and values of medieval erotic chivalry, a tradition which goes back to Guinicelli and the poets of the *dolce stil nuovo*. Castiglione is no pure Platonist, however, and he frequently discusses love or feminine beauty in perfectly mundane terms. In chapter 40 of Book I, for example, we find a portrayal of ideal feminine beauty with many of the customary features of such descriptions which go back to the Middle Ages. But Castiglione includes a discussion of the use of cosmetics. Make-up should be applied with *sprezzatura,* not too obviously or laboriously, and the secret of using cosmetics well is to use them in such a way that the spectator is not aware that they have been used. This is, of course, good sense, but Castiglione offers an interesting explanation of this instruction. People, he tells us, hate artifice when it is used as a snare, for the true purpose of make-up and, by implication, of all adornment and "artfulness," is to heighten natural beauty. We find here, even in this small detail, a manifestation of Castiglione's ideal of the proper relation between "art" and "nature," an ideal so beautifully expressed in some of the lyrics of Jonson, Herrick, and Marvell. Ideal feminine beauty conveys the impression of heightened naturalness by making use of the resources of art. The beholder will have a sense of "delight in disorder," will always be aware of what we might call the "spontaneous" or "natural" element in the lady's appearance precisely because she has used the resources of "art" to heighten them. In this case, "art" is the contrasting background for "nature."

In Book IV, Castiglione detaches beauty, goodness, and love from such considerations, from the realistic or social contexts of the earlier books where the terms are used in perfectly conventional and separate ways. Through the speech of Bembo, Castiglione finally Platonizes, he etherealizes love, and establishes the traditional Platonic identity between beauty and goodness. Goodness, for Castiglione, does not consist in kindness, compassion, and purity alone, but implies other qualities such as excellence—the Greek *arete*—gentleness, good temper, patience, civility, and friendliness. His view of goodness is an encompassing one, and is determined not only by religious tradition but by those qualities a courtier must have if he is to lead his prince to goodness through example and persuasion. These are, after all, the only possible political virtues in a world where all political power is possessed by one man.

Goodness and beauty are finally identified and both become the correlates of love. There is, of course, talk about love in the court of Urbino. Until Book IV of the *Courtier* the talk is of sexual love, whether in or out of marriage. In Book IV, however, Cardinal Bembo gives us his conception of love, a Neoplatonic love which has little to do with sexuality and is therefore—a very realistic note in all this idealism—primarily for old men. In spite of these contrasting loves, the primary definition of love as the desire to enjoy (*fruir*) beauty applies to both the "heavenly" and the earthly Aphrodite. One measure of the wisdom of Castiglione's and Bembo's thought on the problems of love is that the strictly ideal element in love is left for its true embodiment to the aged.

Castiglione's discussion of earthly Aphrodite uses many of the trappings of the courtly tradition: love is ennobling and it involves secrecy and service to the lady. The adulterous element, so prominent in medieval love sentiment, is distinctly played down. Castiglione, like Spenser, incorporates many of the values of romantic love into marriage, a state he values highly (II, 56-57), and it is romantic values which lead Castiglione to advocate premarital chastity. Nevertheless, he is no Puritan, for he is tolerant of adultery in some cases, such as those in which a beautiful woman is forced into marriage with a repulsive old man, or where the marriage is otherwise extremely hateful. He is also quite sympathetic to those lapses from strict morality caused by the strong passion of a deep and genuine love (II, 94). On the whole Castiglione is respectful of traditional sexual morality but reasonably tolerant of lapses under specified conditions.

Bembo's final speech on love, on the love which culminates in religious ecstasy, is not so much a negation of the discussion of sexual, courtly, and marital love which had preceded it but a synthesis of the whole theme. For love exists in a hierarchical structure which corresponds to the hierarchical structure of the soul. The latter has sense, reason, and the most spiritual faculty, "intellect," and the task of the lover is to ascend from the love of sensible things to the love of intelligible things. But unlike some versions of the *scala amoris,* the various kinds of love are to be actualized in one person's life at different ages. Life has its rhythms; the virtues of youth are different from those of age, the latter presuppose the former and should grow out of them.

The core of Castiglione's thought and of his originality is perceptible in a cluster of related and virtually untranslatable concepts: *grazia, gravità, sprezzatura* and *leggiadria.* We can best define them through indirection, starting with the simplest one first.

Gravità is virtually synonomous with dignity, and Castiglione identifies it with the culture of Spain (II, 37). The Spaniards possess a *gravità riposata,* a quiet majesty of bearing which is reflected not only in the physical posture of the person but in his choice of clothes and the materials they are made of. It suggests the kind of impression difficult for us to generate in an age which has seen the virtually complete democratization of men's clothing and in which we can even see signs of the desexualization of appearances.[9] Perhaps what Castiglione meant by *gravità* can be illustrated by Raphael's magnificent portrait of him, in which the figure's expression and clothing reveal a harmonious balance between self-revelation and reticence, between modest simplicity and assertive decoration.

This portrait is a perfect example of one of the great transformations in Italian art of the *cinquecento,* a change which formulated for the eye that particular conception of nobility which Castiglione had formulated for the mind. Heinrich Wölfflin pointed out many years ago in his famous *Klassiche Kunst* that a whole series of gestures and movements disappeared from painting during this era as too vulgar, as perhaps too middle class. We have only to compare the work of Ghirlandaio with that of Andrea del Sarto to grasp the change that Wölfflin was trying to describe, and this change applies as well to religious painting in which the figures came to be much more elegantly posed.

During that era the truly cultivated man had to be as reposed in manner as Castiglione was when Raphael painted him. Although Castiglione is indeed elegantly posed he also appears to be unposed, simply because Raphael somehow conveys the impression that Castiglione is always much the way that he has been painted, always presentable, as it were, always in possession of a modest or measured greatness, a greatness which is not insistent and which appears to be unstudied and "artless." We should not equate this ideal manner with that which goes with habitual understatement, precisely because modern understatement implies inevitably a false humility if only because of the shrill self-assertiveness of the age. What Castiglione—and Raphael—had in mind was that a true gentleman, in their society at any rate, did things with an almost accidental air. He *need* not insist on himself if he wished to convey his own magnificence in a truly human mode. Therefore the possessor of *gravità riposata* did not do anything in haste or anxiously. He avoided fast dances and when he rode, presumably even to war, he did so in a relaxed way, something by the way impossible for a man wearing the heavy armor of the medieval knight.

Whether or not such a gentleman could manifest his magnificence so quietly in contemporary society with its insistent atmosphere is problematic. Perhaps so, but I am reminded of the advice in an old nineteenth-century American etiquette book which cautions ladies against appearing undignified by rushing to catch a train on the grounds that the train will of course wait for a lady!

Sprezzatura and *leggiadria* are both purely social virtues which find their essential manifestation in conversation and in play. *Sprezzatura* is the art of concealing art (I, 26), of giving to whatever is said and done a certain effortless and unpremeditated quality. The root of the word is from the verb *sprezzare*, "to disdain" or "to hold in contempt," and this sense is vaguely present in Castiglione's concept, although without pejorative connotations. A synonym for *sprezzatura* is *disinvoltura* which means "ease," "simplicity of manner," "aplomb" but also can mean "coolness," "cheek" and "impudence." Again we find the elimination of negative connotations, and he uses them both together in the phrase *sprezzata disinvoltura* (I, 26). *Sprezzatura* and *disinvoltura,* with their suggestions of hauteur and disdain, are meant to convey an attitude toward one's own behavior which will save it from affectation, whether the source of that affectation is an excessive haste or eagerness or an excessive artificiality, both avoidable only through a kind of disengagement or detachment. They point to the proper attitude to have if one is to observe the "mean" in one's manner. The "mean" does not imply being blasé, but the manifestation of a kind of rational appropriateness in all of one's conduct. Indeed, *sprezzatura* increases "grace" and is, in a sense, the external manifestation of that grace (II,11).

Leggiadria is close to *sprezzatura* in its meaning, if not identical to it, although it was also used as a synonym for *grazia,* by Della

Casa and Firenzuola. While Castiglione does not give a definition of it, he applies it often to women in reference to what we would have to translate as grace or charm.[10]

Grazia is the most important term of value in the *Courtier*. Grace or the potentiality to acquire it is a gift of nature. In reality it cannot be taught. It can only be learned if the potential courtier— or his lady, for women may also possess it—has at least the germ of it and if he is able to receive proper instruction (I, 14, 25). While it is virtually impossible to define, it can be reached in a flight from affectation, in the use of *sprezzatura* as a kind of easy way of doing difficult things (I, 24, 26), and it flows from good judgment. It is an elusive quality which would disappear in any deliberate effort to obtain it, and is not reducible to any of the more teachable and describable properties of the educated and civilized man. It springs, as we have seen, from *sprezzatura,* from a kind of "recklessness," an unstudied but skillful spontaneity. Grace is, indeed, "beyond the reach of art" and even beyond critical intelligence. It implies what the eighteenth century meant by "felicity," whether of style, phrase, or manner.[11]

Like Machiavelli's *virtù,* Castiglione's *grazia* is essentially ambiguous because both terms finally refer to the conditions of conduct or action, to the intuition, judgment, and skill required if we are to apply general principles to specific situations. The habit of right action like the habit of right manner in conduct requires that practical wisdom possessed by Aristotle's truly ethical man who really can adapt the general principle of conduct to the endlessly varied specific situations of experience.

Grazia, further, can only be the result of the kind of education which avoids what the French call *déformation professionelle,* that degree of expertise in any field which overdevelops one human function or talent at the cost of leaving others in a raw state. *Grazia* is a quality actualized, if at all, only in a self which, like a great work of art, is truly a harmony of parts. This is why, in the careful program of education outlined in Book I of the *Courtier,* there is such insistence on what we would call the "amateur spirit." By all means learn to play chess but don't try to be an expert. Learn

Greek and Latin but don't be a pedant. Castiglione's "amateurism" is not to be understood in the somewhat contemptuous sense we would now give to the word. Since the courtier must advise his ruler, it is necessary for him to be free from any angularity of vision, to be able to adopt a plurality of points of view and not be dominated by any single one of them. The word "amateur" has come to have a bad sense for us because we think of it in connection with artistic work which must, of course, aim at perfection. But Castiglione's amateur is a man in a society, one who must come to know and love many things if he is to function properly in that society. Whatever differentiation and complexity he develops in one region of his personality must not proceed too far and must also be carried over into others, and this process should go on in the service of unifying the heterogeneous elements of the self. The striving for wholeness and a kind of universality is, after all, still the ideal of humanistic education, even if the humanistic temper, its concern for refinement of feeling rather than efficiency of action, its spatial and aesthetic rather than temporal mode of awareness, would seem to have less and less place in the contemporary world.

The attention Castiglione gives to gesture, manner, games, jokes, and anecdotes might seem to some of his readers an extraordinary trivialization of the ideals of true education. But we are the products of years of education in which almost no attention is given to nonverbal modes of communication and expression, or to the non-referential uses of language. The result is the production of "experts" with extraordinary capacities in certain well-defined areas and no grasp of the meaning of human actions, activities, gestures, or of the varieties of emotional expression. Such are those who cannot distinguish between what men say and do and what they mean by what they say and do, who cannot truly understand speech because speech is much more than the words it uses. What the modern reader may see as trivia in Castiglione's program of education are after all the vehicles of those subtle and feeling interchanges between people which do as much as anything to give them the sense that they are really alive. Castiglione knew that gestures, actions, and objects—the clothes you wear, for example—are modes of language, ways of making statements, and that these languages are not substitutes for one another. It has become essential for modern mass societies to create in all of us the sense that we live in a verbal world, for the governing of such societies demands the incessant generation of verbal messages, laws, edicts, regulations, and promises. Castiglione's society was not tempted to confuse statements with events, nor had the floods of words manufactured by the so-called mass media become the primary instruments of political control and social discipline.

Modern civilization with its tendency toward uniform dress and uniform recreations has severely limited expression to verbal statement and has tended to denigrate action language, object language, or sign language. This has had the result of blocking whole ranges of emotional experience simply because what can be said in one such language cannot be said in another. I am not attributing this analysis to Castiglione as his conscious possession any more than it was the conscious possession of any other exponents of the great tradition of humanistic education. It was, rather, so deeply held a presupposition of their thought that only we, who have lost it, can be fully aware of it.

Grace presides over all the activities of man, whether important or trivial, and it is grace which makes the self into a work of art. It is no accident that in the generation after Castiglione, Vasari made the concept of grace central to his art criticism. It had been applied to painting before Vasari, but largely as a synonym for beauty or to describe a quality differing from beauty only in degree. Vasari not only distinguished grace and beauty, but at times he drew a really strong contrast between them. Grace was a quality impossible to define but which was a function of the artist's judgment, of, as it were, his "eye," while beauty was a quality a painting might possess as a result of the artist's carefree observance of the rules or the "science" of his art.

Grace is Vasari's major critical term in his evaluation of paintings, and for him it points to refinement, elegance, and delicacy. Correctness of composition may produce beauty but not grace, nor can the artist make his painting graceful through effort. Effort will only destroy grace although every artist needs training and hard study, whether he will come to possess grace or not. Vasari also suggests that the painter should execute his work with dispatch if he can advise grace at all so that the real work of preparation is not revealed in the final product.[12]

The easy transfer of a vocabulary expressive of an ideal of human cultivation to works of art does much to focus for us the true subject of Castiglione's book, the creation of the self as a work of art through education. A modern reader may note the absence of any consideration of childhood in a work which has the delineation of an ideal human as its goal. But, like the ancient Greeks, Castiglione did not believe that the child was father to the man. The Greeks did not develop a child psychology simply because the child was not regarded as inhabiting a complete but differently structured universe than the one adults inhabited. He was an adult in potency, the raw material of a protracted educational process which would turn him into a man, a kind of *tabula rasa* on which a consistent ideal of personal development would be engraved by his educators.

Julian Huxley in his book *Religion without Revelation* distinguished three ideals of personal development: specialization, all-roundness by summation, comprehensive wholeness. The first is obviously necessary to success in any occupation, but Huxley points out that it can be as dangerous as biological overspecialization. The second attempts to account for the different kinds of fulfillment open to man, some of them, at least, mutually exclusive, either entirely so or as simultaneous possibilities. Thus the same man may at different times find high fulfillment in chastity as well as in sexual love, in war as well as in the pursuit of knowledge. This conception of life is surely one of the meanings at the heart of Greek polytheism. To organize the personality around the sequential alternation of disparate modes of self-realization corresponds, according to Huxley, to the organization of behavior in lower animals around separate and mutually exclusive instincts. While this method of utilizing conflicting impulses can work successfully, it succeeds by avoiding the task of harmonizing contradictions, not by reconciling them. Like Castiglione, Huxley suggests that we make ourselves whole and implies that the task of doing so is analo-gous to the making of a work of art, for "the personality is a spiritual and mental construction, a work of art like other human constructions." But, he also points out that the perennial quest for wholeness exposes mankind to a different kind of overspecialization in which the values of unity and harmony may serve to overshadow excessively those of richness and variety in experience.[13]

Castiglione, I think, can be said to offer us an image of self as both various and comprehensively whole. The aim of education is to develop our consciousness, to make us aware of a wide range of different kinds of human possibilities and activities, and to unify thought and action, learning and feeling, by imposing on them, as it were, *a common style*. This remains a unique human possibility because only in man are contradictory impulses and disparate, fragmented experiences brought together in a single consciousness, only man can impose those relations, rhythms, accents, and sym-metries on experience that are the essence of style itself. As men may turn the contents of consciousness into works of art, so may they manipulate and form themselves into works of art.

The only alternative to style of life is to be the prisoner of con-vention, and I mean by convention not that indispensable set of social habits we all need to exist in the world, but those ritualistic, rigid, and stereotyped patterns of response to the multiplicity of experience which finally serve to deny it. Style is, of course, social and must be if it is to be meaningful. Nevertheless, it is finally intensely personal, the possession of a unique personality, capable of infinite variations within its overarching patterns of order.

A man with style in Castiglione's sense will be most various yet recognizably one in all the contingencies of life. He will be morally solvent, as it were, able to handle any transactions of life in such a way that morals and manners will be one thing. He is *kalokagathos* in that he grasps that no moral act is ugly, and that flexibility and variety of response will not endanger his identity.

I suppose that every age presents us with its own version of the true gentleman as well as with the mock gentleman, the one the subject of epic and romance, the other the butt of the satirist. So too, Castiglione throughout the work has his characters distinguish the true coin from the false. I think we can say that, for Castiglione, the true gentleman is finally marked by that sense of personal dignity and value of which all his actions have become the vehicle. Of the others, he might have been able to make the amusing and cynical remark of La Bruyère: "L'honnête homme est celui qui ne vole pas sur les grands chemins, et qui ne tue personne, dont les vices enfin ne sont pas scandaleux."

I have treated Castiglione's book as a work about the formation of the self, as a work which embodies one of the great ideals of personal development, a vision of what the self may be made to be. In this light, he perhaps should be read along with Montaigne, the great explorer of what the self actually is. It would be illuminating at this point to glance briefly at Montaigne's enormous achievement and establish the other current, as it were, of subsequent speculation about the nature and development of the self. For Freud became the heir of Montaigne, and Nietzsche the heir of Castiglione.

As an artist Montaigne has always received his due, so it is with some surprise that we discover how little attention most of our standard histories of thought and culture give to his work. In a world where we are constantly bombarded with ultimata in the form "either/or," not only from the political and religious orthodoxies but also from the coteries of the "liberated," the works of the man who most powerfully and richly answered, "Both!" have a particular relevance.

As a thinker Montaigne is usually neatly labeled a "pluralistic skeptic" or a "Renaissance neo-Pyrrhonist" and the historian rushes on in his anxiety to reach Descartes, a "real" philosopher. (Is it Montaigne's professed amateurism or his marvelous literary skill that leads so many professional historians to neglect him?) Yet his inquiry proceeds on a prevalent modern assumption that philosophy is centrally concerned with the realities and problems that a man confronts daily, that its task is the reflective analysis of all the modes of human experience, and that it can state its findings in ordinary language.

When he adopted the motto "What do I know?" Montaigne found a truly new standpoint for thought, new at least in the way he applied it. He bypassed the dilemma of ancient skepticism which foundered on the contradictions implicit in the assertion that the only truth is that no truth can be known. Nor did he ever accept the central philosophic assumption of the past that particular truths inevitably point to a single system. In Montaigne's view, the rationalistic system builder rejected most of reality for the sake of mere consistency when the true aim of inquiry is inclusiveness. He thought that every system dealt with experience, as Procrustes dealt with his victims.

From another point of view, Montaigne completed the revolution in autobiographical realism begun by St. Augustine. Of course, St. Augustine's self as he surveys it in the *Confessions* is not entirely a mundane one. Ordinary events—the theft of pears, for example—are recounted only because God endowed them with a special significance, because they are in reality crucial episodes in a drama of salvation, revealing in one way or another man's depravity and God's mercy. In Montaigne, the sense that everyday experience is charged with latent significance remains, but it has been secularized and its range has been immeasurably broadened. Conversion to Christianity as the principle for the selection and ordering of events has disappeared, and all of experience demands interpretation. The result is that Montaigne is the first thinker to take all of daily life seriously, simply as itself, to see ordinary life as both typical and tragic, and to grasp fully the insecurity of everyday existence and its problematic character.

Thus Montaigne's skepticism was really a way of discovering the truth in everything. He saw that those facts of nature and the self which make them seem so untidy are nonetheless real facts, and that man, with all the contradictions of his experience, somehow issues from the all-inclusive unity of nature. Similarly, the apparently irreconcilable antitheses within consciousness actually cohere in the unity of the self. However incompatible, the extremes of experience are in one way or another true of the experiencing subject.

Thus we can come to know something after all, if only in the form of tentative "essays." We can learn something of what we and the world in our variousness are like, and what we discover when we exhaust the contents of a single consciousness—including what is mean and trivial—will be a more universal truth than the constructions of the philosophers. Such a process has a beginning but it can have no end short of the extinction of consciousness itself. Its results can have no final shape, nor can they be molded into a symmetrical structure. They may possess a unity, but it is the mysterious unity conferred by their origin in a single personality.

Montaigne, his book and his world, are all of a piece and they present us with a paradoxical fusion of the intensely personal and the universal. He usually begins an essay with a simple event—a mood or an encounter—or with something which captured his imagination while he was reading in his beloved library, perhaps an ancient custom or some lines of Virgil. Then, in what is best described as a free improvisation, or a set of variations on a theme, he expands the significance of the particular personal datum of experience until it finally includes us all. Perhaps the keenest pleasure in reading Montaigne is to follow his graceful, powerful, controlled mind in a process which is one of self-discovery in both the author and the reader.

By being intensely personal, by reflecting passionately on every shred of his own experience, Montaigne becomes truly universal. And this paradox, in the last analysis, is true of all great writers. Montaigne, like any artist, really never expounds anything, and does his work somewhere beyond the familiar categories of rhetoric and logic. He tells us that life is given to us in an endless series of concrete situations, each of them unique and each of them presenting a challenge.

This, I believe, is what Gide meant when he said that Montaigne teaches us liberalism. But I would add that it is a liberalism free of any simplified view of man's nature and his condition. Few men have been more acutely aware of the relative character of the absolute claims of culture, but he also was aware that tradition and culture were the strongest bulwarks against barbaric anarchy. In a time of violence and ghastly cruelties he keenly desired the peace and well-being of his contemporaries, but he knew that the ideologies of reform often coupled "supercelestial thoughts and subterranean conduct." He could admire the nobility of many of the customs of the cannibals who inhabited the New World, but he did not sentimentalize them or turn them into "noble savages." His sense of the relativity of culture and knowledge was always in the service of moral self-awareness.

Perhaps the most compelling and exciting aspect of Montaigne's work is his exploration of consciousness at the point where it rises from the deeper levels of mental life, and his conviction that the depth of the soul manifests itself in the trivial, the everyday, and the biological, all of which in his hands become clues to the major problems of existence. Indeed, his conception of life is a profoundly biological one. Men, in Montaigne's view, turn life into a comedy when they forget that they are animals and try to behave with the rigid precision of mechanisms, or the detachment and omniscience of angels. They turn it into a tragedy when they make a partial truth absolute and harness the deepest bestial passions to the service of this superhuman claim. More than any other writer, Montaigne reminds us who and what we are, what it is to be human.

Montaigne and Castiglione share one great conception of life whatever their differences: that man properly resides in a "mean" state and that his goal is to modulate and harmonize the antitheses of self; indeed, that the goal of any system of education is quite literally to make men. Castiglione would have agreed with Montaigne who distinguished between able and learned men, between men who possess what they know and men who simply carry the burdens of erudition, between men who make books their authorities and those who find in the great world that book against which all books are judged, or that mirror in which alone we can survey ourselves from the correct angle. So too, he advocates a certain nonchalance, the absence of affectation in speech and manner, the retention of the qualities of naturalness within the results of dis-

cipline, of spontaneity within order, of a certain candid and innocent vision of reality along with the fruits of experience.

Montaigne, of course, is an immeasurably greater intelligence
than Castiglione, and the substrate of his educational ideal is, in a
sense, his whole discovery of the self and its expression in that
great work of art which is the *Essays:* the self as a world much like
the great world which is our measure and guide, which contains
analogous complexities and contradictions, which is, like culture, a
historical deposit, undulating and diverse, a paradoxical unity of
the grossest infantilisms and the most sublime subtleties.

We might say that both Castiglione and Montaigne were concerned with the making of the self, but that Montaigne was aware
of a self that had to be explored and discovered. These two themes
have been related in various and subtle ways in the history of modern literature, and one of the most interesting has found its expression in the theme of the artist who is torn between "perfection of
the life or of the work." For the artist is a man and, as such, should
set himself the goal of making himself into a work of art, but his art
demands a dedication and a devotion to its perfection which precludes the development of his own. The artist too—at least the
modern artist—is committed in one way or another to the exploration of the self. But the self is an ocean and its depths are endless.
Indeed, Montaigne himself implicitly posed the modern problem as
to whether "essays" are not the only honest form for a literature
concerned with the self when the artist wishes also to make himself
a work of art.

Nietzsche, in *The Genealogy of Morals,* asked what the ascetic
ideal might mean to the artist and could give no definite answer. It
might mean many things, nothing, or too much. For the philosopher and the scholar it was clear that it led to the creation of those
special conditions necessary for achieving intellectual distinction.
Perhaps the shock of *Parsifal* was too much for him, but Nietzsche
did not explore the possibility that "renunciation" may be one of
the conditions for achieving artistic distinction or artistic vision.
Artists, according to Nietzsche, had always been at the service of
some morality, philosophy, or religion. They served the myths of

culture and ultimately the structures of power. In a way, no artist had ever done any real thinking, had ever been independent enough intellectually to warrant our taking any of his ideas seriously.

There is, I think, truth in this statement if we refer "thought" and "truth" to speculation and scientific inquiry alone; however, Nietzsche did not see that the artist's intellectual subservience solved the problem of form for him, limited the infinite multiplicity of experience so that he could begin to modify whatever myth or ideology he served. A work of art, a *systematic* philosophical structure or a myth cannot be made out of everything, and some principle of order, however absurd or primitive it may be, must be the point of departure for the achievement of the formal qualities which are the essence of art and structure. Nietzsche grasped that philosophy had become psychology, that the true subject of philosophy had become the self. In a way, philosophy is still possible under those conditions. Even modern linguistic and logical analysis is finally committed, according to Wittgenstein, to the liberation of self from slavery to meanings. The case with art is more problematic, since it must aim at a kind of formal completeness, whether the form is open or closed, which should carry no hint of arbitrariness.

Myths, masks or *personae,* the subphilosophical use of philosophical ideas, have always been indispensable to the artist, and his greatness has never had any necessary relation to the quality of his beliefs or the honesty of his assumed identities. In a perhaps ironic way, Plato's old question is still relevant: Can the artist be an honest man? Can he be trusted in view of the absurdities he frequently seems so fond of?

From another point of view there are really two questions in Nietzsche's single query on what the ascetic ideal might mean to the artist. A work of art, such as *Parsifal,* may celebrate the ascetic ideal, but the artist-ascetic may also celebrate ideals belonging to quite a different mode of life. His personal renunciation of love or action may be the condition for the artistic rendering and celebration of the very life he renounces. Renunciation may be necessary if he is to become the "true spectator" who, like Stendhal, sees beauty as "the promise of happiness" and if he is going to capture that beauty for us.

This, at any rate, is the paradoxical mode in which the theme of the self as a work of art, and the theme of the exploration of the self as the subject of art, have come to be related in our own time. "The wound and the bow" necessarily imply each other and the artist can only truly see his homeland in his exile. His refusal is not simply *of* life but *for* life, and for the sake of beauty he may renounce creation of the self for endless exploration of the self, participation for observation, the quest for the ultimate structure of experience for its texture. This is the gist of the decision made by Mann's Tonio Kröger and by Joyce's Stephan Daedalus; and the decision for art, once made, is irreversible. When, like Aschenbach in *Death in Venice,* the artist attempts to find his way back to participation, to leave his order of truth for truths of another kind, he is destroyed. The very creative gifts which make him what he is become corrupting and destructive. What is his bow in "alienation" is his wound in "participation."

The fantasies and dreams of Aschenbach all turn on the ancient myths concerning the nature of passion in both art and life. First in fantasy, then in dreams Aschenbach considers the first and greatest artist fable of all time, the *Phaedrus* of Plato, and dreams the paradoxical position of the artist with brilliant clarity just before he dies. The artist cannot walk the way of beauty without Eros as his guide, but Eros continually tempts him to the ugly extreme of frenzied participation in the sensual, breaks through the Apollonian discipline of simplicity and largeness, the discipline of detachment and form. The artist thus needs an excess of passion to be an artist, but the very excess he must have is a flaw in him as a man. Only art can discipline it and only art can use it. It cannot be applied to participation precisely because it is an excess. The artist's eyes must feed on beauty from a distance, and the discipline of art is precisely the distance which he must maintain.

The countermyth to the *Phaedrus* is presented in Aschenbach's terrible nightmare in which he has a vision of the "stranger god," Dionysus, who drives out Eros, and conquers Aschenbach's soul. It is the advent of the Thracian god in all his power, as in that moment when he came sweeping down on Hellas from the north destroying all who did not acknowledge the reality of his power. The artist is vulnerable to this fate, Mann suggests, precisely because he repudiates knowledge. Knowledge is all-knowing, understanding, forgiving, but the artist repudiates it because it sets no store by form: "It has compassion with the abyss—it *is* the abyss." It is also that which is the instrument of whatever inner harmony can be obtained, the means for achieving excellence, *arete*. But the artist must reject it because the artist is disposed to excess in spite of the terrible burden he bears of dedicated concern with detachment and form, a concern which exacerbates his very sensuality. Art is, after all, an extraordinary defense, a sublimation which is always on the verge of breaking down precisely because art, for Mann, excludes knowledge. Eros and Dionysus are finally not two separate gods but the same power in different aspects. It is only Apollo—if we may change Nietzsche's myth—who can turn Dionysus into Eros.

Tonio Kröger is successful in his renunciation because his Eros has become charity. Other artists, however, call him a *bourgeois,* and the *bourgeois* try to arrest him. What makes him a poet and artist is precisely his love of what is ordinary and usual in life. His love for the creatures of his imagination is great, but it is informed by and rests upon a love for those who happily participate in life, those who are fair and alive, happy, beautiful and, in the last analysis, quite commonplace. He does not envy those great Dionysiac spirits who seek a demonic beauty and despise mankind. He is, perhaps ironically, an artist precisely because he is a kind of *bourgeois manqué.* No grand conception of the artist this, but a comfortable one, more comfortable than that latest version of the artist fable which is that of the artist *manqué,* of the artist as barren and sick only in the service of his illness.

For two thousand years the *Phaedrus* affirmed the artist as the seer and the visionary, the artist as the lover and pursuer of beauty who flies to the absolute that the metaphysician struggles to reach through the processes of thought. With the revival of this conception in the Renaissance more and more human activities begin to fall under the category of art. The artist again took on the characteristics of a demiurge, of a co-creator of the universe, the man who frees forms from marble and paints the world as it really ought to be. The elaborate theology of art which had been usually the prerogative of the poet came to encompass the painter, architect, sculptor, and musician. For the first time in history, these other arts came to be reckoned, as Castiglione does, liberal arts, studies appropriate to a free man.

In turn the idea of the artist or of art came to be applied to the prince and the courtier and, finally, to the self. Whatever corrections subsequent scholarship may have made of Burckhardt's views of the Italian Renaissance, his brilliant intuition of the aestheticizing of all human activity in that era endures. Vasari tells us that the artist was a hero, for what else do all those biographies finally say? But he also tells us that the artist could, at least in death, be a prince. This we know when we read his thrilling description of Michelangelo's funeral, an artist honored as only princes had ever been honored. And if the artist was a prince, the prince in turn was an artist whose work was the state. With the cruelty of any giver of forms, he used people as if they were words, arranging and canceling them to perfect his creation. So too, the self came to be conceived as a deliberate creation. When the conception of art came to include the conception of self and of life, the terms were set for a new debate even though it had to wait many years to articulate itself. For centuries the debate had been between the artist and the thinker, nor is that debate entirely over. The new debate implied different questions from those of who possesses truth. Rather, men asked how life, collective or personal, may be made to achieve the condition of art, and artists asked how dedication to art might be made to include artistic perfection of life. In effect, the new argument was between the artist and himself and the artist and his environment.

Notes

*

1 Erich Loos, *Baldassare Castigliones "Libro del Cortegiano: Studien zur Tugendauffassung des Cinquecento, Analecta Romanica II* (Frankfurt/ Main, 1955), pp. 84 ff. This work is by far the most useful and thorough scholarly interpretation of Castiglione we possess and I have drawn on it heavily in this chapter.

2 Cf. Loos, pp. 85 ff. and Napoleone Orsini, *Bacone e Machiavelli* (Genoa, 1936), pp. 118 ff., 137 ff., who points out that a similar shift from concern with the active citizen to concern with the courtier took place in England after 1550. This is reflected in the contrast between the doctrines of More, Ascham, and Elyot, with their notions of moral training for active service, and the courtly ideals of Raleigh, Lyly, Sidney, and Spenser. Of course, this contrast is a matter of emphasis and not of opposition. Not until Bacon, however, does the defense of the *vita activa* appear again with all the strength of the classical emphasis on the pursuit of the common good.

3 *Il Cortegiano*, I, 4. All references to this work are to the edition of Bruno Maier (Torino, 1955), which is a more accurate text than that of Vittorio Cian first published in 1894 (Florence) and which was for many years the standard text.

4 On courtesy and nobility in Italy see the two short studies of Aldo Vallone, *La cortesia dai Provenzali a Dante* (Palermo, 1950), and *Cortesia e nobiltà nel Rinascimento* (Asti, 1955).

5 See the acute remarks of Aldo Scaglione, "Chivalric and Idyllic poetry in the Italian Renaissance," *Italica*, XXXIII (1956), 252-260.

6 *Ibid.*, p. 255.

7 Johan Huizinga, *Homo Ludens: A Study of the Play Element in Culture* (New York, 1955), especially pp. 46, 101 ff., 181 ff.

8 *Ibid.*, p. 186.

9 See the interesting study of J. D. Flügel, *The Psychology of Clothes* (London 1930).

10 Cf. Loos, p. 117.

11 Cf. Edward Williamson, "The Concept of Grace in the Work of Raphael and Castiglione," *Italica*, XXIV (1947), 316-324; on "felicity" and "grace" in more recent literature see the references in M. H. Abrams, *The Mirror and the Lamp* (New York, 1953). Castiglione may have derived his use of the term "grace" from Alberti's *Trattato della Pittura* (II, 23) where it is used as an aesthetic term.

12 Cf. Anthony Blunt, *Artistic Theory in Italy 1450-1600* (New York, 1956), p. 92.

13 Julian Huxley, *Religion without Revelation* (New York, 1959).

IV

BACON:

The New Philosophy

Alfred North Whitehead was of the opinion that the two most revolutionary centuries in the history of Western civilization were the fifth and the seventeenth, the former because it saw the Christianization of the empire and the latter because of the phenomenal and portentous development of modern science described in that arc of achievement which starts with Galileo and ends with Newton. Of course, history is continuous and nothing of this magnitude happens without a long process of preparation. The scientific accomplishments of the seventeenth century would have been unthinkable without the gradual recovery, during the Middle Ages and the Renaissance, of the great texts of Greek mathematics and science. Nevertheless, the seventeenth century marked a qualitative change in the history of science as well as a quantitative one. The invention of the telescope and of the calculus mapped a course, for physics and astronomy, of brilliant discoveries, and they were to follow it for more than two hundred years without radical alteration; the invention of the microscope and the revolutionary observations of Leeuwenhoek, Grew, Hooke, Malpighi, and Swammerdam laid the foundations for modern biology and medicine, while Boyle can rightly be called the father of modern chemistry. New instruments, methods, and techniques made a massive increase in scientific knowledge almost inevitable but, as important as these substantive contributions to science were, there are two aspects of the development of modern science which mark it off from science in the ancient world and which have helped to make it the most potent instrument of change the world has ever seen.

In the first place, what we might call the ideology of modern science, unlike that of earlier science, was markedly utilitarian. Traces of this attitude concerning the usefulness of investigating nature can, of course, be found among the alchemists, the scientist-artists of the Renaissance like Leonardo da Vinci, the enthusiasts for natural magic like Agrippa, and among the various craftsmen and engineers whose numbers began to increase with the economic growth of Europe. But the utilitarian attitude toward scientific research, by the seventeenth century, had come to dominate the thinking of some of the very greatest scientists and spokesmen for science, and it was especially acute where the influence of Francis Bacon (1561-1626) guided scientific investigation. Of course the ancient traditions of disinterested intellectual inquiry and of the contemplative pursuit of understanding for its own sake remained strong, often even in the hearts and minds of those who were vigorous utilitarians. Nevertheless, from Bacon on, the strongest argument for science becomes the promise it holds for giving us new knowledge which will be of benefit and use to mankind.[1]

A second characteristic of great importance if we are to understand the difference between earlier science and that of the late Renaissance and the seventeenth century becomes obvious when we reflect on the remarkable growth of scientific academies during our period. Science came to be a distinctly co-operative enterprise, for it was generally understood that it would be the work of many men, not just of a few men of genius, of many men working for generations. Investigators met regularly at newly founded institutions like the Royal Society to perform experiments and to present the results of their researches to one another. More important still, the results were published regularly and made available to the widest possible interested public. While such associations for intellectual purposes were not without a kind of precedent in the philosophical schools of antiquity or the literary academies of the Renaissance, the scientific societies represent something new in the social organization of knowledge. They were free of the esoteric, secretive or religious character of some of their predecessors and were, unlike traditional learned academies, devoted primarily to intellectual innovation and to the discovery and dissemination of new scientific knowledge.[2]

Before we consider the new science, or the "new philosophy," as it was then called, in greater detail, we might take a retrospective glance at the "old philosophy" if only to try to understand why many intelligent and honest men were so reluctant to relinquish it.

Perhaps the most spectacular achievement of ancient science and the imaginative core of the "old philosophy" was Greek astronomy. Certainly the Ptolemaic synthesis of centuries of Greek observations and discoveries, of speculations upon and measurements of the course of the heavens, was a masterly intellectual accomplishment. Moreover, it "worked," even if it was cumbersome at times. It enabled men for centuries to predict eclipses, locate their own positions in space, and calculate the passage of time. It was not merely practical, however, but a religious and magical system as well. The astrology and astral religions which dominated the spiritual life of late antiquity had transposed to the heavens all the secret fears, hopes, and passions that buffet mankind, with the result that the Ptolemaic astronomy came to share in the enormous spiritual prestige and power of the astral faiths.[3]

The resurgence of Pythagorean number mysticism which accompanied the diffusion of astrology in antiquity led men to discover in the symmetries of the heavens types and patterns of regularity and order which could also be found here below. Correspondences between the earth and the heavens abounded, between planets and minerals or plants, or between the planetary spheres and the seven liberal arts and seven virtues. And a multitude of facile parallelisms of this kind seemed to many men for centuries a safe bulwark against the meaninglessness of events. The Ptolemaic astronomy, with its religious, astrological, and magical accretions, had all the force and power of a living myth as well as scientific value. Deeply rooted emotional needs had become attached to it over the centuries and, however unintelligible and puerile much of the old analogical thinking may seem, it gripped the imagination because it worked at a level below that of pure reason. It satisfied the profound human need for order, made the universe seem intelligible, and thus carried in its symbols many of the highest values and aspirations of civilization.

Yet the system was an impressive answer, mathematically and scientifically sophisticated, to the fundamental problem of Greek astronomy in terms of the conditions the most brilliant scientific minds of antiquity had set for its solution. How to describe, in a unitary system, all of the visible motions of the heavenly bodies in such a way that the position of any star or planet, whether in the past or the future, could be calculated?

The Greek astronomers began with the assumption that the earth was fixed and that all other heavenly bodies revolved around it. Further, every heavenly motion was assumed to be circular and uniform. Thus the "appearances," the motions, of any heavenly bodies not apparently moving in a uniform circle—the sun and the planets for example—were to be "saved" by being resolved into two or more circular motions. While these assumptions were incorrect, they are nevertheless brilliant examples of scientific work, and the rest of the Ptolemaic system follows rigorously from them.

Given these two assumptions, the classical solution to the cosmological problem was achieved by Hipparchus and Ptolemy with two remarkable theoretical devices: the theory of eccentrics and the theory of epicycles. The theory of eccentrics assumed, for example, that the center of the presumably uniform circular revolution of the sun about the earth was not the earth itself but a fixed point in space at some distance from the center of the earth. Such an "eccentric" center for the sun's annual revolution about the earth will explain why the sun is close to the earth in summer and further away in winter. A second assumed circular motion of the sun about the earth, a daily one, goes on at the same time that the sun is revolving annually about the earth. These two motions together will appear to an observer on the fixed earth as a spiraling motion which causes the sun to shift the position on the horizon at which it rises and sets. It will also explain the reversal of its path along the horizontal plane of the horizon which takes place during the solstices.[4]

The theory of epicycles assumed that each planet circulated uniformly around its own particular center which in turn circulated around another center and so on. The system of circulations—the number of them was determined by the apparent motions and speed of the planet in question—ended with a circular motion around the fixed center of the universe which, let us recall, was not exactly the earth but the eccentric. The circle around the fixed cosmic center, the widest circle and the one the planet traced in its "eccentric" revolution around the earth, was called the deferent. All the other circles were called epicycles. A first epicycle would have its center on the circumference of the deferent, while a second epicycle would have its center on the circumference of the first, and so on.

This ingenious but rather cumbersome system of wheels within wheels accounted admirably enough for the fact that the progression of the planets through the heavens is not a uniform one but is apparently interrupted by a regular sequence of retrograde motions so that Mars, for example, appears to zig-zag across the sky. By positing a sufficient number of epicycles for any particular planet and appropriate speeds for its deferent as well as its epicycles, the ancient astronomers were able to give a mathematical account of the apparent movements and structure of the heavens to whatever degree of exactitude might be demanded.

Such were the theoretical devices of ancient astronomy to account for the long-term appearances of the heavens. The short-term appearances, which we now know are caused by the earth's daily rotation on its own axis, were accounted for by supposing that the heavenly systems of planets and the great circle of the fixed stars rotated as a unit, with all of their relative positions and motions unchanged, every twenty-four hours around an axis drawn through the poles of the earth.

This system, understood as a mathematical solution to a mathematical problem, is a marvel of thought. The great difficulty with it came at the very beginning of Greek astronomy when astronomers tried to imagine a physical model of the universe along the lines suggested by their mathematical solution. The mathematical circles then became transparent spheres which somehow interpenetrated and which, in some more fanciful versions of this cosmology, were believed to generate notes of music at those points where they came into contact with each other. This was in fact the very music of the spheres, a rare melody which could only be heard by the inner ear when the listener was transfigured in a mystical state of consciousness.

Lest we be prompted to smile at all of this complex celestial machinery, let us recall that even Copernicus and Tycho Brahe could not relinquish circular orbits and epicycles, and that it was not until Kepler reluctantly abandoned the assumption that the planetary orbits had to follow the circle of "perfection" and contented himself with ellipses that epicycles disappeared forever from the astronomical imagination.

The "old" physics had less in common with the new physics than the old astronomy had with its successor, for ancient physics had little to do with weighing and measuring. The distinguished achievements of a few Greek mathematicians, such as Archimedes, in the realm of physics did not set the main direction of physical speculation for the classical and postclassical world. The master in this branch of knowledge as in most others, for centuries, was Aristotle. With the twentieth-century revolution in physics and a renewed interest in the philosophical implications of physical theories, Aristotle's *Physics* has again come to be of interest. But it is neither mathematical nor experimental, and its great ideas failed for centuries to stimulate progress. Indeed, his authority often impeded it. Moreover, the main tradition of Aristotelian-Scholastic physics drew far more heavily on Aristotle's treatise *On the Heavens (De caelo)* than on the far more mature and subtle *Physics*. The earlier work was far more accessible and usable in spite of, or perhaps because of, its inferiority.

The traditional Aristotelian-Scholastic physics rested on an assumption analogous to the astronomical assumption of a fixed central earth, namely, that the directions "up" and "down" have an absolute significance. There is thus, *ex hypothesi*, an absolute center to the universe and "up" is motion along a radius drawn from this center to the circumference of the universe, while "down" is motion in the opposite direction. Moreover, the world below the sphere of the moon is radically different from the world above that sphere. This is a second physical assumption analogous to the astronomical one that all celestial motion must be circular.

The world above the sphere of the moon is made of a "fifth essence" or element, unlike any of the four which comprise the sublunary world, and the natural motion of the translunar world—the largest part of the universe—is circular and uniform. Our world is composed of those famous four elements called Earth, Air, Fire, and Water. Although the names of the elements were derived from the familiar objects, the elements were not generally thought of as identical with the substances we call by those names. There was a distinction, rather obscure, between water and elementary Water, even if the latter was the main component of the former.

Each of the elements could be analyzed into two mentally distinguishable categories, that of substratum and that of quality. It is important to bear in mind that this was a metaphysical and not a physical distinction. No quality existed without a substratum and no substratum without a quality. The substratum of the four elements was the same "stuff" or "matter," and it was called, in Latin, *materia prima.* Each element, however, varied in quality and was qualitatively defined by a union of two of the four basic qualities of hot, cold, moist, dry. Thus the element Earth had, inhering in its substratum of *materia prima,* the two qualities of cold and dry, the element Air was hot and moist, Fire was hot and dry, and Water cold and moist. These four elements, moreover, were convertible into one another through a process of qualitative transformation, and all natural processes, biological and physical, all of the phenomena of change and transformation, generation and corruption, rested on the motion and interconversion of the elements. On the canvas of *materia prima* with a palette of qualities, nature made the four elements and with them the rest of the sublunary world.

Each of the four elements has its own natural position or *topos* in space. In its natural place it does not move and remains at rest, but when it is not in its natural place, it will tend to move along a radius of the universe to that place where it belongs. Thus the natural place of Fire is at the circumference of the great sphere which encloses the sublunary world and so it will always tend to move upward. Earth belongs at the center, so that it will always tend to go down if it is not already in its natural place, while Air and Water lie between these termini of elements. It is clear that this conception of motion is ultimately biological. Indeed, much that was comprehended in Aristotelian physics we would call biology, for it is the study of all processes of change including development and morphogenesis as well as change of place or state.[5]

The "old" physics was closely related to the traditional Aristotelian-Scholastic metaphysics, that remarkable body of speculation and minutely systematic argumentation which took its main axioms of thought from the philosophical treatises of Aristotle. Scholasticism, the major philosophical tradition of the later Middle Ages, persisted well into the Renaissance and, indeed, into our own times, when it continues to be the more or less official philosophy of the Roman Catholic church. It is less a single system of thought than a group of related assumptions and concepts which guided the way its adherents interpreted the world. Although the primary categories of Scholasticism were Aristotelian, they were usable, and were used, in ways which were flexible enough to allow for considerable diversity in the results which various thinkers achieved.

Albertus Magnus, St. Thomas Aquinas, and Duns Scotus shared a common set of conceptual conclusions on the great problems of philosophy.

The great Scholastic metaphysicians would all have agreed that reality could be understood in terms of the following pairs of concepts: essence and existence; matter, i.e., "stuff" and form; potentiality and actuality. These terms have become so much a part of our vocabulary that we may think we understand them when we do not. They are technical terms with specific meanings quite remote from the meanings we confer on them in ordinary language. Thus the essence of any substance was the whole system of qualities, functions, and powers which, in a unity, make up its nature and which distinguish it from other substances. When you know the essence of any substance or species of substance, you are in possession of its definition. That man is a rational animal, for example, is both a definition of man and his essence.

However, there are also essences, such as "unicorn" or "hobgoblin," which are certainly definable but nevertheless do not exist. Therefore in any concretely existing substance we can always differentiate between essence and existence. The Dodo certainly is an essence but he does not exist anymore, although he once did. Except in God there is no necessary relation between essence and existence. His essence is to exist while the existence of all other substances in the universe is contingent, that is, they do not exist *by necessity*.

The concept of matter and form was used in various ways and with varying meanings depending on the context. Thus the sculptor's block of marble was the matter for the form of the statue he would make with it, but the block itself possessed the form or essence "marble" in relation to the substratum in which those qualities constituting the essence "marble" inhered. We might think of these two terms as roughly translatable into the term "possibility" for matter and "pattern" for form, if we grasp that the same substance can be analyzed, as in the example I have just given, in terms of matter and form more than once.

Perhaps the terms may be further clarified if we recall that Aristotle was a great biologist and that many of his philosophical ideas were generated by his attempts to interpret living matter. Each living thing seems, during its life, to impose its form on the alien materials which it ingests and to perpetuate that form in the process of reproducing itself. When it fails to impose its form on other substances it dies and is resolved into its elements. This process is a kind of striving, and something like it takes place even in inorganic nature. The four elements themselves manifest the prototype of this striving in their tendency to move toward their proper places in the universe whenever they are displaced from them. Whereas we would be inclined to reduce the organic and biological realm to the inorganic and mechanical, Aristotle viewed the latter as an imper-

fect version of the former. The inorganic world possessed, in a rudi-
mentary form, those properties which the organic world has in a
complete state of development.

This analysis into form and matter can be applied to all substances in the universe except to angels and to God. The angels,
like God, are spiritual beings, but they differ from him in being
finite and in being "composite" in regard to essence and existence.
While they have no "matter," their essence does not of necessity
entail existence and they are therefore contingent.

The third pair of correlative terms, potentiality and actuality, is
dynamic in that the terms refer to processes of change, or more
accurately perhaps, to processes of growth and decay, since the
fundamental models for potentiality and actuality are biological.
Every substance, organic or inorganic, enters into processes of
change and may be understood as manifesting through change particular powers and tendencies. These powers and tendencies may
be part of the natural endowment, so to speak, of the substance, or
it may have acquired them; they may enable a substance to act
upon other substances or be acted upon by them. Now any particular sum of powers a substance possesses may remain latent or un-
actualized, or one or more may be manifested in a particular number of definite ways. No substance, at any time, will have all of its
powers in action simultaneously and therefore every substance will
always have some unmanifested potentialities. The one exception
to this, as to so much else in the Scholastic metaphysics, is God. He
is "pure act," that is, he is always fully realized. At the other end of
the universal scale of being is *materia prima,* which we have already encountered in our discussion of the elements. It is pure potentiality, utterly unformed "stuff," which is nowhere existent as
such but merely as the substratum for some form or other. It is, in
fact, merely a conceptual limit.

One further instrument of philosophical analysis fundamental to
Scholastic philosophy was the famous four causes of Aristotle:
formal, material, efficient and final. In Aristotle's thought, the four
causes are not really as complicated as they became in the hands of
some of the Scholastics. They are, for Aristotle, the answers to four

rather simple questions we can ask about any substance insofar as we regard it as the outcome of a process of change or development. First we may ask what it is, next out of what it is made, then what agent was operative in making it, and finally for what end it was made. Final cause, the end or goal of a process, is the causal category that made a lot of trouble in the Aristotelian tradition. It does not mean "purpose" except when it refers to those products that humans make, whether epic poems or pencils. The final cause of an acorn is, to be sure, an oak, but Aristotle would have denied that there is anything "purposeful" in that outcome of the process of growth, if we mean by "purpose" the fulfillment of someone's conscious intention or need. Similarly, modern evolutionary biology posits myriads of adaptive and "purposeful" structures in living things without in the least compromising its naturalistic principles or positing a mind or conscious spirit hovering over the evolutionary process.

However, when Aristotelian philosophy was placed in the service of Christian theology, the Scholastics tended, at the most abstract level of their thinking, to conflate the idea of providential governance of the world with the notion of final cause. Although the greatest medieval thinkers were by no means naïve about the absurdity and irrationality of making God preside directly over all of the myriads of processes of change which make up the world of nature, in the final analysis, and at that point at which their philosophy spilled over into theology, they encouraged the tendency to think of nature as purposive in a way quite alien to Aristotle. For Aristotle, the fact that the lilies of the field neither toil nor spin had little to do with their gorgeous raiment. Their beauty no less than their indolence is simply the outcome of a natural process. It would not be an exaggeration to say that a medieval Scholastic would have finally thought of their beauty as intended by God, who, although he works in nature through secondary causes, still intends that his creation should embody the symbols and paradigms of moral or religious truths. When, as late as the seventeenth century, Sir Thomas Browne finds the quincunx everywhere in nature, he sees a divine deliberateness and intention in the ubiquity of this figure, a purposiveness which is as alien to the authentic thought of Aristotle—though not to Scholasticism—as to that of a modern scientist.

These habits of allegorizing nature, of finding purposes and intentions everywhere, became more pronounced within some of the important traditions of medieval thought as it continued into the Renaissance, even though the nominalists and Occamites, working within similar traditions, were cutting the ground from under the old metaphysics and preparing the way for some of the earliest developments in modern philosophy and science. Renaissance Neoplatonism and the renewed interest in ancient occult sciences such as magic reinforced the tendency to see nature as everywhere purposeful by divinizing it. Thus the traditional philosophical systems, ancient and medieval with their Renaissance elaborations, which Bacon, Descartes, and other great thinkers of the seventeenth century attacked, were permeated with a supernaturalistic kind of teleology, with an essentially religious or animistic conception of final causes. They rightly saw such a conception of nature as thwarting scientific inquiry before it even begins, for men were simply too prone to assume that, once they had grasped what they thought of as the divine intention of any process or event, they had real knowledge about it. While the new philosophies were by no means prepared to deny that the visible things of this world imply the existence of God, or that the firmament reveals his glory, they were agreed that such propositions were scientifically irrelevant.

Perhaps the most important master idea of the Aristotelian-Scholastic philosophy, the final model for the organization of thought and experience, was the idea of hierarchy. In its metaphysical application, the idea of hierarchy shaped all of being into a scale or ladder, and each higher rung on the ladder, each order of existence, possessed more of being itself, more value and more beauty. At one end of the scale was *materia prima,* the mere possibility of being and value, while at the other end was God, being and value in infinite degree. Everything else lay arranged in between in its due rank and order.

The idea of a ladder of being goes back to Plato, although the

Neoplatonists first gave it a truly crucial role in their systems, and it had a life which went well beyond the life of the Scholastic hegemony in Western philosophy. Indeed, it plays an important role in the philosophy of Spinoza and Leibnitz and, in modified form, is a crucial idea in the Hegelian tradition. Some modern philosophers such as Bradley and Collingwood have made brilliant use of it in their works and it truly seems to be one of those philosophical ideas which are endlessly usable.

In its philosophically most sophisticated form, the hierarchy of being is conceived of as structured according to two principles. Each entity higher on the scale possesses all of the powers and functions of the one next below it plus greater and higher powers of its own. Thus, for example, an animal can perform all of the essential functions of plants. It has, in the traditional terminology, a vegetative soul, which means that it can grow and reproduce itself. In addition, however, it has a sensitive soul and can perceive the world through its organs of sense. Man possesses a still higher faculty in rationality, the rational soul, a faculty which presupposes and rests on the lower souls of vegetative function and sensation.

The second principle is a bit harder to grasp, for it seems to reverse the modern notion of evolutionary change as proceeding from the simple to the complex. Each higher being on the ladder possesses a greater degree of all of the potentialities of living beings, a greater capacity to perform more of the functions and activities that life is capable of, from eating to thinking. However, the higher beings are really characterized not by complexity but by a much greater unity and simplicity, according to this way of thought. In a sense, of course, Aristotle would have agreed that a man is much more complex than a sponge, but his definition of simplicity or complexity is really different from our own. For Aristotle, it is a mark of a being's imperfection if, in the performance of any function, it must use cumbersome means. Thus the pure immaterial intelligences that moved the heavenly spheres—later identified with biblical angels—could come to know without the cumbersome use of the media of sensation and by an act of pure intellectual intuition. They were therefore both simpler and more perfect than man.

In turn, man surpassed the animals because his reason enabled him to perform many of the animal functions with greater efficiency, greater flexibility, and more directness. In this sense, man is both more perfect and more simple than the animals. In other words, simplicity means something like efficiency and power of functioning even though the substructure of the function may be somehow complex.

Man's position on this universal ladder is a peculiar one. He occupies a place of critical importance on it, for he is a bridge between the world of sense and the world of thought, between the world of animality and the world of pure intelligence, well above the animals and a little lower than the angels. Further, since his body is made up of the four elements which compose the universe, and he possesses in addition an immaterial rational principle, we may think of him as an epitome of the universe itself. He is a microcosm, as Donne said, "a little world, made cunningly of elements and an Angelike Spright," and occupies a semianimal and semiangelic position on the ladder of being, subsuming the various kinds of souls, or organized sets of functions, from the highest to the lowest.

Whatever the scientific or philosophical value of this conception of man it symbolized a profound psychological truth about him which we have recovered in modern times with the new model of the mind furnished by depth psychology. Man is, in both views, a paradoxical creature who is a fusion of potentially warring principles, reason and biological drives, animality and spirituality, atavistic impulse and imperfectly realized ideal restraints. Many of the extraordinary psychological insights of that tormented genius Blaise Pascal flow, like those of Freud, from the central perception that man is, indeed, *ni ange ni brute* but a puzzling mixture of both.

Yet if man's peculiar position on the ladder of being was for many a tragic one, others found a cause of exaltation therein. Pico Della Mirandola rejoiced in his vision of man as microcosm occupying a central position in the scheme of things because it gave man a unique freedom to dwell at any of the levels of the hierarchical reality he epitomized. Where Pico saw freedom, Pascal saw contradiction and the very cause of man's tragic grandeur and misery.

The history of ideas affords many instances of what the late A. O. Lovejoy in his classic work, *The Great Chain of Being*, called "metaphysical" pathos, whereby precisely the same interpretation of the world or the same idea, objectively considered, could nevertheless give rise to directly opposed valuations or emotional responses. Thus, when Giordano Bruno revived the ancient doctrine of the infinity of worlds and set it in the framework of the new astronomy, leaving the earth floating in an infinite uninterrupted sea of space, the idea generated remarkably different reactions. Pascal again gives us the negative side of response to this new cosmology, for the silences of infinite space terrified him. Thomas Traherne, on the other hand, exulted in a sacred rapture at this newly discovered manifestation of God's power and glory.

There is doubtless, at any time, a kind of intellectual claustrophobia as well as an intellectual agoraphobia, and the roots of such attitudes lie well within the recesses of the mind. Nevertheless, there seems little doubt that the great cultural transformations of the Renaissance and the seventeenth century generated an especially rich number of instances of "metaphysical" pathos. The comprehensive claims of medieval Christianity to prescribe correctness of belief in many areas of life which, to us, are essentially secular, had much to do with the intensity and diversity of responses to the breakup of that medieval synthesis enshrined in the old science and philosophy. Only an ideological complex which had demanded, promised, offered, and threatened so much could have created such extraordinarily varied, passionate and intense reactions, pro and con, to the increasing threats to its authority.

The first of the attacks on the old philosophy began early and were from two quarters. Within Scholasticism itself, the fourteenth-century nominalists and Occamites subjected traditional metaphysics to a thoroughgoing critical analysis and did much to undermine it in philosophically sophisticated circles. The more influential, if less thoughtful and expert, attack came from the humanists. From

Petrarch on down they never tired of attacking the Scholastics and Aristotelians in the interest of a purer religious life, a more elegant Latin style, or in defense of the new humanistic curriculum of study. But they were scholars and men of letters for the most part and, if they were interested in science at all, it remained a rather bookish interest with no attempt to uncover new knowledge of nature. They might prefer one ancient scientific authority over another but were unconcerned with initiating an independent inquiry into scientific subjects.

Nevertheless, they helped to recover more of the records of ancient science in their general search for all of the available literature of antiquity and, by undermining the prestige of the medieval curriculum of study, opened the door to a fresh consideration of the scientific achievements of classical times. More positive contributions to the development of scientific thought in the Renaissance came not from the humanists but from artists and artisans, and this for a fundamentally simple reason. The artistic conquest during the Renaissance of realistic representational techniques, the mastery of mathematical perspective, was the indispensable presupposition for the development of all of those sciences which rest on observation and description.

It is difficult to imagine a time when there was no knowledge of those representational techniques, not to mention photography, which would enable a biologist or an anatomist to make a permanent and accurate record of his observations. The great work of anatomists like Vesalius would have been an impossibility without the existence of highly trained and skilled illustrators. Even physics benefited from the work of the artists since some of them, like Leonardo, undertook the study of mechanics in order to understand and represent motion, while all of them were involved in thinking about optics in one degree or another because of their interest in perspective. The sophisticated union of theory and practice, science and art, which was to be found among so many of the great artists of the Renaissance was an essential part of what one distinguished scholar has called the "tangibilization of science," a process complementary to and concurrent with the intellectualization and upgrading of the so-called "mechanical" arts, especially painting, sculpture, and architecture.[6]

How important for science perspective, the techniques for representing three-dimensional space were, can be grasped by the simple perusal of any anatomy text after Vesalius. The elucidation of anatomical structure requires not merely a surface outline but the construction of imaginary cross-sections of the object in various planes so that a complete representation may be given of its structure and outer contours. Only by such a complete graphic record can observations be preserved and tested by other observers. It is no accident then, that we find in Italy a long line of painters who were also anatomists, and the list includes some of the greatest names in the history of painting: Pollaiuolo, Leonardo, Rosso Fiorentino, and Michelangelo. Nor is it any accident that some of the most magnificently illustrated books during the Renaissance and the seventeenth century were scientific treatises: the botanical studies of Nehemiah Grew, the anatomical studies of Vesalius and Malpighi, and the microscopical observations of Swammerdam and Hooke, to mention but a few.

Even photography, as important as it has been for scientific research, has not entirely displaced the artist, and medical illustration is still a flourishing profession. Moreover, students of biology are encouraged to draw specimens because as the great naturalist Louis Agassiz once said, "The best aid to the eye is a sharp pencil." Wherever in science, accurate observation, as distinct from experimentation or analysis, is the fundamental procedure, accurate representation is not merely an illustration of the result but the result itself.

Accurate drawings can educate the eye of the student in many cases, as in anatomy, more effectively than a photograph, and the very attempt to draw what one sees, however unskilled the attempt, literally opens the object to the understanding. The mind and the eye are not antithetical, for intelligent vision is informed vision. In a way, we think *because* we see and see *because* we think. It is thus no exaggeration to say that the Renaissance painters taught men so to look at the world about them that a detailed knowledge of the structure and function of the things natural became possible. If the modern sciences of observation are unique in history for the minuteness and particularity of their studies, they owe much of their success to the great artistic observers and experimenters, and in some respects the ancestor of the modern laboratory was the artist's *bottega*.

The only comparable revolution in vision in human history took place soon after the artistic energies of the Renaissance began to ebb, with the inventions of the telescope and the microscope. We cannot overestimate the importance of these two inventions, the two fundamentally simple instruments which excited the curiosity and wonder of mankind at the same time that they have been of incalculable value in extending our knowledge of the world in which we find ourselves. Interestingly enough, these two aids to the eye, which as instruments of research depended on the existence of adequate representational techniques to illustrate and report their disclosures, also marked the beginning of the end of the Renaissance union of art and science.

The microstructure of the human body, or magnified appearance of the surface of the moon, was of no value to artists as artists, for they were seeking, as they must, to represent reality as that reality appears to the natural vision, however educated or informed. To look at the human world through a telescope or microscope is to see it from a strange perspective, to enter, in fact, the world of Swift's *Gulliver's Travels* where the Brobdingnagian beauties have, in their "magnified" existence, coarse and pitted skin, and the minuscule Lilliputians are horrified at the elephantine proportions of the human race. Moreover, the new mathematics of the great Renaissance and seventeenth-century mathematicians soon went far beyond what artists or even architects needed to know. Science and art thus parted company. Whether this divergence was unnecessary or inevitable, desirable or a misfortune, has long been debated. It took place, and is one of the root causes of the numerous absurd confusions on the supposed enmity of science and the arts.[7]

The incredibly rich and varied creations of the Renaissance artists not only actualized utterly new sets of potentialities for art, they educated the vision and powers of perception of their contemporaries, and as these powers grew, men found new uses for the past and also found that nature revealed herself in a new light. These artists did for the language of vision what the great poets have done for language itself: created a vocabulary which turns diffuse impressions into intelligible experiences and raised thereby the general threshold of consciousness.

I should explain, at the risk of repetition, that the sort of vision I am talking about is a structured vision, vision guided by the intuition of an intelligible order in some datum of experience, of the relation of parts to whole or of function to structure. Whether in art or science, deep in the mind of the observer lies some "ghostly paradigm of things." It is interesting to note that some eminent contemporary scientists are worried about the effects of the fantastic progress in instrumentation so characteristic of contemporary science. It is beyond question that progress in instrumentation marked monumentual stages in the progress of science, but the sheer flood of data which these extensions of the senses produce creates a situation in which we see so much so fast that we inevitably risk understanding less.

Goethe has been criticized for his rejection of Newton's work in optics and for his statement that the use of the microscope and the telescope confuses the mind, in spite of the fact that he made important observations on the growth and motion of microorganisms! (The way a chance remark of the "sage of Weimar," like the one about the microscope, can be inflated beyond all importance finds its only parallel among Johnsonians.) Flatly stated and out of context, this sounds like obscurantism, yet Goethe was a scientist of distinction, and he may well have simply been afraid of empiricism run riot, of being deluged with data which, however accurate, could obscure the structure of things and the regularities in natural phenomena.[8]

From the point of view of the historian of science surveying the peaks and looking for the watersheds, the centuries of humanism and artistic innovation were preparatory, however indispensable that preparation and however permanent their nonscientific contributions to the human enterprise. This point of view has its own kind of vitality, even if it sometimes obscures the vital links between science and the rest of the culture, and simplifies the relations of a genius to the lesser men around and before him. On the other hand, it permits us to define the truly critical moments in the history of science and to identify the crucial figures who changed its direction. If we adopt it, the commanding figure in the history of modern science is Galileo.

And what an extraordinary figure he is! A scientific genius of the highest order, who is read in the Italian schools as a literary classic; a cultivated humanist and musician who wrote verse, studied with minute care the great Italian poets, knew many of the Latin classics by heart, and so loved painting that it is said that his earliest ambition was to be a great artist. Moreover, he is of special cultural interest because he has also entered history with the imaginative power of a great mythic figure, as a heroic martyr to free thought. The facts about Galileo's confrontation with the Italian Inquisition are more complex than some rationalists are willing to admit and the events more tragic, motives more blindly stupid than clerical apologists will often acknowledge. His personal tragedy was partly the result of ignorance, fanaticism, and ecclesiastical power politics; but Galileo also seemed to some of his judges to be toppling, for obscure reasons, that whole quasi-sacred picture of the world which had been the belief of the most venerable ancient authorities and had endured for ages.[9]

If one must select which idea of Galileo's was most threatening to his traditionalist contemporaries and his persecutors, we would probably have to say that it was Galileo's assumption of the complete uniformity of the whole of the natural world. With one stroke, this idea, an indispensable foundation of modern science, sweeps away the spheres, the quintessence, the circles of perfection, indeed, the whole physical image of hierarchical order, of a value-saturated physical universe, of the tangible tokens of traditional beliefs concerning God's governance of the world.

Galileo did not come upon this idea, or any other of his leading ideas, by pure acts of intuition. Diverse influences operated to create the view of cosmic uniformity. Historians like Machiavelli viewed events from the perspective of both a historic and a cosmic continuum. The universe is always the same throughout, as mankind in its fundamental motives and desires has not changed since it first appeared on the scene of history. Even the animism and panpsychism so popular among the Neoplatonists and the practitioners of magical pseudo-sciences like alchemy helped in this regard, for, if the world is one great, perfect, living organism, a *zoon,* as Plato called it, then the Aristotelian distinction between a sublunary imperfect world and a perfect celestial world became invalid. Equally important, Galileo drew upon a long tradition of important scientific work, especially in mechanics, which went back to the Middle Ages.[10]

Perhaps the most crucial period for the formation of Galileo's scientific ideas occurred during the years he spent at the University of Padua. It had long been an important one in Italy, and its medical school was reputed the best in Europe. There are two important reasons for the scientific vigor of Padua and for the stimulation and encouragement Galileo enjoyed there. One of them is political, for Padua lay within the Venetian domains and, however aristocratic the government of Venice may have been, its rulers were not tyrants. The university enjoyed great liberty of thought and utter freedom from ecclesiastical interference. Indeed, the domains of Venice were among the few regions in Europe where heretics and would-be heretics were safe from persecution by inquisitors of any creed whatsoever. Venice had never, like Geneva, burned a Michael Servetus or, like Rome, a Giordano Bruno.

A second reason for Paduan pre-eminence in science derives from its earliest tradition of studies. The study of Aristotle at Padua was a propaedeutic for a degree in medicine and not, as at the Sorbonne, for a degree in theology. Padua thus developed a strong tradition of critical study of the scientific thought of Aristotle. Physicians were less interested in rationalizing Christian theology than in learning how the organism worked in health and illness. Moreover, the military and nautical interests of Venice encouraged the development of mathematical and physical studies, and some of the earliest and most fruitful attempts to assimilate the newly recovered texts of the great Greek mathematicians took place within the sphere of Paduan intellectual life.

Aristotle has so often been blamed for stifling the development of science, that we need to remind ourselves that there has always been more than one kind of Aristotelianism in the history of Western philosophy. A tradition of critical reflection on his scientific and methodological works which started in the medieval universities was one of the indispensable foundations for the development of modern science. Galileo descends in a straight line from those medieval physicists who were groping their way to formulating a physics of "impetus." [11]

At Padua, scholars would not only have agreed that the mysteries of revelation should be pondered, but they maintained with more than ordinary emphasis that God's other book, the great book of nature, should also be read. The notion of God's two books, one sacred Scripture, the other the natural world before us, has a long history reaching back into patristic times and before. Its ultimate source in the Christian tradition can be found in St. Paul's reminder to pagans that the visible things of this world show forth the God who is their creator and who lies behind appearances. The theme comes up again and again during the Middle Ages and played a conspicuous role in that rationalization of Franciscan piety which was the work of St. Bonaventura. The Franciscan vision of the natural world as both a theophany and an object of fraternal love found its philosophical counterpart in St. Bonaventura's doctrine that through mystical contemplation we can behold in nature the "footprints" (*vestigia*) of God and, in the human soul, His image (*imago*).

At the close of the Middle Ages, Nicholas of Cusa gave a mathematical turn to the idea of reading God's book of nature, and found in mathematical symbolism a disclosure of the mysteries of God's being. Galileo, too, drew upon the metaphor when he urged men to understand that the book of creatures was written in mathematical language; not, however, the mystical mathematics of Pythagoras or

Nicholas of Cusa, but the chaste and sober language of quantity and order. Its letters, Galileo proclaimed, were triangles, circles, and other geometrical figures, and without mathematics, the book of nature would remain forever unintelligible.

At a stroke, Galileo repudiated the long tradition of a mystical-religious reading of the book of nature, whether in terms of mathematical or nonmathematical symbolism. In the same act, he relegated all sensory qualities—color, smell, sound, and the like—to the subjective world, leaving to the physical world only those properties capable of mathematical interpretation: extension, figure, position, motion, mass. As to God's other book, the book of Scripture, it was not intended to be a source of scientific information about the physical world, but was intended for the salvation of our souls and should be read for truths of that order. This sharp division between the world of quantity and the world of qualities, between scientific knowledge of the world and revealed knowledge marks off the views of Galileo from those of any of his predecessors even when, as with Nicholas of Cusa, they dimly grasped the special importance of mathematics in understanding the natural world. Indeed, Galileo expressly denies that the mathematical interpretation of nature will give man any special knowledge of supercelestial truths. On the contrary, the science would uncover and teach relatively few truths, but those would at least be certain. It would replace the many grandiose promises of the traditionalists with sober knowledge.

Galileo's specific contributions to science were many and of fundamental importance. He did more than any single individual, including Copernicus, to destroy medieval astronomy. His observations with the telescope disclosed "imperfections" in the surface of the moon which were utterly shocking to traditionalists convinced of the symmetry and "perfection" of the celestial world. His observations of the satellites of Jupiter not only revealed new heavenly bodies, but also showed that these new bodies stood in the same relation to Jupiter as the moon does to the earth. With this sort of evidence, and more, he was able to argue conclusively against both the Ptolemaic system and the system of Tycho Brahe according to which the sun moves about the earth while the remaining planets move around the sun.

Perhaps his most important contribution, if we must select one, is in the very manner in which he conducted his investigations into the law of falling bodies. It remains to this day a great and utterly lucid example of the way in which science can combine both reason and experimentation. As we shall see, method was the central concern of all of the "new philosophers" of the Renaissance and seventeenth century, and the contributions of Vesalius, Bacon, Harvey, and Descartes to the theory of practice of scientific method were of the greatest importance. Yet Galileo's example took on a paradigmatic value and can still tell us more about the way a physicist works than speculations, however impressive, about the way he ought to work.

Starting with alternative hypotheses about falling bodies, Galileo tried to *deduce* mathematically what *observable* consequences would follow from each of the alternative hypotheses, *before* conducting any experiments at all. One of the alternative hypotheses was found to lead to impossible consequences, for the mathematical deductions derivable from it would not fit any possible set of observable phenomena. The other alternative led to the consequence that the distance traversed by a falling body would be proportional to the square of the time which has elapsed from the moment the body began to fall. Then Galileo ran some experiments to test this hypothesis and they confirmed it.

Galileo's actual *modus operandi,* like that of other eminent scientists, was actually far closer to an authentically Aristotelian procedure than to anything Baconian. Nor does the later, more sophisticated, empiricism of a Hume or a Mill help to explain it. Aristotle had taught that the *arche* or universal, what in science we would call a law, is intuited by a kind of intellectual sight. Earlier, Plato had pointed to the element of insight in knowledge by his theory of *anamnesis,* by describing knowledge as a kind of remembering. Galileo began by studying a few instances of a phenomenon in an attempt to determine which of the elements in the data of experi-

ence could be given the most complete mathematical formulation.
This first step in his method he called intuition or resolution, and if
successfully carried out, the result would be a set of quantitative
formulations. The next step, which he called demonstration, was to
work these formulations into equations, sets of mathematical rea-
sonings, which would both describe phenomena already known *and*
suggest fresh and more inclusive mathematical propositions. Experimentation, the final step, is really a way of testing the "demonstration." Indeed, Galileo often devised experiments as a way of convincing his opponents rather than as a way of convincing himself.
In any case, he realized clearly what Bacon was often obscure
about: that mountains of experimental or observational data will
reveal no more than a few well-selected instances, that the "law"
has in principle been grasped during the process of what Galileo
called "intuition." Whitehead once expressed this fact by saying
that one good deduction was worth a thousand experiments, and
Darwin meant much the same thing when he said that ten specimens for a biologist were too many.

Galileo's whole procedure beautifully demonstrates the fact that
experiments do not discover a law, they test a hypothesis and, if it
is verified, the experiments *illustrate* the operation of the law.
Moreover, the gifted experimenter does not test all the conceivable
hypotheses. He first eliminates those hypotheses which would lead
to *unobservable* consequences. The elegance and power of Galileo's reasoning and method, the brilliance of his example, did more
to guide other researchers in concrete scientific investigation than
many of the contributions of the methodologists, however gifted.

One reason for this lies in the fact that the great methodologists
in this period were not always themselves gifted scientists, but a
much more important reason is that the search for method was the
search for a general method which would be a flawless instrument
for the making of certain and unlimited progress in theoretical and
practical knowledge of all kinds. Obviously, this goal was impossible, but the variety of ideas about method and the urgency with
which they were frequently advanced exerted a fruitful and varied
influence on general progress of science, even if such speculations

could not have been as exemplary as the concrete procedure of a Harvey or a Galileo.

The history of scientific methodology in modern times would take us back at least to the nominalists of the fourteenth century who, having relinquished metaphysics and having reduced universals to words, began to think about weighing and measuring. We would also have to include some consideration of the speculations of the medical faculty at Padua, the influence of the alchemists and magicians, the work of some of the medieval investigators in optics who were the sources for some of the most interesting ideas advanced by Leonardo da Vinci and the contributions of artisans and engineers.

However, what is important for us to grasp about that complex story with all of its interwoven strands is that, while it was dominated by the quest for a single general method, the variety of its speculations and results were more important than its unitary aim. There is no one method, in any precise sense of the word, for all of the sciences, and the variety of methodological ideas generated in the course of time permitted individual investigators to draw their guidance, or at least their inspiration, from the sources they found most useful.

Methodological speculation on science during the Renaissance reached its high point in the work of Bacon and Descartes. Both were enormously influential in fostering the progress of science, although only one of them, Descartes, was himself a scientist, and even though it is very doubtful if any scientific discovery of the first importance was ever made by a strictly "orthodox" Baconian or Cartesian.

In spite of the differences between these two great thinkers, they both shared a profound conviction that they had discovered a general method of finding new and certain knowledge of the nature of things. Moreover, both were convinced that correct method is more important for attaining to the proper understanding of the workings of nature than the genius of any particular individual no matter how spectacular. Neither Bacon nor Descartes felt that there were any really great intellectual differences between men of an intrinsic sort. Men are born mentally much more alike than different, and the great differences which later appear are much more the result of education and training than heredity. Even the greatest thinkers of the past, an Aristotle or a Plato, fell frequently into error because they trusted too much in the unaided powers of the mind and did not grasp the importance of a proper method.

Both Bacon and Descartes use the same figure of speech to illustrate their argument: an artistic ignoramus with a compass can draw a more perfect circle than the greatest artist working free hand. The correct method would be to the mind what the compass is to the hand and Descartes, even more than Bacon, was convinced that a single "compass of the mind" would solve problems and make discoveries in any field of inquiry whatsoever.

Dr. Johnson is reported to have said that wherever there is mystery roguery is not far behind. Both Bacon and Descartes would probably have agreed with him and extended roguery to include humbug. Ideals of clarity and simplicity as the hallmark of truth dominate their work. For Descartes the sign of a true idea would be its clarity and distinctness, while Bacon enjoined upon the seeker of truth that he write in as lucid and simple a style as possible, without frills or decoration, for the truth, however unexpected it may be at first, will be both simple and luminous.

All this, Bacon and Descartes had in common. However, they part company over mathematics. Descartes was certain that true ideas would be mathematical or approach the conditions of mathematical statement. To those who disagreed, he pointed to the fact that mathematics was the one science of the time, the one body of knowledge both in its methods and results, which commanded universal agreement. It therefore must be the very model of what knowledge is, the truly paradigmatic subject. Bacon, on the other hand, was suspicious of mathematics because it seemed to him to be, as it is, not really empirical. He feared that excessive attention to it would perpetuate the speculative approach to knowledge so characteristic of the philosophers of tradition.

Men needed to escape from bondage to symbols, whether verbal or mathematical, and turn their attention to things. Hence Bacon,

who did so much for the cause of science, failed to grasp the importance of the greatest scientific work of his own time and passed
over the achievements of Galileo, Kepler, and Harvey, not to mention Copernicus. The views of Galileo and Harvey must have
seemed to Bacon unconvincing because they were logically compelling without being based on masses of data. Harvey proved, for
example, that the blood must circulate even though he knew nothing of the capillary system and could not provide a complete physical model for the circulation of the blood. To Bacon, such reasoning, however compelling, must have seemed suspiciously
aprioristic.

Descartes, on the other hand, really grasped the greatness of his
revolutionary scientific contemporaries. He felt that the weakness
of the old philosophy lay less in its divorce from experience than in
the fact that the old thinkers were too trapped in naïve ways of
interpreting the experience they had, or too imprisoned in anthro-
pomorphic ways of looking at the world.

It would be unjust to imply that Bacon was merely a crude empiricist while Descartes was a fantastic rationalist. Bacon saw
clearly that, while some of the old philosophers were "spiders" and
spun great cobwebs of thought out of their own substance, others,
like the alchemists, were "ants" and went on blindly experimenting
and "experiencing" without modifying any of their hypotheses or
assumptions. The true investigator would be a "bee," creating the
honey of useful knowledge from the proper union of his own intellectual substance with external reality.

Descartes, too, had a place for observation and experimentation
in his scheme of science but it was a far more limited one than
Bacon's. The role of experimentation for Descartes lay in helping
the investigator to select between alternative, equally plausible,
mechanical-mathematical explanations. Thus Harvey had to experiment to discover the truth about the circulation of the blood because there was more than one mathematically correct interpretation of the evidence he had at hand. In such cases, experimentation
was crucial. Otherwise, Descartes was convinced that uniform and
coherent mathematical laws of motion governed all of the natural

world and that a complete system of nature could be constructed *a priori* by mathematical deductions from general mathematical principles. It would, in his view, have been a waste of time to derive, laboriously, such mathematical laws through experimentation.

Although both Bacon and Descartes greatly influenced the course of science, Descartes had perhaps the greater influence on the development of philosophy. His formulation of the traditional dualism between soul and body was really a recasting of that dichotomy into a fresh one between the mind and the body. So extreme was his disjunction between the two, and so persuasive his argument for it, that he set the major philosophical problem his successors tried to solve for at least a century. Descartes claimed that all of reality could be divided into matter or *res extensa*, "extended reality," and mind or *res cogitans*, "that reality which thinks." Let us note that "mind," for Descartes, has nothing to do with sensations, emotions, images, fantasies, or desires. It is simply the cognitive faculty, and this is immaterial and unextended.

How such a substance constituted a unity with the body of man presented a real dilemma, since mind and matter by definition had no possible points of contact. Descartes rather lamely suggested that, since the pineal gland was shaped like a cone and ended in a point, the soul may join the body at the apex of that organ, for a point has no dimensions and might well be thought of as the meeting ground for matter and spirit. Spinoza tried to solve this dilemma with a doctrine of psycho-physical parallelism. Mind and matter do not interact directly but nevertheless image each other, for they are but modes of a universal substance. Leibnitz suggested that the monads, all of the individual things which make up the universe, were governed by a pre-established harmony which coordinates the world external to the monad with the world internal to it. Thus, while there is no real interaction between monads, a thinking monad and its "experience" correspond because of a built-in universal system of order.

The influence of the debate over the relations of mind and body long outlasted its philosophical vitality. Even today, when philosophy has long since turned to other questions and in other directions, there is a massive residue of Cartesianism left in the general consciousness and many Westerners probably still experience themselves as dualistically split in a way which is fundamentally Cartesian.

The legacy of Bacon will detain us longer than that of Descartes for it was in many respects more important for the history of science. Bacon was much more the ideologist of science than Descartes and his ideas had a more far-reaching cultural and social impact. His influence is paramount wherever in modern science we find a utilitarian outlook and wherever we find a clear recognition of the co-operative, public, and cumulative character of scientific research. We need not know more about science than can be gleaned from a good newspaper to recognize how important a part of the modern scientific ethos these attitudes are. His ideological legacy has long outlasted his methodological ideas and, although the Baconian (and Cartesian) emphasis on method finds, here and there, a strong echo in modern scientific thought, our contemporary scientists are far less given to underestimating the role of genius and intuition in scientific work and none of them still dreams of a single universal method for all of science.

Other, more subtle, differences mark off modern from ancient science, differences which, in the last analysis, have to be referred to another kind of scientific "sensibility" whose roots go well beyond Bacon but which is clearly visible in page after page of his work. For one thing there exists in the modern scientific consciousness a sense, beautifully expressed in Montaigne, for example, of the importance of the mundane, everyday fact of experience, of the specific, odd, or unique datum, as clues to the nature of man and of the world. In the scientific sphere, this sense of life corresponds to the importance accorded in modern scientific thought to the negative instance or the abnormal and deviant specimen as affording not examples of nature's failures but clues to the way nature really works. "Treasure your exceptions," an injunction of crucial importance to the modern researcher, could not have been carved over the gateway of the edifice of ancient science.

This attitude toward experience is reflected in Bacon's plan to include a history of abnormalities in his projected universal natural history, a revolutionary idea related to his notion of experimentation as frequently involving the abnormalization of nature. In his view, the experimenter subjected nature to a kind of pressure or distortion which would force it to reveal its latent structures and processes.

Greek thinkers, on the other hand, were inclined to see in the abnormal or the monstrous a simple failure of nature, the inability of some form to dominate its matter. The ugly, the irrational, the abnormal were often confined to the cellar of the universe where all imperfect things are stored, as in a well-run household all skeletons are kept in closets. Aristotle's famous definition of a woman as some sort of "failed" man, as an instance where the form of humanity has failed to dominate its matter, has perhaps less to do with misogyny or castration fantasies than with this way of looking at some kinds of differences or exceptions.

In short, a defective specimen, whether truly defective or simply believed to be so, was much like a defective statue. Little could be learned by observing it. Such an approach was less characteristic of the Greek medical tradition which, by definition, was concerned with the abnormal in some sense of the word, but even there, the view of illness as a disturbance in the inner homeostatic balance of the organism did not lead to a search for specific causes or focus attention on those exceptional occurrences which may lead to new knowledge about the causes of illness. Interestingly enough, Greek ideas concerning homeostasis have come back again into medical thinking and are proving useful in interpreting the nature of some functional illnesses. But they have proved useful again only after scientific medicine conquered a vast amount of knowledge concerning specific agents of disease.

This intense concern for particularity and individuality, for arriving at the universal *through* the singular and even the exceptional instance, is a conspicuous feature of the modern literary sensibility as distinguished from the ancient one. Generalizations of this order are going to admit of numerous exceptions and qualifications, yet it is interesting to speculate that Montaigne, Shakespeare,

Bacon, and other great writers of the Renaissance did as much to educate inner vision for the apprehension of the concrete particulars of experience as the painters of the Renaissance did for sight. This is perhaps another way in which poets made a contribution to the progress of science somewhat analogous to the one the painters of the Renaissance made. In each case a language was created to bring more of the richness and diversity of experience within the realm of what can be articulated.

Another Baconian idea, although he was premature in advancing it, turned out to be of crucial scientific importance, and this was his elimination of any absolute distinction between that which is natural and that which is artificial. The laws which govern natural processes and those which govern man-made things are one and the same, just as the same laws of nature govern the normal and the abnormal. Not until 1828, when Friedrich Wöhler synthesized urea from ammonium cyanate, was Bacon's hypothesis validated, and against the general opinion of the scientific world of Wöhler's time. As far as I know, only the alchemists of Bacon's time even came close to grasping the fundamental unity of organic and inorganic nature, but they did so in such obscure terms that their version of the idea did not enter the main tradition of scientific thought.

Aristotle had made a very careful distinction between nature and "art." Nature realizes itself in a finite number of species and these species are, in the last analysis, the intelligible structure of nature itself. Such basic forms are radically distinguished from "exceptions" or abnormalities as also from works of art. The latter come into being when man imposes a man-made "form" upon a natural substratum. However valid Aristotle's analysis may be for some purposes, Bacon performed an important service in breaking the boundaries dividing nature and "art," normal and abnormal.

For Bacon, common universal laws govern the whole material universe. Matter, for him, was not a passive principle but a kind of active corporeality, something already shaped, actually or potentially dynamic. All things whatsoever, however men may want to distinguish them, come into being and change according to the same *material* causes. The sculptor who makes a statue is not, Bacon would have said, imposing a "form" on "matter," but functioning as a kind of active material cause on a material object. He is "obeying" nature's properties as manifested in the stone rather than changing them. Thus, a truly universal natural history would include works of art as well as abnormalities and normalities. It would include accounts of great feats of human ingenuity in making things as well as accounts of vile, mean, or bizarre objects, traditionally thought to be unworthy of the attention of an educated gentleman.

Historians of thought have usually been more interested in Bacon's contribution to scientific method, however critical they sometimes have been of it, than in his speculations on the larger issues of philosophy. However, in recent studies he has come to be considered as more original and distinctive a philosophical intelligence than was once generally thought.[12] In the first place, he constructed a singular kind of pluralistic philosophy which completely separated science from either revealed theology or theological metaphysics, on the one hand, and from politics, on the other.

It can easily be shown that this separation was historically necessary if science, at least in England, was to be set free from the suspicious interference of ecclesiastics and statesmen. Nevertheless, it has been a fateful separation wherever it has occurred. To separate either religion or politics from the disciplined rational inquiry of science can only foster the barbarization of both, and if the scientist in his laboratory should not, *qua* investigator, concern himself with the moral, intellectual, and political implications of his discoveries, the rest of us must. And even the scientist, as a social being, is simply one of the rest of us. But Bacon was a peculiar combination of the radical and the conservative, and was most anxious to demonstrate that the advancement of science would not disturb the religious and political *status quo* to which he was deeply committed. An unusually prophetic man in some respects, he failed to grasp just how revolutionary science was going to be.

Bacon, of course, genuinely felt that what is presumed to come from God, or what flows from the authority of the law, cannot be subjected to the same sort of criticism as what flows from the mind of man. However sincere he may have been in this belief, it is a refusal of the great philosophical demand for a unified vision of all the modes of knowledge. Indeed, Bacon points to this desire for intellectual unity and system as one of the very vices of learning. Far from being a noble ambition, it is the root cause for the failure of knowledge to progress, a delusion which blinded men to the proper way of acquiring new knowledge because it confounded together what should be kept strictly separated.

Other Baconian ideas are more interesting and derive from what is perhaps a purer philosophical impulse. He eliminated all mental properties from nature and from any possible metaphysics of nature. If men wished to construct a metaphysical view of the natural world, they must arrive at it by inductive procedures, and he offered such a naturalistic and materialistic metaphysics in lieu of the traditional Scholastic metaphysics taught in the schools. He advanced the theory of induction, and if he left many problems unanswered, we should remind ourselves that the theory of induction is still a problem, so much so that some modern theorists of scientific method have wanted to scrap induction altogether.[13]

He clearly propounded the notion that observation of the causal processes of nature, whether in natural or experimental conditions, must be the only test for a scientific principle. This notion is related in turn to his modification of the traditional view of logic. For many of the Aristotelians (not, of course, those like the scientifically and critically minded Aristotelians of Padua) logic was nothing less than the laws of reason, while some nominalists, such as Peter Ramus, suggested that it had to do only with the proper arrangement of propositions, and so reduced logic to rhetoric. Bacon thought of logic, on the other hand, as establishing the proper relation between sensory experience and the intellectual elaboration of that experience, as the instrument for the proper conduct of empirical activities undertaken for the advancement of knowledge. Finally, he ordered the branches of learning in a new and fruitful way, and not only gave a most brilliant and persuasive critique of the traditional systems of learning, but undertook to reform the direction of the future progress of organized knowledge.

In spite of the wealth of Bacon's ideas, the strength of his influence, his actual contribution to the advancement of science is
sharply debated. The great achievements of Galileo and Harvey
grew out of the rational empiricism which was the fruit of the brilliant critical consideration of Aristotelian ideas of method which
took place among the late medieval physicists and physicians.[14]
There is, moreover, in spite of the great praise of Bacon among
seventeenth-century scientists like Boyle and Hooke, no evidence
that any scientist really worked along strictly Baconian lines. Yet a
careful study of Baconian influence will show that he had a great
effect, however indirect or imprecise, on those sciences which rest
on observation, description, and classification. Botanists like Grew
and microscopists like Hooke felt themselves to be good Baconians, however deluded they may have been about this. We will take
up the character of Baconian influence in more detail after considering his philosophical views at greater length, but we can say that
his influence on the course of science was immense, if not precise;
ideological, if not technical and strictly scientific: and that he saw
some of the relations of science to technology, industry, welfare,
and other activities and concerns of man more clearly than anyone
before him.

Bacon's philosophy can, from one point of view, be divided into
two parts, a "destructive" or critical part, and a reconstructive part
in which the various proposals of his "great instauration," the
scheme for the reformation of all learning, are advanced. The reconstructive part is incomplete, and of some Baconian projects we
have little more than brief sketches. Insofar as he tried to encompass so monumental a task, much of his work would have been
doomed to remain unfinished even if Bacon had lived to be as old
as Methuselah.

His major philosophical works, *The Advancement of Learning,*
later expanded into the Latin *De augmentis scientiarum,* and the
Novum organum, both have this bipartite arrangement of a critical
and a constructive section. In the *Advancement,* Bacon begins with
a discussion of the enemies of learning, who are divines, politicians, and scholars. He did not think that all such were to be

thought of as necessarily enemies but he clearly recognized that divines had frequently impeded the progress of learning for fear of heresy or irreligion, politicians because they feared that learning might weaken the martial virtues of their people or otherwise create civic problems, and scholars because of the very character of traditional learning itself.

Bacon takes care of the divines and politicians rather briefly and spends the greater part of his criticism on the scholars. In fact, the whole of Bacon's critique of contemporary learning is directed against the universities, the seats of traditional learning, which foster a kind of knowledge shot through with "diseases and peccant humours." In general his accusation is that the learning of the universities, of the scholars they trained and supported, was sterile. Their thought remained entirely within the compass of their books and, far from discovering new knowledge, they spent their time in disputation and commentary. Neither fresh ideas nor fresh observation could possibly arise by such an approach to learning.

There were three main manifestations of diseased learning for Bacon and they were represented by the arid rationalism of the Scholastics, the excessive concern for elegance of style and copiousness of words of the humanists, and the undisciplined empiricism and excessive concern for practical results of the alchemists and magicians.

The Scholastics, said Bacon, erected massive systems of purely verbal character according to the rules of a verbal logic on the slenderest factual foundations. So doing, they were able to persuade themselves that they had answered all questions and knew all things. The very authority over the minds of men that their work commanded was, far from being a sign of its truth, a sure sign of its error, for scientific truth does not lie in authority or universal consent. Moreover, the Scholastic tradition was absolutely sterile. The Scholastics repeated the same formulas over and over again and disputed the same questions afresh in each generation. Unlike the mechanical arts, Scholasticism shows no signs whatever of progress.

The humanists too are wordy, but in a different way and about different things. Their knowledge is grammatical and rhetorical, a bookish knowledge which moves within the closed circle of the commentary or of servile imitation of an ancient text. The alchemists and magicians, the empiricists of Bacon's era, who tried to control natural processes did not, to be sure, spin webs of words but they too had serious defects which made them virtually as sterile as the Scholastics and the humanists. For one thing they worked in too small an area of the great world of nature and could not, even if they knew how, uncover those great general principles and laws which govern the natural world. Their empiricism was so undisciplined, so much in the service of immediate practical results, so lacking in theoretical and methodological guidance, that their efforts, however intensive, were doomed to failure. Where the Scholastics built structures of idle words, the empiricists amassed mountains of unorganized or hastily organized facts. Ironically enough, the two opposed ways of understanding the world meet in their identical pretensions to omniscience and in their fruitlessness.

Bacon, who had a marvelous gift for the explanatory metaphor, describes the Scholastics as being like spiders who spin out great and symmetrically organized webs from their own substance, beautiful and impressive structures, to be sure, but extremely fragile after all. The empiricists, on the other hand, are like ants who laboriously gather mountains of material and leave it entirely unchanged in storerooms. The Baconian method will combine some of the rationalism of the "spider" and some of the empiricism of the "ant." The proper Baconian will be like the bee, who gathers materials from various flowers, adds his own substances to it, and transforms it into honey. Bacon, in fact, is saying that we are not intellectually more gifted than the Scholastics, and if we pursue their methods, we can only produce cobwebs as they did. Nor can we work harder at gathering and amassing data than the magicians and alchemists who, indeed, labor mightily. What mankind requires if knowledge is to progress is a new method, not more labor or more thinking of an abstract sort. This method will, to a great degree, equalize minds. If, indeed, we are inferior in natural endowment to the intellectual giants of antiquity the proper method will more than compensate for this inferiority. It will, as we have seen, be for us what rulers and compasses are to artists: they enable a mediocrity to draw a straight line or circle far better than a remarkably gifted craftsman working free hand.

The new method was the heart of *The Great Instauration,* Bacon's ambitious plan for the restructuring of all knowledge, and the plan was to unfold in six parts. What was required, first of all, was an encyclopedic survey of all the existing branches of learning. Lacunae were to be pointed out, various desiderata suggested, reasons for the bad state of learning were to be clearly expounded, and suggestions for improving matters were to be made. *De augmentis scientiarum* comes pretty close to fulfilling Part I of the "instauration," and we may assume that Bacon felt he had made a complete contribution to this goal with his expansion of *The Advancement of Learning* into *De augmentis.*

The next part of the plan would expand the art of interpreting nature, and this is really the most important part of the whole project. The new art or method would, as we have seen, equalize intellectual differences between investigators to a large degree and would, properly used, generate new arts and sciences without fail. Unlike the existent methods it would not lead to endless disputation and the endless generation of arguments old or new, but would give certain, solid, and useful knowledge. Bacon promised to complete this part of his plan, but all we have that corresponds to it is the *Novum organum.* Of course, methodological completeness in scientific matters, in the sense in which Bacon or Descartes imagined such completeness, is impossible and this part of his plan is still "incomplete."

The third part of the plan called for the compilation of specific data, whether derived from experimentation or observation, arranged according to the rules of the art of interpreting nature. Such collections of data were to furnish the concrete empirical knowledge on which true learning must rest. Bacon's own contribution here was quite small and of minor importance. Some more or less incomplete attempts at natural history are all we have.

Part IV was *The Ladder of the Intellect.* Here again, all we have of Bacon's contribution is a preface, but we know that he meant to offer complete and thorough examples of the workings of his method with different subjects. Part V, *Forerunners, or Anticipations of the New Philosophy,* was to contain useful suggestions derived from the interpretation of the materials of the new natural history of Part III. Part V, nevertheless, would be useful and, presumably, Bacon hoped to aid other workers by suggesting not only topics of research (Part I) but by offering tentative results of relative accuracy which would effectively guide others in the right direction. Part VI of the *Instauration* was *The New Philosophy or Active Science.* Bacon left a preface to this part in which we learn that this was to be natural science brought to completeness in both the theoretical and the practical spheres. This task the great Lord Chancellor bequeathed to posterity, to those future generations of scientific workers who, building on the solid facts of Part III and using the new method described in Part II, would give a complete scientific account of the world and maximum control over all natural processes.

The philosopher C. D. Broad in a classic essay on Bacon said of *The Great Instauration:*

. . . we may compare Part II to a factory full of ingenious machinery, Part III to a store house of selected materials for this machinery to work upon, Part IV to a showroom in which typical examples of finished products are exposed to public view, and Part VI to a warehouse in which all the finished products are to be stored. Part V is a collection of goods made by inferior methods or only half finished, but useful enough for many purposes. Part I is a list in which the directors have noted what goods the public already have and what further needs remain as yet unrecognized or unsatisfied. Unfortunately the machinery is incomplete; and the engineer, instead of drawing the plans for completing it, has to spend his time in collecting raw materials and in penning eloquent prospectuses.[15]

Bacon shared with Descartes and other new philosophers an essential optimism about bringing science to "perfection" or completeness once men adopted the right methods. We know now after some centuries of brilliant scientific achievement that the world is more complex than men had ever thought, and that technological advances have brought immense problems in their train. Looking back on their hopes in the light of history we might be forgiven for detecting a little bit of the "spider" in both of these great men.

Bacon deepened his critique of the impediments to the advancement of learning in the first book of the *Novum organum* with his discussion of the four "idols," the four great sources of human error which more than any other cause, perhaps, prevent the accomplishment of the "great instauration." He meant by the term "idol" much the same thing that Democritus meant by the term *eidolon,* a false image which enters consciousness and which is the cause of erroneous and irrational explanations of the order of things. For Democritus as for Bacon the *eidola* were responsible for all the traditional, conventional ways of looking at things which it was the task of the philosopher to sweep away.

Bacon's "idols" were four, the idols of the tribe, of the market place, of the cave, and of the theater. The idols of the tribe were those causes of error common to all humanity, innate in human nature, and which derive from the nature of the human mind and senses. The intellect of man is, alas, not often what Bacon called a "dry light" but rather the prey to his wishes and fears. Moreover, men's minds are not only unstable and restless, they are also, at the same time, sluggish and lazy. Thus men jump to conclusions which please them, ignoring contrary evidence or misinterpreting it, too restless to think carefully and too lazy to work hard at gathering all the evidence required. They also take fantasies and ideas for realities and treat vague abstractions as if they really existed. Even though the senses are generally more reliable than thought, men frequently also ignore the fact that even sensation may be in error and so err in their observations as well as in their speculations.

The idols of the market place are all of the errors of understanding which arise from the nature of language itself. This was, in Bacon's view, the worst of the idols. Language is a collective invention to which all men, *hoi polloi,* contribute. It is the creation of average minds and therefore embalms and preserves the thinking of commonplace minds of the present as well as the past. It is filled with the false associations and false beliefs which dominated the thought of the past and to which we have been inevitably exposed from infancy on by the very process of having to learn a given language at all. Many of the words we have learned to use enshrine a false conception of reality or, indeed, express nothing but fantasies with no basis in reality whatever. Moreover, unless we learn habits of critical thought, we are totally unaware of the pitfalls of the very language we use. Words, in fact, are inherently misleading and inadequate vehicles of truth.

Bacon's criticism of language is even more radical than that of Hobbes who, at least, felt that some intellectual progress was possible through precision of definition. Bacon's strong distrust of language is perhaps the fundamental cause for his cautious view of the role of hypothesis in science. At times we almost feel that Bacon, although he recognized the role in science of hypothesis balanced by sensory observation, really would have liked to reduce the acquisition of all knowledge to direct observation. The Baconian view of language gave to the development of science in England a particular slant that it did not have elsewhere in Europe. Many of the proponents of the Baconian advancement of learning were also involved in the movement for the reform of language, and men such as John Evelyn, Thomas Sprat, and Abraham Cowley were active in both endeavors. According to the convinced Baconians, the greatest single impediment to the reformation of learning in the past had been the excessively verbal character of that learning, its vulnerability to the idols of the market place. It was inevitable therefore that the reform of learning and the reform of language should have come to be considered as but two aspects of one great reformation.

The idols of the cave, whether innate or acquired, all refer to the particular prejudices or distortions of the single individual. Such idols are literally numberless, for they do not derive from the defects common to mankind as a whole but from the peculiarities of each man's unique constitution or his private diffraction of environmental influences. Bacon tells us that you can be reasonably certain you are being led astray by idols of this sort if you find an explanation peculiarly pleasing and satisfying. Any one of a host of vulgar prejudices might serve as rough examples of these idols. C. D. Broad suggested as a more sophisticated example Lord Kelvin's assumption that all physical theories must be capable of being represented by mechanical models.

The first three classes of idols have one feature in common. They cannot be entirely overcome. Men must use language whatever its limitations. Their minds and senses cannot be turned into perfect instruments of knowledge and each individual will always be subject to the distortions of his own peculiarities. Nevertheless, properly instructed, mankind can reduce the dangers of the first three kinds of idols to a minimum. On the other hand, the fourth class of idols, idols of the theater, those false philosophic systems of the past which we voluntarily construct and believe in, can be entirely eliminated. These systems are simply the result of ignorance of the proper method of using the mind and the senses. They are the productions of false reasoning laboring over insufficient facts, poorly organized evidence or badly selected data. There is no point, Bacon tells us, in trying to argue away each of the authoritative false systems of the past in detail. Bacon saw that to do so would be to waste time in that very same disputatious, verbal learning he so despised. Fortunately, they all bear an infallible sign of their weakness. They neither progress nor do they have any practical consequences. Once men grasp the true method of learning, the proper way of organizing experience and interpreting it, the old philosophy will inevitably disappear.

The idols describe all the snares and pitfalls that beset men in the quest for true and useful knowledge of things. Bacon, however, never merely criticizes but always offers grounds for hope. From the idols he passes to what he calls "ministrations," that auxiliary part of logic which offers assistance to sense, memory, and reason. The senses require instruments to increase their power and accuracy, and whatever tendency they have to error can be greatly reduced by checking the data of one sense with those of another or the observations of one investigator with those of another. In fact, Bacon's conception of experimentation involves reducing dependence on the senses to a minimum, for in a properly conceived experiment there should be little chance for errors in observation. Memory is aided by the keeping of careful records and by intelligent methods of arranging data derived from observation or experiment. The reason is aided by certain methodological instructions concerned both with collection and organization of data and with guiding the careful movement of the mind from particulars to general principles and back again. The investigator—who, to be sure, possesses a mind already purged of idols—must constantly check his conclusions at every stage against experience. He will use an inductive method more complex than that of simple enumeration in that it will be guided by careful attention to negative instances which, in turn, will help to eliminate false alternatives.

Bacon's stress on the negative instance clearly differentiates his method of induction from that of Aristotle. The latter had distinguished between two kinds of induction: one, the theoretically complete but practically impossible kind, which would demand the examination of each particular instance of the class of objects to be studied. We might call this induction by a process of utterly exhausting the subject. The other kind of induction, a workable kind, was induction by definition. Here the investigator defines the nature of the species, for example, by examination of a sample of the individuals comprising it, individuals assumed to be "typical." Even though the notion of species as "types" has, in emphatic form, been something of an impediment in biological thought, we all really do something more or less like this when we arrive at the notion of a species. The danger in this mode of induction came about not only because of the tendency to assume that the species was really a fixed type but because of the subsequent tendency to treat each individual that did not conform to the hypothetical type as an exception or a monster. If, at times, the definition of the type was reworked to accommodate to exception, the more usual procedure was to treat it as an unintelligible abnormality. Bacon's stress of the negative instance, on the positive significance of variation within species, sharply distinguishes his theory of induction from Aristotle's.

One of the most striking features of Bacon's constructive philosophy is his method for the creation of a truly useful natural history. Part of the new natural history was to comprise, traditionally enough, a history of normal and typical natural phenomena. Two other features, however, are original and follow consistently from his insistence on the study of negative instances, on the one hand, and on his obliteration of the distinction between the artificial and the natural on the other. Bacon enjoined upon future investigators that they make a thorough history both of abnormalities and of the results of experimentation and invention. In this injunction Bacon was far in advance of his contemporaries and demonstrates a philosophical brilliance that some of his modern interpreters have wanted to deny him. Moreover, although Bacon had a strongly utilitarian attitude toward knowledge, he insisted that the data for his new history should be chosen essentially for whatever possibilities they seemed to have for affording new knowledge, for providing the factual base for those fresh inductions which alone can advance learning. He grasped clearly enough that an excessive utilitarianism could dry up knowledge at the very root. This caution reflects itself also in his careful distinction between "experiments of fruit" and "experiments of light," and his emphasis on the greater importance of the latter. He also warns the future investigator to avoid being misled by curiosities, however interesting in themselves, for the clue to the secrets of nature also lies in and even rules the commonplace things we usually ignore as well as in the unusual and the exceptional.

Thus Bacon urges investigators to collect their data from all possible sources and to select those facts out of the masses of data which have the greatest potentiality for advancing learning. Such are called "prerogative instances" in the *Novum organum* and Bacon, no more than we, can give a foolproof method for selecting such data infallibly. One thing is certain, however. Investigators purged of the idols will be much more likely to grasp "prerogative instances" and realize the force of "negative instances" than minds still caught in the trammels of erroneous thinking.

As we shall see when we discuss the Baconian influence, many of the self-professed Baconians of the seventeenth and eighteenth centuries distorted the master's teachings in the classic way that second-rate minds distort the ideas of genius: by ignoring the careful discriminations and qualifications of the original. Thus some Baconians carried Bacon's emphasis on the utility of true knowledge to heights of vulgarity and even wished to turn all the schools of Britain into trade schools. Some of the "virtuosos"—gentlemen experimenters and collectors of specimens—exaggerated Bacon's recognition of the importance of abnormal phenomena, and assembled useless curio cabinets of freaks and oddities. Others, like Bacon's "ants," continued to experiment mindlessly.

If some distortions of Bacon's teaching came through exaggeration others came through misunderstanding. In his discussion of the character of true natural philosophy Bacon still uses much of the terminology of the past and some subsequent students of his work failed to grasp that Bacon had truly presented a radically different conception of natural philosophy than the traditional one of the schools. Thus Bacon's "metaphysics of forms" sounds like an old-fashioned discussion of qualities. Heat, color, weight—all are "forms," specific powers which produce certain effects in the external world and on the sensory apparatus. So far Bacon sounds like a Scholastic physicist. They too sought to catalogue the large number of different powers or qualities discernible in the physical world. However, Bacon insists that these forms are not, as they would be for a Scholastic, final structures of physical reality. They are, rather, specifications of a more universal nature, so that heat must be understood as a variety of motion. This in fact is what Bacon set out to prove in the second book of the *Novum organum*.

Thus Bacon's metaphysics of forms has nothing to do with traditional metaphysics at all, in spite of his use of the term. As Broad has pointed out, Bacon is very close to stating what Keynes called the principle of limited variety. This fundamental concept of modern science posits that there are a limited number of substances which can be clearly distinguished from one another in terms of properties that are unique to them, e.g., melting point, density, etc., and that the enormous number of substances we discover in the world are reducible to these primary substances. Moreover, such apparently ultimate qualities as color can be reduced to variations in the frequency of a periodic change, and heat and color both can be assimilated to each other in terms of motion once color is interpreted as the periodic motion of particles of a certain magnitude and heat as the irregular motion of particles of a larger magnitude. Bacon grasped in principle that the scientific understanding of the world involved establishing a particular kind of unity between natures which had hitherto been considered simple and ultimate. This unity is discovered by the study of what Bacon called the latent processes and latent structures of bodies and simple natures. The fundamental processes of the physical world are not only dynamic they are also imperceptible. In fact, while Bacon was not, strictly speaking, an atomist, he accepted the view that particles in motion were the ultimate constituents of matter. When he criticized the brute empiricism of the "ants" he criticized, in effect, the naïve commonsensical view of matter which made it impossible to unify disparate phenomena. The "ants" failed to bring the mind into play, he might have said, precisely insofar as they were unable to infer latent invisible structures which alone would really account for what the senses gave them.

The boldness of Bacon's thought on scientific and philosophical matters was not paralleled by any particular originality concerning either religion or politics. As we have seen, part of this reticence flowed from Bacon's honest conviction that scientific inquiry need not damage either the established church or the monarchy and, in the *Advancement,* he wrote many eloquent paragraphs to reduce the anxieties of statesmen and ecclesiastics on this score. His religion would have appeared to be "genuine," whatever we may mean by this, but not particularly strenuous. It was a matter which was settled and which needed no further discussion. He had, it would seem, the attitude of the conventional believer who makes conventional observances but whose talents and energies are really at the disposal of other interests.

Politically, Bacon would have to be called a conservative constitutionalist. His essay on the "True Greatness of Kingdoms and Estates," for example, presents us with exalted ideals of government, and Bacon certainly believed in the right and duty of Parliament to make good and wholesome laws which would improve the state and correct the defects in the body politic as fast as they arose. Nevertheless, *The Advancement of Learning* assured James that Bacon would never in a thousand years dissent from the absolutism so dear to that monarch, and Bacon conceded the right of rebellion to no man or people, even if the change would have been for the better. Bacon, in fact, was a stanch defender of the royal prerogative, but not at the utter expense of the Parliament. No man who possessed his firm belief in the rule of law, his sense of the unity of his country and people, his belief in certain moral principles of government, however much the actual conduct of affairs might involve expediency, could have advocated any theory of capriciously absolutistic government.

In politics as in religion, Bacon believed in the *données,* what his time and place offered, and he did so with conventional sincerity. Some readers of Bacon have been harsh on him and have accused him of gross hypocrisy. How could the man who wrote a noble essay on friendship have prosecuted Essex? they ask, forgetting that Essex was guilty of treason and that it is only in the modern, brutal, totalitarian state that it becomes truly plausible for a sensible man to put personal loyalties above those of the body politic. Others have rightly noted the utter absence of romantic sentiment in Bacon. In fact, it is hard not to be somewhat amused when Bacon humorlessly points out that young men need women to take care of concupiscence, middle-aged men need them for company, and old men need them as nurses, although his observation that wives and children constitute hostages to fortune and may interfere with enterprises of great pith and moment should scarcely offend anyone with any experience of life. The simple fact about Bacon is that he was completely unresponsive to the heroic, whether to the great lover, the noble warrior, or to the magnificent rebel. His mind and imagination were remarkable but sober, and his measured, beautifully lucid prose is suffused with that "dry light" which he felt a deluded mankind needed so badly.

A brief glance at his views on poetry will perhaps illustrate more clearly what his temper was like. Some of his general views expressed in *De augmentis* derive from Aristotle. Poetry is an "imitation" of life, that is a representation of generalized human action or a specific action under an individualized aspect. Bacon, however, assigns poetry to a special faculty, the imagination, and along with other Renaissance theorists of poetry, derives the poetic activity from man's disappointment with things as they are, with the human desire to create a "golden world." Aristotle, on the other hand, had located the origin of poetry in a natural impulse to "imitate" or make representations of things and, more important from the point of view of literary criticism, in an impulse to represent events as more intelligible than they are in nature where they are embedded in too many contingencies and irrelevancies.

Bacon divides poetry into three kinds. Epic imitates the actions of men as past, while drama imitates them as present. A third category is what he calls "parabolic" poetry, and this is a kind of allegorical poetry, the imaginative representation of a philosophic or moral truth. It would seem that Bacon first attempted a division of poetry into three categories in terms of temporal aspect as related to genre. But the third division introduces a new principle of classification, semantic in nature, and inconsistent with the first. On the other hand, "parabolic" poetry is "typical," or as we might say, timeless, so that a temporal scheme might plausibly govern all three categories. Obviously, from the point of view of time of presentation, there can be no form of representation of events as future, since a writer imagining future events would have to present them as transpiring before our eyes or as having happened, that is as drama or narrative.

Bacon utterly ignores the lyrical forms of poetry, the whole of the literature of subjectivity, in his discussion of poetry, and relegates them either to philosophy or to rhetoric. He reflects in this one of the limitations of neoclassical interpretations of Aristotle which narrowed the meaning of *mimesis* to actions of a rather palpable or visible sort. Thus elegies, odes, sonnets, and so forth were thought of as either like moral essays, in which case they belonged to philosophy, or as persuasive and hortatory proclamations quite properly falling under the rubric of rhetoric.

As we might expect, Bacon was either uninterested in, or suspicious of, the emotional effects of poetry, the sort of effects poetry achieves through an imaginative reordering of the data of experience and the everyday rhythms of language. Bacon felt that poetry should reflect the world of fact, that it should give us that world in generalized and heightened form, to be sure, but that it should not depart too far from it. If it is "parabolic" poetry, then it should embody in its presumably ornamental tropes and figures a literal truth of the scientific or philosophical order. Bacon's great vision of new possibilities for science was certainly not paralleled by a commensurable vision of poetry. Indeed, in his inventory of the state of knowledge in his time, he thinks that poetry as a branch of knowledge is complete and needs no further development.

Bacon's short work *On the Wisdom of the Ancients* (*De sapientia veterum*) offers the reader a remarkably revealing example of just how the Lord Chancellor, along with some of his more sober-minded contemporaries, read poetry. It is a set of allegorical interpretations of ancient myths, some quite ingenious and others hopelessly far-fetched, and what Bacon discovers in the ancient poetic fables is nothing less than some of his own most cherished philosophical, scientific, and moral opinions. Obviously, allegorical poetry and allegorical interpretations of poetry had been among the dominating traditions of Western literature from antiquity, and there is nothing peculiar in Bacon's allegorizing of myth as such. What is revealing, however, is his utter insensitivity to anything we can identify as their literary and aesthetic value.

His few remarks on the drama are so "unliterary," even below his remarks on nondramatic literature, that it is utterly impossible to imagine how a small and industrious group of people could ever have thought that Bacon really wrote Shakespeare's plays. Bacon was keenly aware that the drama could have a powerful effect on its audience, but he does not follow Aristotle in thinking of that effect as a benign catharsis. Indeed, he seems inclined to fear that the drama lends itself too readily to corrupting the people and to the dissemination of evil. It was for him, apparently, a very ambivalent form of literature, too easily adapted to the purpose of manipulating the mob by pandering to its appetite for rhetoric and spectacle. I do not suppose that Bacon would have disagreed with Jonson, that the good poet must be a morally good man and that the function of drama was to elevate the moral awareness of the audience. He does not, however, say anything to indicate that he lived during the greatest period of dramatic art after the ancient Greek theater.

One feels that although Bacon may have reflected on poetry with the aid of Aristotle, he really sided with the Plato of the *Republic*. After all, the idols which delude mankind are largely the result of the emotional elements in human nature and language. With perfect consistency Bacon rejected the emotional side of poetry. The man who pursued knowledge illuminated by a "dry light" and whose reflections on the practical conduct of life are coldly prudential, would hardly be carried away by aesthetic raptures.

Bacon's distrust of the emotions, his essential suspicion of heroic values of whatever sort, were not unrelated to some limitations of an intellectual kind. Certainly one motive for his absolute separation of divine and natural knowledge lay in his suspicion of "enthusiasm," of that passionate concern with religion which, in his era, so often led to political turbulence. Bacon accepted revealed religion, as we have seen, and firmly refused to relate it to other realms of thought and imagination. Indeed, he insists that the sign of a genuine divine revelation will be its unintelligibility. The philosopher with the consuming sense of having a revolutionary and rational intellectual mission, ends up in the same boat with Tertullian who believed precisely because revelation was absurd! Did Bacon really think this? Of course, but one cannot help but feel that this abdication of inquiry was prompted by that cool, often ruthless, prudential temper which so exasperated his political enemies and still exasperates some contemporary readers of his *Essays*.[16]

Whatever Bacon's limitations may have been as a man and as a thinker, however little he may have had to do with fostering the great scientific discoveries of the seventeenth century in any direct way, he had enormous impact as the "statesman of science" on shaping the developing sense of what science was about, what it might be used for, and how it was to organize itself. His influence did much, for good and for evil, to create many of the elements in that cluster of values and attitudes which surrounds scientific work in our own time. To that influence we now turn.

The influence of Bacon on English civilization in the seventeenth century reached into every important aspect of cultural and even political life. In a general way, we can detect the Baconian influence whenever we encounter the phrase "experimental philosophy." This was the current of scientific thought which, however much it may have varied from Baconian principles in some respects, nevertheless was true to the spirit of its author in advocating the accumulation of great amounts of new, accurate information, whether derived from observation or experiment. Running parallel to it was the Cartesian current of thought, and it went by the name of "mechanical philosophy." The Cartesians accepted Descartes' mechanical model of the physical universe and his mathematical model of scientific knowledge. However different, both traditions agreed in giving to experimentation a crucial role in the advancement of scientific learning.

The English "virtuosos," the enthusiasts for the new philosophy, were all committed to the experimental method, whether or not they accepted the mechanical model of the universe offered by Descartes. Even those "virtuosos" who were not Cartesians were quite prepared to agree that many of the results of observation and experiment were best stated in mathematical terms, and they pointed to the great affinities between Descartes and Bacon in that both advocated the direct study of nature and both rejected authoritarianism in scientific matters.

As we shall see, only particular aspects of Bacon's thought became greatly influential. On some matters of great importance to him his advice was ignored. For example, Bacon was firmly opposed to specialization in science. In fact it was among the major obstacles to the advancement of learning that had to be overcome.

Bacon thought it very unfruitful to investigate the nature or "form" merely of a particular thing or instance. A specific form will also be found elsewhere in nature, and cannot be understood unless it is studied in all of its characteristic manifestations. In the light of this notion we can understand why Bacon looked with such mistrust and misunderstanding upon the work of Harvey and Gilbert, for example. To be sure, they did not accumulate heaps of data. They seemed much too theoretical, deductive, or too attached to mathematical or verbal demonstrations. But they were also, in Bacon's view, overspecialized, too confined to one small section of the universe.

The great scientists of the era certainly do not seem overspecialized to us moderns. On the contrary, the versatility of some of the greatest scientists from Galileo to Newton and beyond seems to us to be simply staggering. Nevertheless, their scientific work was accomplished through what would have appeared to Bacon to be narrow specialization. In Bacon's scheme of things, the great achievements of scientific thought would come when the universal natural history would be complete or near completion. Unless most of the facts were in, how could men know the nature of things? Clearly, Bacon's empiricism, with its considerable sophistication, led him to overestimate just how much data a scientist may need to make his contribution to knowledge.

In the final analysis, the Baconian influence was not in any precise sense of the word scientific, but ideological. Bacon was, as R. F. Jones called him, the "spiritual leader" of scientific thought. His great program of reform, his hopefulness concerning the advancement of learning, his inspiring vision of the practical benefits which the new science would bring to alleviate the miseries of mankind— all of these attitudes generated devotion and emulation in many who could not be called Baconian in any strict sense of the term.

In specific ways, the Baconian influence appears not only in experimentalism, but even more precisely wherever men sought to contribute to a universal natural history inspired by the belief that this achievement would lead to a knowledge of all the laws of nature and enable man to reproduce, at will, all of the processes and results of which nature is capable. Bacon and his followers were, from our point of view, rather sanguine, to say the least, about the amount of time it would take to complete this task. In a few generations, all the data will have been accumulated and man will find himself on the threshold of becoming master of nature. However misconceived this task may have been, theoretically and practically, Bacon's vision had the effect of channeling an unprecedented amount of human energy into scientific work. But the greatest work was done by people who knew when to ignore him, whether consciously or unconsciously.

The experimentation and observation that Bacon advocated was not new to science nor did Bacon, as we have seen, give a really satisfactory account of the role of these procedures in uncovering new knowledge. His advocacy of experimentation became, rather, the heavy artillery in the attack on ancient science and philosophy. The new philosopher must remain in physical contact with the multiplicity of nature and not yield to the temptation to spin words and theories as the ancients and the Scholastics had done. It was to the great credit of thinkers and experimenters that they gathered new data and tried to make useful discoveries and inventions. Bacon himself had pointed to the heroes, largely unknown, who had invented the compass, gunpowder, and the printing press, three inventions which in his eyes symbolized what even a random, unsystematic search for discoveries might accomplish.

The high value Bacon put on the contributions to knowledge of practical craftsmen, of mariners and of artisans became very strong in many of his followers and helped to complete a much needed redefinition of the nature of knowledge which began among the artists and craftsmen of the Renaissance. Traditional views of knowledge had doubtless been too aristocratic and contemplative. Bacon, from one point of view, simply gave a powerful and convincing summation of the arguments against the aristocratic and purely intellectualistic view of knowledge that had been worked out by several generations of artist-anatomists, architects, and engineers. In addition, he clarified the relations which obtain between technology, industry, and commerce, on the one hand, and knowledge, on the other, and brilliantly grasped that this relation was a reciprocal one. Practical and economic needs help to generate new knowledge and knowledge in turn can serve to change man's physical and economic environment. The greatest blow which Bacon gave to the older traditions of learning lay in his insistence on the fact that even average minds and uneducated men could make contributions to the store of learning and invention of the first importance when they adopted other methods for dealing with the world than the educated and cultured were accustomed to use.

Perhaps the outstanding characteristic of the Baconian current of thought in the seventeenth century was its emphatic utilitarianism. Bacon himself was not as extreme as some of his followers in this, and as we have seen, carefully distinguished between those "experiments of light" which would reveal general principles governing natural processes and "experiments of fruit" which would issue in practical results. Bacon knew well that the "ants," indefatigable experimenters that they were, achieved little precisely because they sought too eagerly for immediate practical results. Centuries of alchemical experimentation motivated by the desire to make gold had led nowhere. Nevertheless, the primacy of experiments of light over those of fruit does not mean that Bacon valued pure understanding for its own sake. On the contrary, the principles that man would discover from disinterested inquiry were precisely the ones which would give him practical dominion.

The careful balance that Bacon tried to preserve between theory and practice, the quest for understanding and the quest for power, was lost in many of his followers. The Baconians of the latter half of the seventeenth century at times inflated the utilitarianism of the master to the point of vulgarity and made it virtually identical with an attitude of resentment of intellectual activity pursued for its own sake. A debased Baconianism became part of the ethos of those newly literate, emergent classes, mostly Puritan, who confronted the ancient, aristocratic cultural traditions with that peculiar form of *ressentiment* which Max Scheler found to be characteristic of eras of rapid social change, those eras when economic and political power shifts from "haves" to "have-nots."

As R. F. Jones put it in his classic study of the Baconian influ-ence, *Ancients and Moderns:*

The utilitarian spirit is everywhere evident in the twenty years pre-ceding and following the Restoration, that is, among the Baconians, not among the atomic scientists. The effects of it are seen in the attitude of the age toward what we call pure science. The satisfying of intel-lectual curiosity through scientific inquiry is regarded as a legitimate activity, but it is associated with the proud speculative man in contrast to the humble experimenter working for the good of mankind.[17]

By and large, then, the Baconians fostered an attitude hostile to speculative reasoning, for such reasoning in their view divorced the mind from sensuous observation of phenomena. We have seen how Bacon considered all of the intellectual monuments of ancient and medieval thought as sterile, however impressive, and however gifted their creators. They had been prodigious efforts of the mind and will which had nevertheless done nothing to alleviate the lot of mankind.

Bacon, above all, encouraged the belief that no great qualifica-tions of intellect were necessary for scientific work. The use of the senses, with which men are quite uniformly endowed, and the co-operation of large numbers of investigators, would more than com-pensate for genius, imagination, and intuition. The aggressively democratic political elements among the Puritan rebels found this doctrine, needless to say, quite congenial. Bacon would have been horrified to see it, but he became the ideological father of a new historical fact of the first importance: the fusion of social and in-tellectual egalitarianism in a single political movement of great in-fluence and power. The new movement differed *toto genere* from anything earlier. Protagoras and other theorists of democratic gov-ernment in the ancient world had argued that all men possessed the requisite degree of *eidos* and *dike,* "reverence" and "justice," to live in a free state and to make democratic institutions work. Men did not, however, possess any other form of equality. Indeed, the whole agonistic ideal of ancient Greek culture, the striving for *arete* or excellence that dominated the ancient *polis,* was predi-cated on admiration for the subordination to the superior man, the man with rare gifts of mind, spirit, or body. The most crucial scenes in Thucydides are precisely those which describe the corruption of the Athenian people when they turn from the Periclean ideals of excellence within freedom, of respect for leadership and order within a democratic constitution, to the demagoguery and mindless egalitarianism of Cleon.

The novelty of Puritan intellectual egalitarianism lay in the belief that a certain method and certain kinds of activity canceled out most, if not all, intellectual differences between men. Never before had men been provided with a coherent rationale and a set of "instruments" for the task for intellectual self-assertion. For many people, Baconianism came to be the possession of a marvelous thinking machine which always gave the right answers and which permitted one to ignore the views of those misguided enough not to use it.

This conviction frequently found expression not only in the utilitarian outlook but also in the assertion of the primacy of sense over thought in the acquisition of knowledge. In a way, this is an authentically Baconian idea, for Bacon had frequently argued that men had relied too much on pure thought and not enough on observation. The distinction between him and some of his followers is again more a matter of the spirit in which this conviction was used than the meaning of the letter.

Since the most articulate and influential spokesmen for Baconianism were generally to be found among the Puritans, it might be useful before proceeding to point out that generalizations about Puritanism are quite risky. The term could be applied to a common soldier in the Parliamentary army or to a great gentleman like Fairfax, to an agitator like Lilburne or to a poet, thinker, and statesman of the order of Milton. Moreover, attitudes characteristic of the main stream of Puritan conviction early in the century are frequently held by Anglicans and Royalists later on. Thus, the plain style in preaching originally associated with Puritanism finds champions among the prelates of the Restoration, and the very center of Baconian thought, the Royal Society, received royal sanction and numbered important noblemen among its friends and supporters.

Nevertheless, it is true to say that the major Puritan sects, regardless of differences, did share in some common political principles and certain common cultural attitudes.

Revolutionaries, even mild ones, are by definition optimistic, and Puritans of whatever variety were to one degree or another revolutionaries. Bacon, although the stanchest of conservatives in matters political and religious, was nevertheless a revolutionary in the intellectual sphere and an optimist in an age in which the major English thinkers and writers were so pervasively pessimistic that historians can refer with some validity to an age of Jacobean melancholy. It is hard for us who have been raised on ideas of progress, however challenged by the momentous events of the twentieth century they may be, to conceive of a time in which the prevailing outlook on man and his destiny was based on the conviction that mankind had decayed. Bacon's meliorism and his hopes for material progress did much to undermine the force of this idea among those who dare to hope for an improvement in their political and economic destinies.

Along with his attack on pessimism and his offer of hope, Bacon's utilitarianism, his emphasis on the kind of knowledge which would ameliorate the lot of mankind, his attacks on the ancient thinkers whose works were the basis of the aristocratic and prelatical culture, his conferring of great importance on the works of artisans, mechanics, and agriculturists—all of these elements in his thought endeared him to many of the leaders of the revolutionary elements in England, the spokesmen for change who led, or spoke for, Cromwell's armies.

Those who for one reason or another were alienated from the traditional humanistic and religious culture, so deeply identified with the wielders of established power, found in Bacon an ideology which conferred dignity on their aspirations, values, and vocational activities. Not all of the uses made of Bacon's thought by the disaffected were self-justifying, however. Bacon's genuine, if unemotional, humanitarianism, his democratization of the ideals of learning, spurred the formulation of constructive social and educational changes. Yet the irony remains that a princely Lord Chancellor who lived sumptuously should have become the patron saint of so many semicultured intensely pious merchants, half-educated thinkers, and iconoclastic divines.

In a country like England in the seventeenth century, so riddled with sectarian conflict, the Baconian philosophy aided the progress of science in a special way. Bacon, as we have seen, sharply separated science from any involvement with religion or politics, and the Puritan intellectual, in general, accepted Bacon's conviction that scientific activities could be cultivated without in the least modifying the religious beliefs of the investigator or subverting the political order to which he gave his allegiance. Both Baconianism and puritanical Calvinism agreed in repudiating the great philosophical effort which aimed at the rationalization of religious belief and the relation of it to other activities of the mind and imagination. Both too, repudiated the great tradition of classical thought which obliged the philosopher to assume an overriding ethical and political responsibility. John Milton, in these respects, was more classical than Puritan. If he found in the work of "our sage and serious Spenser" a teacher of ethics the superior of Scotus and Aquinas, less poetic Puritans more often were content with the guidance of conscience as it confronts the Bible unadorned, uncritical loyalty to their leaders and an uncomplicated enthusiasm for scientific and technical progress. Science, in short, could remain out of the religious and political conflicts of the age. Such a blissful state of innocence or aloofness available to scientists has long since disappeared, although from time to time one hears nostalgic remarks about it from the scientific community.

The reader will doubtless recognize in the amalgam of Baconian and Puritan ideas we have been discussing the "pragmatism" and that generous moral faith in the capacities of scientific and industrial progress to alleviate the miseries of mankind which are among the outstanding characteristics of modern liberal humanitarianism. Modern "progressives" would perhaps prefer to find their origins entirely in the Enlightenment of the eighteenth century or among the Comtians and optimistic Darwinists of the nineteenth, but their rhetoric frequently betrays an unacknowledged seventeenth-century heritage.

This pragmatic and meliorist faith which directed so much human energy down to our own time achieved much of the substance of what it hoped for, and the Baconians would doubtless have been very pleased at much that they would find in the England and the America of the twentieth century, both in our material conditions of existence and in the organization of so much of our lives to achieve even greater material progress. Some of them, however, might have been pleased by trends in our culture which have long disturbed our more thoughtful contemporaries. They were, after all, the fathers of that peculiar form of modern anti-intellectualism which regards thinking as such, even very hard thinking, as a covert form of idleness or egotism. While the Puritans, theologically speaking, felt justified by faith and not by works, they more and more came to insist that true intellectual effort had to be associated somehow with a virtually physical struggle with material objects.[18]

By the third quarter of the seventeenth century the Baconian Puritans came to be in as sharp antithesis to the upholders of traditional learning as possible. The latter continued to seek the truth in the mind itself and in libraries, reacting to Puritan insistence on "works" by an aristocratic contempt for any contact with the variety of palpable realities which are the object of scientific inquiry. The humble, simple investigator working on God's creation with his hands was poised against the elaborately trained scholar in his book-lined study interpreting the wisdom of the past, the doer with his eyes turned toward the world and toward the future was pitted against the thinker, with his devotion to the records of tradition and the experience of the past. Finally, in a political version of this antagonism, the "democratic" man was opposed to the "aristocrat." The defenders of the old learning especially encouraged this last political and social opposition by insisting that the old learning was so bound up with religious and political orthodoxy that it should be supported for that reason if for no other.

If today there are important voices raised in the expression of concern over the isolation of the scientific culture from the humanistic one, and we hear some *mea culpas* from both sides, the attitudes in the seventeenth century were frankly polemical. How deep the antagonisms were between the Baconian and Puritan reformers, on the one hand, and the traditionalists, on the other, becomes strikingly clear when we reflect on the fact that, in 1653, Parliament actually considered the possibility of suppressing the universities and other institutions of traditional learning as at best useless, and at worst pagan.[19]

At its best, the spirit of pious utilitarianism was informed with an operational sense of secular truth and a humanitarian sense of its uses. At its worst, this attitude led to a denigration of humanistic culture and disinterested inquiry and sometimes fostered a love of invention hardly distinguishable from the mindless enthusiasm of some of our modern gadgeteers. Similarly, Bacon's emphasis on method over individual genius, his insistence on the co-operative character of progress in knowledge, contained hard kernels of truth and did much to alleviate the unwarranted pessimism of his time. In a debased form, however, it led to the view that the sum of contributions of any large number of mediocrities would somehow lead to more truth than the results of the labors of one genius.

The authoritarian attitude toward truth needed the strong blows that Bacon gave it, but his influence also served to damage a traditional conception of learning which, whatever its faults, did foster high standards of scholarship and intellectual discipline. His desire to democratize knowledge, to seek everywhere for it, and to disseminate it widely among other investigators, found its negative form in the vulgarization of learning, in the attack on that kind of knowledge which, because of its complex or subtle character, could not be popularized, or in the pernicious tendency to dilute an idea in order to make it simple enough to be generally understood.

The heterogeneous character of Bacon's ideological influence, both positive and negative, took in the over-all view two distinct forms. During the Cromwellian regime, his influence was most conspicuous among educational reformers, whether among those who wished simply to enlarge the traditional curriculum to suit it to changed conditions of life, or among those who sought to use the schools as the lever for radical social and political transformations. By the time of the Restoration the ideological side of Baconianism greatly diminished. The revolution had failed and the Baconians of that era were almost entirely scientists absorbed in their intellectual and professional concerns. The interest in educational reform along Baconian lines did not entirely disappear, however, although it was no longer politically revolutionary in character. Cowley's famous essay, "A Proposal For the Advancement of Experimental Philosophy" (1661), made the then novel suggestion for the scientific training of the young school child, a proposal of a purely pedagogical nature.

The conflict between the upholders of traditional learning and the Baconian enthusiasts was, as we have seen, part of a larger conflict involving opposing political and social ideals. At a deeper level, it reflected the conflict between a pessimistic and an optimistic current of feeling, a struggle between those who looked to the future with hope and others who looked to the past with nostalgia. It was a struggle between temperaments as much as minds, between spiritual "arcadians" and "utopians." [20] A fully developed notion of the idea of progress had to wait until the eighteenth century to find prophets prepared to proclaim it unambiguously, but some of its most important features first appeared in the seventeenth century among the varied followers of Bacon.

Bacon's *New Atlantis* is his contribution to the utopian literature of the world. Brief and incomplete though it is, it remains a remarkable distillation of Bacon's leading ideas and convictions, and it shares with the *Essays* the distinction of being among the most widely read of Bacon's works. The first draft of this work was probably composed between 1614 and 1617 during a time when Bacon had little time for writing and was very active in his political career. It was probably brought to the state in which we have it in 1623, although it was not published until after his death in 1627.

In spite of the fact that the *New Atlantis* is incomplete, it seems fairly clear that Bacon intended in this work to delineate both an ideal commonwealth and a scientific organization—virtually a brotherhood of scientists—which occupied a central role in the community. The scientists are crucial to the society of Bacon's ideal commonwealth because it is dedicated to achieving dominion over nature through progressive discoveries and inventions. The rulers of Plato's ideal state, we may recall, were philosophers, and they regulated the welfare of the people through the implementation of immutable philosophical principles. While Bacon's scientists do not directly govern, they continually alter the conditions of life of their country by uncovering and using new truths about the workings of nature. To this degree, Bacon's commonwealth is dynamic in contrast to the ideal societies of Plato or More. Nevertheless, it did not come into being through a historical process of development, but its laws and constitution were framed by an extremely wise original legislator, Salamona, just as More's Utopia was founded in all of its essential features by Utopus.[21]

Bensalem, the heart of Bacon's Atlantean community, is the site of Solomon's House, the brain and nerve center of the kingdom, where a highly organized group of scientists labor continually for the improvement of the lives of all the inhabitants of the kingdom. Different aspects of scientific work are there assigned to different officers, and we discover a close correspondence between the stages of Bacon's theory of induction and the work of the various functionaries of Solomon's House. Thus, the gathering of data, of carefully made observations, is the task of officers called Depredators, Mystery-Men, and Merchants of Light. These last travel around the world, quietly and secretly, and bring back reports of whatever they find that is good in the outside world. Be it noted that they bring nothing to that world, which remains ignorant of their very existence, some indication, perhaps, that Bacon took a more or less nationalistic view of the role of science.

We may recall that the universal natural history which was to be the foundation of the new philosophy rested not only on data acquired through observation but also on data acquired through experimentation. In Solomon's House experimental data is provided by functionaries called Pioneers. All data gleaned by these two major categories of investigators are then examined in order to discover those "forms" which Bacon talked of in his "metaphysics of forms." These are, as we know, not metaphysical entities but the modes of action of nature herself. To understand fully such a form, to discover it, is the same as being able to superinduce it in nature. Among the forms which Bacon enumerates are not only physical qualities such as heat, color, cold, scent, but attributes such as longevity, toughness, and generative power. In order to arrive at the form, the data acquired through observation and experimentation must first be carefully ordered in tables of different kinds and this is the task of a new category of scientists, the Compilers.

As Bacon explained in the *Novum organum,* if we wish to find the form of heat we must first compile our data in three tables. The first table will list instances of heat itself, the second table will list instances resembling heat except that they are not hot. Thus something luminous but cool would appear in table two. The third table will contain instances in which heat is present in varying degrees. The Compiler will not only set up these tables but will, through a process of elimination of instances, order the tables so that they can be used for a first generalization concerning the nature of heat. In the *Novum organum,* the first level of generalization is called the "first vintage" and the functionaries in charge of it in Solomon's House are called Dowry-Men or Benefactors. In the terminology of John Stuart Mill, they are experts in framing temporary hypotheses by the use of the method of concomitant variations.

The temporary hypothesis which is the "first vintage" is then rigorously tested against fresh instances not previously listed in the tables, and special weight is given to "negative instances," those cases which contradict it. At this point in the process there is a second phase of experimentation, "new experiments of a higher light." The experimentation of the Pioneers was in the service of adding to fundamental information. This new phase of experimentation, the duty of Lamps and Innoculators, is in the service of testing a hypothesis.

We have so far proceeded carefully up a ladder of induction, from less certain generalizations to more certain ones, each step taking us closer to the "form" we have been seeking. The final generalization is the work of special officials called Interpreters of Nature. They are responsible for the final stages of the process. Since they have a clear grasp of the "form" and its operations derived from all of the processed data their subordinates have submitted to them, they are able to superinduce it. They thus have complete control over color or scent, heat or cold, toughness or weakness, or any of the other properties of things, and can bring them about where they did not exist before or modify them in different ways. At this point the labors of the brotherhood begin to pass over into useful and fruitful discoveries and inventions.

This remarkable society of scientists, each with his proper function and title, is inspired by a vision of the incalculable benefits which their work will progressively bestow on mankind. In Bacon's *New Atlantis* we can see one of the earliest and most powerful statements of what we might call the "scientific faith," the belief which has inspired the activity of many scientists since Bacon's time, that their labor will make the future progressively and steadily better than the past has been. In this respect Bacon's ideal commonwealth is more truly a "Utopia" than most of its predecessors, if we give the term its usual modern meaning of an ideal society set some time in the future which the men of the present may achieve through their own efforts. Of course, Bensalem is imagined as distant from Europe but contemporary with Bacon's own time, and he does not explicitly point to it as a future society. Nevertheless, it is a vision of a society some of whose most important features can be understood as emerging from Bacon's contemporary world once mankind organized itself to promote the advancement of useful scientific knowledge.

The relation of Bacon's ideal commonwealth to its predecessors is an interesting one, and a comparison of them with Bacon's will serve to mark more precisely the degree to which Bacon is original. The name "Atlantis" itself goes back to Plato's *Critias* in which he describes a fabled country of that name which rose to a great height of civilization but was finally destroyed for its arrogant pride. Bacon imagines a *New Atlantis,* a land which has reached unprecedented heights of progress but whose leaders are dedicated to the humble pursuit of truth and knowledge and whose citizenry live temperately, observing due measure in all things. Bacon doubtless wished his readers to understand that the New Atlantis was able to escape the fate of the old one precisely because it cultivated the true moral virtues of Christianity and the true intellectual virtues of the pursuit of useful scientific knowledge.

Sir Thomas More had little if any influence on Bacon, as famous as his *Utopia* had become, for excellent reasons. There was too much of the social critic and reformer in More for Bacon's taste, and Bacon never for a moment would have tolerated the very idea of revolutionary political and social changes as indispensable prerequisites for ameliorating the condition of mankind. On the contrary, Bacon, as we have seen, was often at pains to assure the authorities that scientific progress would bring nothing but benefits to the established order of things.

Bacon's *New Atlantis* has a number of significant features in common with Tommaso Campanella's *The City of the Sun,* even though Bacon never mentions the work of this contemporary Italian philosopher. He did know the work of Telesio, however, and the latter had a profound influence on the thought of Campanella so that the channel of influence may have flowed from the older thinker whose works both Bacon and Campanella had carefully studied. *The City of the Sun* is like the *New Atlantis* in being an imaginative epilogue to the author's philosophy elsewhere prosaically expressed. Both give an important role to science and scientists in their respective ideal states, both communities have elaborate institutes for scientific work, and the citizenry of both accord to scientists the highest honors, such as statues, normally reserved for kings and conquering generals. This last is a striking idea for its time, a time when scientific activities of the sort both Campanella and Bacon wished to foster were still generally regarded as "illiberal" and "mechanical."

Other points of resemblance between Bensalem and the City of the Sun are even more striking than these. The citizens of both realms refuse to take money for services or courtesies, and among them can be found individuals who know thoroughly one or an-

other of all of the languages of mankind. In spite of the fact that
they seek to protect themselves in all possible ways from the influence of foreigners, they know a good deal about them and, if a
stranger turns up among them, they are hospitable and will even
keep him as a guest of the state for three days. In neither land have
they been able to avoid the problem of war completely, but they
seem invariably to win whatever wars they have and to treat their
vanquished enemies with such generosity that conflict is kept to a
minimum. In their personal habits they live chastely and pay careful attention to matters of diet. They are quite prudential about
matrimonial matters and choose their mates according to eugenic
principles, evidently feeling that marriage and raising a family is
much too serious a venture to be left to the unguided winds of
passion for decision.

It is hard not to suspect that Bacon may have known Campanella's work after considering this long list of resemblances, and I
have already suggested that a good many of these ideas may well
have a common source in the work of Telesio. What is far more
important than the matter of influence, however, is the fact that the
new science, in the work of these thinkers as well as others, was
understood as a social fact of the highest importance, even if all of
them underestimated just how important it was to be. Moreover,
scientific work was conducted in an ethical atmosphere of the
greatest sobriety and of high moral elevation. The scientists,
ideally, are also sages, and radiate the aura of a semisecular priest-
hood. The people they serve are uncorrupted, morally sound, and
worthy of the dedication of the investigators of nature.

The people are thus worthy because they have been justly governed for centuries by a wise code of law under an unchanging
constitution. Indeed, the laws of Bensalem are so good that the
constitution of King Salomona, the founder of the commonwealth,
has lasted for 1,900 years. Bacon apparently agreed with the Machiavellian dictum that a good state is the work of a single individual and that a state flourished to the extent that it was able to
preserve or renew its original ethos, for one of the aims of the
Atlantean monarchy is to preserve an original virtue. The other

aim, of course, is the furthering of material progress by the subsidy and regulation of organized scientific research. Bensalem is remarkably conservative on the moral, social, and political side, even if it is very progressive in all that concerns scientific and technological advancement. It has a traditional sort of class structure based on the ownership of private property, and a traditional family structure based on monogamous marriage. As against Plato, More, and Campanella, Bacon repudiates communism, and as against Plato and Campanella, he repudiates community of wives.

The lower orders of Bensalem are organized vocationally in companies or guilds pretty much like the ones in the England of Bacon's time. There are rich people in Bensalem, to be sure, but they are not selfish and, like the wealthy in classical Athens, they are obliged to provide for public services at their own expense. Bensalem is certainly not the Garden of Eden for there exists some crime or vice, and some misfortune. However, the degree of this sort of misery or unhappiness is quite small, so small that it is usually handled by family councils. Unlike ordinary family councils the ones in Bensalem have the backing of the state and can call upon it to enforce whatever decisions they come to. This is seldom necessary, however, for the inhabitants of Bensalem are so much in tune with the order of nature that the state seldom has to exercise force, whether directly or through the family councils.

The Bensalemites have an established religion, which to no reader's surprise, turns out to be Christianity, miraculously introduced in the apostolic era. They are not fanatical, however, and tolerate Judaism. Public morality is as high as private morality in Bensalem. Their officials are completely incorruptible, and even the customary giving of gifts to justices, the very practice, universal as it was, which brought Bacon into disgrace, is not tolerated. To use Bacon's own phrase, there are no "twice-paid" officials in Bensalem. This is perhaps the only conspicuous instance where Bacon specifically alludes to a particular moral evil of his own time and country, the very one in which he became embroiled, and uses his utopian construction for the purpose of moral and social criticism.

In the last analysis, the social and political order of Bensalem is a heightened version of the order of Bacon's own time and place, a vision of the realization of the ideal order implicit in the actual one. It reflects his thoroughly conventional political ideas and loyalties and, from time to time, it reflects his own taste, as in the love of Bensalemites for elegant pageantry and for refined appearances, in notable contrast to the barrackslike egalitarianism of Plato and More. But then, these two distinguished predecessors framed mythical states not primarily to suggest programs of action but to serve as instruments of moral vision. Any Utopia of that sort, whatever its intended uses, is less an exact model of a possible society than an open exploration of different ways of ordering the interactions between social institutions.

Solomon's House, the scientific brotherhood, is the very eye of the kingdom, Bacon tells us. Its splendor, its atmosphere of dignity, courtesy, and reverence, suggests the aura of a sacred college. There dwell and labor the men who continually regenerate the society, not through drastic legislation, for they are not legislators nor is further legislation necessary for an uncorrupted and wisely governed people, but through the power of scientific technology. They combine in their persons both the progressive and the conservative aspects of the Atlantean civilization. They labor as scientists to advance the growth of useful knowledge for the benefit of present and future generations, and they incarnate, preserve and implement the moral and social ideals of their ancient constitution.

The organization of Solomon's House bears a striking resemblance to the organizational changes Bacon introduced into the administrative arm of government during his political life. He clearly believed that political administration and co-operative scientific research could be carried on by a minutely structured hierarchy whose ranks had very specialized and delimited tasks. He discovered that the instrument of government he helped to create along such lines was not very workable, but he never had the opportunity to discover that the scientific organization of Solomon's House would not work either. One cannot distribute stages of a general method of scientific investigation to different individuals and ex-

pect them to come up with anything. Scientists co-operate through
pooling expert knowledge of a particular science or of its branches.
Bacon, as we have seen, had an intense mistrust of specialization
but, in attempting to avoid it, he introduced a form of specialization which was peculiarly unworkable. Any scientific work, however specialized, will demand of the scientist that he both observe
or experiment *and* interpret his data. If a cytologist calls on a bio-
chemist for assistance, he does not expect him to think for him, but
to give special information which will help him, the cytologist, to
understand his problem.

In organizational matters, whether they involved politics or science, Bacon tended to think too much in terms of subordination
and superordination, in terms of the detailed articulation of a
method, neglecting the personal factor in both politics and science.
Gorgeously arrayed hierarchs maintained in splendor by the state
cannot create those results in science which have been the fruits of
a lifetime of patient dedication by intellects of the highest order
and most remarkable gifts.

The strikingly utilitarian ideals of Bacon's *New Atlantis* have
been noted by Bacon's admirers and detractors. Both Plato and
More, in the last analysis, place their hopes for amelioration of the
human condition in the limitation of human desire. One way or
another—even through coercion and deception, as in Plato's case
—mankind's inordinate greed and lust for power must be curbed.
In a sense, Bacon takes an opposing direction. He proposed to gratify human wants as much as possible, including those desires for
status, splendor and possessions, that desire for relative difference
and superiority which More and Plato wished to eliminate.

It was Macaulay, in a celebrated essay on Bacon, who imagined
the horror Plato would have felt had he seen his ideal republic
developing along the model of Bensalem: "With what vehemence
he would have ordered the brew-houses, and the dispensatories to
be pulled down; and with what inflexible rigor he would have
driven beyond the frontier all the Fellows of the College, Merchants of Light and Depredators, Lamps and Pioneers. . . . The
aim of the Platonic philosophy was to raise us far above our vulgar

wants. The aim of the Baconian philosophy was to supply our vulgar wants."

Macaulay's quietly scathing comment on Bacon is, after all, somewhat unjust. Bacon did acknowledge the claims of moral culture as well as those of technological progress. However tiresome the joys and pursuits of the Bensalemites, they do express an ideal of restraint and decorum, even in the pursuit of the gratification of "our vulgar wants." But Macaulay is also right to the degree that he defines Bacon as one of those thinkers who place the growth of human felicity in the increase of material possessions, in the results of a kind of technological dominion over nature. Neither Plato nor More ignored the problem of poverty, of the human misery engendered by the sheer lack of the necessities of life. But, for them, the problem of poverty was essentially the problem of avarice, of human selfishness. Hence the communism they both postulated for their ideal commonwealths. They assume that the world already contains all that men truly need in sufficient abundance to give each and every one of them a dignified, if not luxurious, existence. Men must therefore learn to conquer avarice and to distribute the wealth of the world more equitably. This transformation does not require an increase in the quantity of knowledge at the disposal of mankind but an increase in moral self-awareness, an expansion of consciousness in the service of moral self-development. Moreover, men do not need new *kinds* of knowledge, much less new objects, inventions, or new powers over nature in order to promote their true welfare. They need to know themselves, and any new knowledge should promote this end. For Plato, even the knowledge of the natural world would serve to further this goal.

One may be tempted to sympathize with Macaulay's judgment more deeply when he considers the multifarious and heterogeneous activities of the researchers of Solomon's House in isolation from the rest of Bacon's writings, without the memory of the richness and power of that mind as it has expressed itself in some of the finest pages in the history of English literature and thought. The resplendent functionaries of Bensalem labor in brewhouses as well as in laboratories for medical research. Bakehouses and kitchens stand near perfume houses; suggestions for technological creations of the first importance are proposed along with "dainty works of feathers of wonderful lustre." They labor mightily to improve the agriculture of the land as well as the production of "papers, linens, silks, tissues." Macaulay was quite right in assuming that Plato would have been horrified at this heterogeneous collection of activities, proposed to mankind as worthy of the dedication of its finest minds, without the slightest attempt to distinguish important from unimportant researches, and with the naïve assumption that man's true welfare will flow quite simply and uncomplicatedly, one way or another, from activities of this character.

It is perhaps unfair to read back into Bacon the undreamed of excesses of modern gadgeteering, of which Macaulay only glimpsed the beginning, but it is hard when we read that long and heterogeneous list of enterprises, arranged as they are according to the senses they correspond to—touch, sight, sound, taste, and smell—not to think of the swollen catalogue of some modern universities where, it would appear, absolutely everything is studied with little explicit indication of what it might be important to know and do in a single finite lifetime.

On the other hand, none of us who enjoy the increased health, leisure, and comfort which modern technology has made possible can really afford to take too austere a view of our "vulgar wants." Much that we have come to value as among the necessities of civilized existence, and properly so, would doubtless have seemed quite unnecessary or even shoddy to Plato. The technological transformation of the world has raised the whole general level of demand and of need. Our sense of what is necessary for a decent existence, of what is "excess" or "waste," has been so altered that Macaulay's sweeping generalization concerning "vulgar wants" can no longer command general assent even among those sympathetic to his view.

Moreover, Macaulay failed to grasp that the heterogeneous character of the investigations of Solomon's House symbolizes something much more important than gadgeteering, than providing literally everything for everybody. Bacon grasped, as Macaulay did not, the interrelatedness of all natural phenomena. Bacon would not have been surprised to have learned that Pasteur, who saved the wine and the silk industries of France from enormous losses, developed an effective vaccine against rabies using knowledge of precisely the same order. The desire for silk and wine may seem vulgar to some, but the same forces are at work throughout nature whether or not men prefer some aspects of it to others. Behind Bacon's democratization of knowledge lay a clear perception of this principle as well as utilitarianism.

Bacon could avoid the whole problem of the moral uses of the knowledge which gives us control over the forces of nature by locating his scientific community in a moral society with good customs and habits, as well as good laws. He could not foresee that technological progress would outstrip, in many cases, man's capacity to use new inventions and discoveries for his own true good. Still less could he have even dreamed of a time when the kind of knowledge he advocated would place at the disposal of warring nations the power to end the very existence of the human race.

Notes
*

1 For a distinguished collection of essays on the nature of modern science with special reference to its relations with other aspects of modern culture see Parts II and III of *Roots of Scientific Thought: A Cultural Perspective*, ed. Philip P. Wiener and Aaron Noland (New York, 1957). See also A. Wolf, *A History of Science, Technology and Philosophy in the 16th and 17th Centuries*, 2 vols., 2nd ed. rev. by Douglas McKie (London, 1950; Harper Torchbooks, 1959, 1961), and *Toward Modern Science*, 2 vols., ed. R. M. Palter (New York, 1961). This last is an anthology of important studies of ancient, medieval, and Renaissance science.

2 See Martha Ornstein, *The Role of Scientific Societies in the Seventeenth Century* (3rd ed., Chicago, 1938).

3 See Franz Cumont, *Astrology and Religion Among the Greeks and Romans* (New York, 1960).

4 It should be noted that the theory of eccentrics posited a fixed point at a fixed distance from the center of the earth for all of the ultimately uni-

form circulations of the cosmos, not only for the sun. A good account of the Ptolemaic system can be found in J. L. E. Dreyer, *A History of Astronomy from Thales to Kepler,* rev. by W. H. Stahl (New York, 1953), and in Giorgio Abetti, *A History of Astronomy* (New York, 1952). See also T. S. Kuhn, *The Copernican Revolution: Planetary Astronomy in Western Thought* (Cambridge, Mass., 1957).

5 The doctrine of natural place, the notion that every physical object has *its* place, is not the only Aristotelian conception of place. Aristotle advanced it in *On the Heavens* and it became the authoritative one for centuries. In the *Physics,* however, he dealt brilliantly with the notion that the universe is one in which everything has, not *its* place, but *a* place, a notion of place which is that of modern physics. See Friedrich Solmsen, *Aristotle's System of the Physical World: A Comparison with His Predecessors* (Ithaca, N.Y., 1960).

6 Erwin Panofsky, "Artist, Scientist, Genius: Notes on the 'Renaissance-Dammerung,' " in *The Renaissance: Six Essays* (New York, 1962), pp. 121-182, especially p. 140.

7 Cf. the remarkable essay by Agnes Arber, *The Mind and the Eye: A Study of the Biologist's Viewpoint* (Cambridge, Eng., 1954). See H. H. Rhys (ed.), *Seventeenth Century Science and the Arts* (Princeton, 1961), especially the essay by J. S. Ackerman, "Science and Visual Art." Cf. the penetrating remarks of J. Bronowski on the creative interaction between science and the arts and the affinities between scientific and artistic activity in *The Common Sense of Science* (New York, n.d.).

8 See Rudolf Magnus, *Goethe as Scientist* (New York, 1961), originally published in German in Leipzig, 1906. For the reference to Goethe on the microscope see Panofsky, "Artist, Scientist, Genius," p. 181. On "paradigms" in science see T. S. Kuhn, *The Structure of Scientific Revolutions* (Chicago, 1962).

9 See the brilliant study of Giorgio De Santillana, *The Crime of Galileo* (Chicago, 1955). For some idea of Galileo's humanistic side see the essay by Erwin Panofsky, *Galileo as a Critic of the Arts* (The Hague, 1954).

10 See, for example, the important essay of E. A. Moody, "Galileo and Avempace: Dynamics of the Leaning Tower Experiment," in *Roots of Scientific Thought: A Cultural Perspective,* ed. Philip P. Wiener and Aaron Noland (New York, 1957), pp. 176-206. Cf. also the article by Alexander Koyré, "Galileo and Plato," in the same collection, pp. 147-175.

11 See J. H. Randall, Jr., *The Career of Philosophy: From the Middle Ages to the Enlightenment* (New York, 1962), "The Padua Tradition of Method and Greek Mathematics," pp. 284-307, and "The Medieval Roots of Galilean Science," pp. 256-283.

12 See F. J. Anderson, *The Philosophy of Francis Bacon* (Chicago, 1948) and his *Francis Bacon: His Career and His Thought* (New York, 1962). My account of Bacon is heavily indebted to Anderson's two important studies.

13 See, for example, K. R. Popper, *The Logic of Scientific Discovery* (New York, 1959).

14 See the sections cited, in note 11, in Randall's *Career of Philosophy*.

15 "The Philosophy of Francis Bacon" in Broad, *Ethics and the History of Philosophy* (London and New York, 1952), pp. 117-143, especially p. 121.

16 Descartes and Bacon, for religious reasons, left psychology in a peculiar condition, the one through a radical dualism which left the mind theoretically beyond investigation, and the other through self-contradictory views of the soul, with tendencies toward both naturalistic and supernaturalistic accounts of various of its specific functionings.

17 R. F. Jones, *Ancients and Moderns: A Study of the Rise of the Scientific Movement in Seventeenth-Century England*, in "Washington University Studies" (2nd ed., St. Louis, 1961), p. X.

18 Jones, p. 108.

19 Jones, p. 114. For my account of the interrelations of Puritanism and science I am greatly indebted to the classic study of Jones.

20 I have adopted the distinction between "Arcadians" and "Utopians" from René Dubos' brilliant study of medical "Utopias," *Mirage of Health: Utopias, Progress and Biological Change* (New York, 1959).

21 We can detect the influence of Plutarch in the theme of the original wise legislator who sets a state on its essential course. His accounts of Solon and Lycurgus probably provided the inspiration for figures like Salomona and Utopus. The tradition of the original legislator persisted, and even Harrington, in his *Oceana*, echoing Machiavelli, argued that a commonwealth should be the work of one man.

V

HOBBES:

The Scientific Secularization of the World

Close to the end of his life, Thomas Hobbes (1588-1679) wrote a brief autobiography in Latin couplets, two lines of which are justly famous:

> Atque metum tantum concepit tunc mea mater
> Ut pareret geminos, meque metumque simul.
>
> [At that time my mother conceived such great fear
> That she gave birth to twins, to fear and myself at one time.]

It does not require a very extensive acquaintance with Hobbes's writings to recognize in this observation an acute piece of self-analysis. We would, however, be misinterpreting him if we took this to mean that Hobbes was merely fearful in some mundane way, or that he lived his life tormented by irrational anxiety. He was, on the contrary, a bold and courageous thinker, quite capable of enjoying life, a man who attracted and held the affection and regard of his friends.

The fear that beset Hobbes was that which observant and thoughtful men might feel when they are compelled to notice how close to the surface of civilization lie anarchy, savagery, and chaos. Some generations, living at certain times, may not be constrained by events to reflect very hard on the irrationality of mankind, but Hobbes was not so fortunate. Fear was, for him, not so much a personal affliction as the dominating passion of mankind. If Dante could view the universe, including hell, as governed by the ordering principle of love manifesting itself in Protean forms, Hobbes placed fear at the heart of his vision of the life of mankind, fear as it creates order by engendering submission, and fear as the passion which, in another form, drives men to destroy each other when it engenders desperate rebellion.

Hobbes's long life had begun in the glorious reign of Elizabeth I, in a time of general buoyant optimism, for the great queen had quieted the religious and political discords of her country and even seemed, in the eyes of many, to have created a durable solution for the problems she had inherited from the past. In his maturity Hobbes witnessed a terrible civil war which overthrew customs, pieties, institutions and "solutions" apparently as durable as nature herself, a physical conflict foreshadowed by that "Jacobean melancholy," which marks the temper of the opening decades of the seventeenth century. Hobbes lived into the Restoration and witnessed the reinstatement, in modified form to be sure, of political and social structures which had apparently disappeared forever. *Omnia mutantur,* "all things change," and the changes, political, social, intellectual, had been so great that any clear-headed observer of the age would, like Lear, have been forced to conclude that much that appears to be "nature" is really convention and much that appears to be truth is really illusion.

Underneath this flood of metamorphoses marked by the cruelest kinds of violence, by every variety of religious and political fanaticism, by revelations on every hand of all forms of the pathology of conscience from savage self-righteousness to the utter absence of principle, Hobbes discerned one constant truth: man is a creature driven by intense egoistic passions and prone to use all of the ambiguities and uncertainties of thought and language to rationalize his own self-seeking. His much vaunted conscience is nothing more than his own good opinion of himself and its concrete content is infinitely various. Like Machiavelli and Montaigne before him, and Nietzsche and Freud after him, Hobbes was a great psychologist whose knowledge is in the service of unmasking mankind, a master diagnostician of the various forms of the pathology of conscience.

Hobbes was also a great clarifier, and his intellectual posture is that of one who cuts through the accumulated cant of centuries to get at some few certain truths. Like other men of this kind, he disclaimed erudition or profound scholarship. Aubrey reports that Hobbes "was wont to say that if he had read as much as other men, he should have known no more than other men." However, his claim of being unlearned must be accepted with a few reservations. His first published work, in 1629, was a translation of Thucydides, one of the most difficult of Greek authors, and at the age of eighty-nine, he translated both the *Iliad* and the *Odyssey* as a kind of recreational activity. Hardly the work of an unscholarly man!

Hobbes, in fact, was erudite enough, but his attitude toward knowledge was that of an independent and vigorous mind who made a personal use of the books he read, whether for profit or pleasure. For example, among all the possible uses of Thucydides, Hobbes makes a rather tendentious one and claims that the essential lesson the great historian taught was the superior wisdom of one man to that of any body of men. Indeed, Hobbes tells that he was prompted to translate the work to warn his contemporaries against the blandishments of orators, those spellbinders who subvert good government and give their countries over to corrupt rule by the many. This is an early example of Hobbes's lifelong intellectual practice, to use what he learned to reinforce the essential structure of his own thought.

Hobbes did not claim to have learned anything from the recreational exercise of translating the Homeric poems, but his intimacy with those texts did not prevent him from having excessive admiration for Davenant's unfinished epic *Gondibert,* perhaps the most unreadable poem of the seventeenth century to a modern reader. This enthusiasm was less the result of eccentricity of taste than of adherence to certain principles of what a contemporary epic poem should be. To Hobbes, *Gondibert* embodied the emergent neoclassical standards of the nature of poetry, standards which harmonized with his own sober view of the imagination. The function of poetry, especially epic poetry, was to educate men in those political and moral virtues which made for a peaceful civic society. Poetry should offer not only exemplary actions, it should also be written in an "exemplary" language, one reflecting social standards of civilized restraint in expression and thought. Wit and judgment, fancy and clear thought, had to be blended in just those proportions that would please a reasonable, sober, urbane man without violating his sense of reality. The last thing Hobbes wanted a poem to do was to ravish its reader, and while Homer was doubtless the most admirable of poets, he was no strict model for another age.

The reader of Hobbes may well be startled to find recurrent attacks on the great classical authors, including the very giants of antiquity, Plato, Aristotle, Cicero, and Seneca. In part, these attacks have a Baconian motive, and are prompted by the wish to reform the structure of knowledge, free it from the dead hand of the past, and liberate men to acquire new and useful knowledge of real things. Hobbes, however, also had a political motive, for the classical authors, with all their talk of liberty, had contributed mightily to encourage those elements in society who wished to subvert the state and destroy civil peace.

His attacks on the ancient cultural heroes were not prompted by obscurantism or ignorance. Hobbes was quite free from the spirit of envy and resentment, of class hatred, of self-assertive ignorance, which lay behind much of the Puritan polemic against traditional humanistic learning. Indeed, his ironic attacks on the theological squabbles of both the orthodox and the heterodox far exceed in importance his battle against the classics. In fact, he condemns both of the two prestigious traditions of learning and moral culture, the Christian and the classical. Both carried a great deal of meaningless and useless cultural freight, and both had become, in one degree or another, the vehicles of political and social disorder, ideologies, windy words for orators who would erode the power of the state. Hobbes's judgment and learning were governed by his convictions concerning the overriding interests of mankind in the present. No authoritative voice from the past could deflect Hobbes from his mighty effort to instruct his contemporaries as to their actual condition in the world and the only available remedies for their political and social ills.

All we know of Hobbes's life would show that his mind was molded by a few such passionate convictions and by a few deeply felt moments of intellectual insight. Aubrey tells us that Hobbes learned geometry at the age of forty, when, quite by accident, he looked at a proof in Euclid. At first puzzled, he pondered it, and then exclaimed, "By God, this is impossible!" More delighted than puzzled, he immediately began to work back from that proof to the earlier ones it presupposed. Whether or not this anecdote is true, Hobbes's mind seems to have worked this way, and geometry did become for him virtually the only real knowledge possessed by the human race, the very model of what knowledge should be. Such moments of intellectual excitement were evidently not moments of "conversion." Hobbes's enthusiasm for mathematics did not make him a thoroughgoing Cartesian. On the contrary, he always retained a great deal of admiration and respect for Bacon, who had been the great intellectual influence of his youth. Hobbes, in fact, had known Bacon and had probably accompanied the Lord Chancellor on his contemplative walks at Gorhambury with those other youthful attendants who took down Bacon's ideas as they struck him.

We have now sketched out three of the predominating elements in Hobbes's thought, those interests and attitudes which molded the shape of his specific inquiries: his "fearfulness," his interest in mathematics, the importance he conferred on the study of the psychology of the passions. His fears over the fragility of civilized order led him to advocate strong government, one which would unhesitatingly secure order, peace, honor, and security for the individual. To those goals Hobbes was perfectly willing to subordinate some liberties and, although he believed that a strong monarchy was the best form of government, he was quite willing to agree that other forms of government would do, providing they were sufficiently powerful.

Hobbes's interest in mathematics, his enthusiasm over the spectacular results of the new physics in applying mathematics to the understanding of bodies in motion, convinced him that the ultimate causes of all phenomena, even of the psychological and political order, were to be sought in the differing movements and relations of bodies. Hobbes, in effect, reduced philosophy to science, and he was convinced that the true philosopher, like the scientist, reasoned in terms of cause and effect in interpreting experience. Indeed, the philosopher could expect to foresee effects and predict events, once he was free of the verbalisms of the systems of the past, of Bacon's idols of the theater. Thus Hobbes, in principle, offered to give a completely secular and naturalistic interpretation of man and the universe, in spite of some apparent inconsistencies on matters religious. Moreover, Hobbes's naturalism differed from that of his predecessors not only in being more thoroughgoing but in the fact that it was based on the new science, on the claim that the methods which had been so successful in mechanics and astronomy could be extended to man, his mind and his society.

Hobbes's interest in the psychology of the passions, in the complex and numberless ways in which men rationalize their desires, dominated his interpretation of both the past and the present, of history and of politics. History is simply the story of how political order is gained and lost, a tale of how human beings have tried, with varying success, to control their own destructiveness in order to preserve their lives and possessions. A knowledge of history or politics is really a knowledge of the passions of men, the story of the various ways in which a changeless, anarchically disposed human nature has dealt with the problem of its own survival. It teaches two important lessons, if it teaches anything at all: man's infinite capacity for self-deception, his blind egotism; and the difficulty of securing stable political order.

These conclusions are traditional enough, and they would have commanded assent from St. Augustine, Machiavelli, and Calvin, among others. However, Hobbes's great strength and originality lies not so much in his conclusions but in two characteristics of his work. His many brilliant insights gain greatly in relatedness and coherence because of his effort to derive them, however imperfectly, from a few metaphysical postulates, and they are set in a framework of a scientific account of the world and of man. The inadequacy of Hobbes's science for his purposes is irrelevant from this point of view. He is the first great thinker to attempt to gain the kind of knowledge of man and society which had predictive value and which was, in principle, reducible to the postulates of natural science.

It can easily be argued that Hobbes's materialism and determinism, his "scientific apparatus," were not really necessary for much of his psychology or for any of his politics, and it is true that Hobbes was not much of a scientist or mathematician in spite of his claims. He insisted, for example, that he had "squared the circle," although we should remember that contemporary mathematicians of high gifts were making the same claim before we judge him too harshly. A more severe limitation was his failure to grasp the significance of the work of his mathematical opponents, much of which was to lead to the development of the calculus. Other ventures into science proper, against the great Robert Boyle, for example, were again conspicuous failures.[1]

In spite of these shortcomings, Hobbes did have an excellent grasp of the nature of mathematical reasoning and of its application to physical phenomena, even if he would not admit his errors when it came to specific scientific and mathematical problems. Unlike Bacon, Hobbes really understood the work of Kepler, Harvey, Gilbert, and Galileo, not only because he knew mathematics well but also because he did not share Bacon's great distrust of hypothesis. Like Bacon, he believed that science must rest on observation and experiment. He also agreed that hypotheses must be carefully framed and cautiously used. But Hobbes had far more insight than Bacon into the complex relations which exist between hypothesis and experiment, mathematics and physics.

However, Hobbes's influence on the course of science, in spite of his efforts, was far less than that of Bacon. Neither of them possessed the special gifts required for first-rate scientific work, but Bacon was the better practical statesman of science. Hobbes's devastating critique of religion, however much he disclaimed the charge of atheism, would have made him an unwelcome ally of the scientists even if he had been a first-rate scientist himself. The major scientists of the time and the leading apologists for the Royal Society's plans for the advancement of science were at least con-

yentionally devout, and some of them, like Newton, were quite absorbed by theological reflections.[2] Hobbes's practical atheism and
his obvious contempt for theological debates probably had a good
deal to do with the fact that he was never elected to the Royal
Society, one of the great disappointments of his life.

After all, a Baconian empiricism which would leave both religion and politics relatively untouchable was precisely the sort of
ideology the Royal Society's members needed to free them for their
work, however different their scientific practice may have been, or
however unwilling or unable they were to consider the larger implications of the new science. After decades of political and religious
conflict, they simply needed to stay out of trouble. Neither in that
time nor in our own are scientists necessarily political reformers or
philosophers, nor can they always give a logically rigorous account
of what, in fact, they actually do as scientists.

Whatever his limitations as a scientist or a mathematician,
Hobbes was a great political philosopher, and much of his interest
in the new science was surely motivated by the desire to re-create
the certainty and real knowledge of that sphere in the myth-
burdened worlds of psychology and politics. He was, to say the
least, rather sanguine about the ease with which this passage, or
"reduction," could be made, but it was clear to him that no political and psychological knowledge of enduring validity was possible
within the conceptual framework of Christian theology or humanism. Scientific knowledge of the workings of the mind would yield
the key to the workings of the state. New knowledge in turn might
persuade mankind to enter those paths which will ensure civic
peace and that minimum of security necessary for a civilized life.

Inspired by the model of knowledge offered by mathematical
physics, Hobbes treated many of the old problems of psychology
and politics in a new way and with fresh insight. On the other hand,
the very model which enabled him to see so much that was new, led
to its own obscurities. Thus Hobbes, who distrusted metaphor and
analogical thinking so much, could not escape them any more than
any other thinker. The methods of the new science were not strictly
applicable to Hobbes's political subject matter and images like

"motions of the mind" or descriptions of the body politic as if it were composed of discrete physical particles are quite as metaphorical as many of the guiding concepts of classical political philosophy. Of course, Hobbes was well aware that the mind of man and his political activity were far more complex phenomena than the motions of the planets, and he was not naïve enough to try to use the mathematics at his disposal to interpret them. Mathematical physics was a paradigm, hovering far above such phenomena, a pattern which was their ultimate explanation. Contemplating the newly discovered order of nature one could find clues for the interpretation of society. A new image of order may serve as a new paradigm or model for the interpretation of experience, opening our eyes to things we had never noticed before or making us see old things in a new way. By the same token, it may lead us to overlook what it cannot include.

Thus Hobbes's model led him at times to offer explanations of complex psychological and political processes which sound oversimplified, if not crude. The influence of the new physics may even have marred his masterly analysis of the emotions, for Hobbes virtually omits any consideration of human gregariousness and of those libidinal ties which do serve, however imperfectly or ambivalently, to bind men together. Mechanistic physics offered no analogue for love, it would appear, although Hobbes doubtless might have found one if he thought that *eros* was really operative in the affairs of men.

Unlike Machiavelli, therefore, Hobbes sees little hope of the greedy wills of individuals or disparate interest groups in the state limiting each other through the very desire of each single will to enjoy the fruits of its own cupidity. Not that Machiavelli was an optimist about this possibility, but he did believe that, when good laws and customs existed, men might be seduced into preserving order in the state if they each got some, if not all, of what they wanted. While the human quest for possessions was a disruptive force, the desire to enjoy those possessions was cohesive and made the liberal state possible. Machiavelli's enthusiasm for the mixed constitution, which Hobbes disliked because it segmented the sovereign power, rests in part on the fact that such a political structure allows all citizens to share in wealth and power without giving too much to any one group. Such a state could well have great social differences within itself, but since all shared in governing, those differences would not grow to the point where they became disruptive.

Hobbes, on the other hand, placed little trust in self-limitation of this sort, and relied on external coercion or the threat of it to secure civic peace. To be sure, Hobbes posits a primitive social contract in which external coercion was voluntarily and irreversibly assumed by mankind, but this only proves, in a way, how essentially coercive the state is and must be. Machiavelli would have been the last man in the world to deny that the state rests on force and on the monopoly of the right to use it, but his reading of history and his ardent desire for liberty led him to find some hope of creating large areas of freedom in the eternal tug of war between the ruler and the ruled.

Hobbes's pessimism may well have been a result of his "fear," but it also issues from a certain one-sidedness of intellectual temper. Machiavelli not only found some great examples of political success in the history of antiquity, he also accepted some of the basic assumptions of ancient political philosophy. He would have agreed with Aristotle, generally if not in detail, that man is by nature a political animal. Machiavelli's devotion to liberty, to his own great *polis* of Florence, his exhortation to his compatriots to free Italy from the barbarian—all these stamp him as one who loved his homeland and saw it as the place for the realization of ideal citizenship, at least potentially. Hobbes has little patriotism of this sort and, unlike the ancients or Machiavelli, never seems to grasp that man is bound, however imperfectly, to his family and society by erotic ties. For Hobbes, the ancient heritage of Greek political philosophy, the great Roman republican rhetoric of liberty and love of country, were largely pernicious fictions masking self-interest, and in rejecting them he threw out the baby with the bath and left some crucial social and political facts unexplainable.

Moreover, Hobbes never quite grasped that men do frequently

love their superimposed authority, however ambiguously, and that this is a political fact of the first importance. Nevertheless, his "physics of politics" illuminates more of the dark corners of political life, tells us more about the anatomy of power, than anything in the formal political philosophy of antiquity. It is no accident that Hobbes's favorite ancient author was Thucydides, and what Thucydides saw and understood could not really be contained within the intellectual and moral categories of Plato or Aristotle. A Plato, after all, might well have told Thucydides that he was finally wasting time with the shadows of reality, while Aristotle might have failed to see what contribution to thought of lasting importance the record of a war could make. Indeed, when the main stream of Greek moral and political philosophy took its course from the Socratic claim that nothing evil could happen to the good man, it left all the paradoxes and ambiguities of concrete moral experience and political existence to the tragedians and historians. Hobbes was interested in the concrete actualities of social and political life. He wanted to raise the raw material of actual history and actual political struggle to the level of philosophy. His distrust of traditional learning was, to this degree, well founded.

This distrust was part of a more inconclusive distrust of language itself. Traditional learning was largely verbal. Men had been deceived by metaphors, myths, and symbols into thinking they knew and understood much when in fact they knew little. "Words are wise men's counters: they do but reckon with them, but they are the money of fools." If the wise man could be said to have any intellectual "money" it would be mathematics. Even the names of things, the most immediately referential kinds of words, are slippery. Every phrase of Hobbes's famous definition of names radiates mistrust: "A name is a word taken at pleasure, to serve for a mark which may raise in our mind a thought like to some thought we had before, and which being disposed in speech and pronounced to others, may be a sign to them of what the speaker had or had not in his mind."

Hobbes's nominalism has political as well as scientific motives. He frequently reminded a brutally contentious age that men were

destroying each other ostensibly over words, inherently meaningless myths, and unintelligible or unverifiable politico-religious dogmas. At times, his account of this stupidity will remind the reader
of Thucydides' superb and terrifying description of the rebellion in
Corcyra, when the degradation and corruption of language went
hand in hand with the decay of moral and civic order. Hobbes
learned from Thucydides that the state of language is intimately
related to the state of political and social life, although neither of
them shared the naïve view of some contemporary semanticists
and psychologists that all conflict is merely verbal. They both knew
too much about the energies of mankind and about our remarkable
capacities for self-deception to offer any simple solution for the
predicament of man in society. An ideology may well be nonsense,
but the massive and destructive forces it may capture are real
enough.

In spite of his distrust of language and metaphor, Hobbes was,
paradoxically enough, one of the great prose stylists in the English
language. Sprat, the historian of the Royal Society, contrasted the
styles of Bacon and Hobbes acutely: "Bacon is short, allusive, and
abounding in metaphors: Hobbes, round, close, sparing of similitudes, but ever extraordinarily decent in them. The one's way of
reasoning proceeds on particulars and pleasant images, only suggesting new ways of experimenting without pretence to the mathematics. The other is bold, resolved, settled upon general conclusions, and in them . . . dogmatical." It would be hard to better
this description of the styles of the two philosophers. Bacon's superb didactic metaphors are precisely what the reader carries away
from a reading of his works, and to remember them is to remember
the gist of Bacon's thought. The four "idols," the "diseases and
peccant humours of learning," the three kinds of intellectual work
symbolized by the spider, ant, and bee, the bee exemplifying the
proper relation between external facts and internal thought blended
in the service of making something useful for mankind—all these
metaphors carry the weight of Bacon's thought.

We are much more likely to remember of Hobbes, phrases like
his definition of laughter as "sudden glory," of curiosity as "a lust

of the mind," or his marvelously eloquent description of man in a
state of nature in chapter 13 of *Leviathan:*

> Whatsoever therefore is consequent to a time of war, where every
> man is enemy to every man; the same is consequent to the time,
> wherein men live without other security, than what their own strength,
> and their own invention shall furnish them withal. In such condition,
> there is no place for industry; because the fruit thereof is uncertain:
> and consequently no culture of the earth; no navigation, nor use of
> the commodities that may be imported by sea; no commodious build-
> ing; no instruments of moving, and removing, such things as require
> much force; no knowledge of the face of the earth; no account of time;
> no arts; no letters; no society; and which is worst of all, continual fear,
> and danger of violent death; and the life of man, solitary, poor, nasty,
> brutish, and short.

Hobbes's metaphysics is perhaps the weakest and certainly the
least important part of his system. It is really much more a simple
"form" supporting a great wealth of content than the foundation of
his thought. The essential principles of his metaphysics are few.
The universe is nothing but matter and there is no other reality
than body. Spirit is nonexistent. A material God made the cosmos
and imparted motion to it, thereafter retiring from any active involvement with his creation. The properties of body are extension,
which we experience in the mind as space, and motion, which we
experience in the mind as time. Whatever knowledge we possess of
the universe is entirely sensory, either immediately so as in all acts
of perception, or derivatively in all subjective processes of the
mind. Moreover, knowledge is primarily of sensory particulars, and
universals are merely names, something that the brain does with
language. The whole system of reality is governed by laws of cause
and effect, by an iron system of determinism governing matter, and
that specification of matter we choose to call mind, is itself only a
special case of matter in motion.

Unlike Spinoza, who gave in some respects the most consistent
and thoroughgoing expression in the history of seventeenth-century
thought to the emergent scientific view of the world, Hobbes did
not try very hard to deal with the inconsistencies of his thought or
of the great philosophical problems he raised. Indeed, he seems

hardly to be aware of them. He claimed that thought is nothing but a tissue of phantasms that external bodies generate in us but also claimed that these same phantasms could give us real knowledge of the external world in spite of the fact that, like the external world, they are no more than the motions of matter. In Hobbes's system, consciousness or self-consciousness is as much or more of a mystery than ever, and Hobbes simply chose to leave it at that and get on to more important things.

It may seem a paradox that Hobbes should neglect the problem of consciousness and nevertheless be the remarkable psychologist he was. But this omission was not important, for his psychology was of the passions, of the role of emotion and fantasy in the history of human error and misery. Moreover, since all knowledge and thought is finally sensory, we cannot transcend any aspect of the process of knowledge in order to explain it, and it would be futile to try. Thought cannot "explain" sensation, for thought is no more than a trace left by sensation, an image which has become less clear and less exact by its detachment from the external object which engendered it. Imagination, which we have come to think of as a valuable creative faculty, is, like thought, merely "decaying sense," and it is even less reliable because it lacks the logical structure which informs thought. It is identical in its fundamental character with memory and dreaming, two more subrational ways in which the brain manages sensory impressions.

Hobbes therefore reduces the self to a tissue of sensory impressions, whether clear and immediate in the presence of objects, or vague and less vivid in their absence. Sensory impressions may be compounded, to be sure, as when men imagine a Centaur, for example, but such compoundings are no more than fictions of the mind. The flood of images which is the mind itself is, however, no simple chaos. There are two ways in which men experience the contents of consciousness. First is the flow of images *"unguided, without design, and inconstant; wherein there is no passionate thought, to govern and direct those that follow, to itself, as the end and scope of some desire or other passion. . . .* And yet in this wild ranging

of the mind, a man may oft-times perceive the way of it, and the
dependence of one thought upon another."

The "wild ranging" of the mind has a minimum degree of organization, one which is usually unconscious and rests on principles of
association. This state of consciousness has little if any apparent
coherence and yields meaning only upon introspection if at all.
There is, however, a second state, when the contents of consciousness are *regulated* by some desire, and design." That this controlling passion may not be immediately conscious is clear from the
following passage:

And because the end, by the greatness of the impression, comes
often to mind, in case our thoughts begin to wander, they are quickly
again reduced into the way: which observed by one of the seven wise
men, made him give men this precept, which is now worn out, *Respice
finem;* that is to say, in all your actions, look often upon what you
would have, as the thing that directs all your thoughts in the way to
attain it.[3]

Men may forget what it is they desire and, when they do, their
thoughts lose direction and efficacy. If they remind themselves of
what it is that is the true goal of their activity, their thoughts will
again become appropriate: "For thoughts are to the desires, as
scouts, and spies, to range abroad and find the way to things desired." [4]

This welter of sensory impressions, all with different intensities
of vividness and each with a different emotional charge, is the mind
itself. How then, given this confusing state, can men arrive at the
truth? Fortunately we are able to define words, we can discipline
the mind by subordinating it to sensory reality, and we can exercise
care in correlating words to their proper external referents.

Seeing then that truth consisteth in the right ordering of names in
our affirmations, a man that seeketh precise truth has need to remember
what every name he uses stands for, and to place it accordingly, or
else he will find himself entangled in words, as a bird in lime twigs,
the more he struggles the more belimed. And therefore in geometry,
which is the only science it hath pleased God hitherto to bestow on
mankind, men begin at settling the significations of their words; which

settling of significations they call *definitions,* and place them in the beginning of their reckoning.[5]

Having reduced all mental life to the relations between sensory impressions, to phantasms, and having greatly emphasized the role of emotion and wish in the functioning of the mind, it is natural that Hobbes should have been much interested in that most "fantastic" of mental processes, dreaming. In sleep, the mind is no longer under the discipline of the immediate impact of objects upon the senses. Therefore, it reveals the life of the mind without the continual ordering effect of sensory reality. In sleep, the images and phantasms shift and move, meet and part, according to their own laws, laws derived from physiological principles. Dreams make sense, Hobbes contends, if we understand the kinds of relations which obtain between sensory impressions and emotions. For example, in the waking state, when we are frightened, we feel a chill. If, however, we become cold when asleep, we will experience fear and therefore dream of fearful objects; "In sum, our dreams are the reverse of our waking imaginations; the motion when we are awake beginning at one end, and when we dream at another." [6]

Hobbes, it is clear, has no theory of dream symbolism or of what Freud called the "dream work." However, he has many acute things to say about them. They proceed from internal physiological stimuli and have an emotional basis, for appetites and aversions generate phantasms just as phantasms generate various feelings. Since the function of memory is not operative in sleep, dreams have no time and always occur in the present tense. The quiescence of memory in sleep also explains why the dreamer is not shocked by the oddities of dreams, for memory is the basis of comparison, and the capacity to be surprised rests on being able to compare what you see with your usual experience. Since the dreamer cannot do this, nothing surprises him.[7]

These remarks on the atemporal character of dreams, the concept of the dream as occurring in a peculiar state of consciousness in which the dreamer has no memory and therefore no history, is a brilliant anticipation of Freud's view of the atemporality of unconscious processes. Hobbes was one of the few men before contem-

porary times who attempted to give a rational account of some of
the peculiarities of dreams, and especially of the dreamer's attitude
to the events of his own dream. He was struck, evidently, by the
complacent and passive attitude with which the dreamer may observe the most extraordinary and bizarre events produced by his
own mind. While his explanation is not as complete, or as subtle,
as that offered by modern psychology, it is brilliantly correct in
attributing these peculiarities of dream to their different temporal
and causal structure.

Hobbes's view of the memory is that it is a critical faculty, imperfect to be sure, but nevertheless the means by which events and
objects are ordered in temporal sequence through comparison.
Thus the widespread conception in the seventeenth century of
memory as the vehicle of both poetic and religious inspiration, a
conception with the prestige of ancient authority, falls under
Hobbes's attack. For him, the notion of inspiration, poetic or religious, was absurd, as if the mind were a bagpipe inflated by another's wind! The grand conception of the faculty of memory which
was contained in the Platonic-Augustinian tradition had claimed
that if memory were plumbed to the depths, we would return to
that "plain of truth," or God himself, from which we have somehow been separated, and that we would, in that act, enjoy a vision
of ultimate truth. How important Hobbes's repudiation of this doctrine was is clear when we consider that it undercut all the claims
of prophets and poets to the possession, in myth and metaphor, of
"higher" truths.[8]

Hobbes had no more grasp of the psychological meanings of
myth than his contemporaries and he takes a solidly rationalistic
view of these productions of the mind, relegating them with no
hesitation to the category of nonsense. His treatment of the passions is his true psychological masterpiece, and to that we can turn
now.

Men are endowed with essentially limitless desires, and the ends
of willing and desiring, its goals, may be proximate or remote.
Those which are close to us, so to speak, we call means, and those
further off are ends. There is, however, no ultimate end, no infinite

object, which is the final resting place of desire, no Utopia which can still the striving of the human will. As long as a man lives he is in a state of desire, and his satisfactions come, so to speak, en route, in a quest terminated only by death. Happiness is the actual enjoyment of specific things you want, not the by-product or aftermath of having known or enjoyed something.

Man, like everything else, is in continual movement. He is one kind among many of dynamic systems of "body in motion," and he too obeys the universal laws of motion which transform one structure into another. Rest, changelessness, Utopia—all are ideas which really imply death. Certainly they have nothing to do with life. Human striving, which Plato and Dante saw as a sign of man's transcendental destiny, saw as directable toward an infinite good which could quiet a commensurable craving, is now turned loose upon the world to seek continually after an endless succession of finite objects. Marlowe's Tamburlaine fits with equal ease in the universe of both Machiavelli and Hobbes.

Desire, however, is only a curse when it is excessively frustrated. A high degree of contentment, if not bliss, may be available to men in the continuous and gratifying exercise of vital functions within the optimum limits of tension. In spite of Hobbes's emphasis on human rapacity, he does not measure the value of life by possessions but by the manner in which human energies are deployed in the act of possessing. A good life is one in which there are durable and lasting conditions for pleasurable activity and man, therefore, seeks not only particular goods, food, clothing and the like, but also for those circumstances which will enable him to continue to have pleasure and avoid pain. He therefore needs the security and the protection of his life and possessions. Thus, to achieve "felicity" man needs at least some power. The excessive lust for power which dwells in the majority of men is, in essence, no more than the desire to get as large a share of the pleasures and good of this world as one can and for as long a time as one can.

Hobbes's prudential ideal of "felicity" is not one that he thought was widely actualized. Indeed, we might regard the sovereign as coercing all men to behave outwardly, at least, as if they were prudential, and providing those conditions which would permit some men to truly realize that degree of "felicity" the world can grant. We must be careful not to accuse Hobbes of a crude hedonism. His view of pleasure is no more riotous than that of Spinoza, in whose *Ethics* the word *gaudium,* joy, appears so often to describe the most pleasurable emotion a man can have. Whatever their differences, both Spinoza and Hobbes meant by "pleasure" that particular intensification of vitality which makes life worth living for individuals and furthers the survival of mankind.

Hobbes, of course, does not offer men any form of beatitude. His felicity is tame compared to the degree of exaltation possible in Spinoza's universe, and it rests, not on the achievement of moral and intellectual perfection, but on the prudential conduct of life. For Hobbes, man cannot transcend himself, but he can find fulfillment in the proper exercise and management of the passions. The ordered state simply makes it possible for individuals to achieve this condition for themselves. It is not an educational or a remedial institution and Hobbes, unlike modern totalitarians and utopians, never dreamed that it could offer mankind any higher salvation than peace.

Not only does Hobbes emphasize the importance of the emotional life in itself, but he grasps the essential relation of emotional life to intellect and intellectual excellence. Too much or too little passion are both bad for the working of the mind. The mind needs steadiness and calmness, but it also needs energy to function and to perceive quickly the relations between things or events. Both fancy (facility in perceiving similitudes) and judgment (facility in perceiving differences) rest on the right degree of emotional tone as well as on the proper disposition of emotional energy. The multitudes do not possess a finely equilibrated emotional identity and they are therefore not far from madness. Indeed, madness is nothing more than the subjection of the reason to those passions which can cause strange or unusual conduct.[9] In madness or in sanity, in order and disorder, human life is primarily governed by emotions: fear and hope, desire and aversion, love and hate. We must never lose sight of this fact, in Hobbes's view, if we are to understand the essentially coercive nature of all political and religious institutions.

Hobbes's analysis of religion, as of politics, rests on his conviction of the often fearful but always passionate egocentricity of mankind. In this he could have agreed with St. Augustine or Calvin. But religion, for Hobbes, neither explains nor remedies this state of affairs. On the contrary, it is a reflection of it, born from the union of fear and ignorance. Moreover, Hobbes argues forcefully against the theocratic policies which were frequently derived from such pessimistic views of man's sinfulness.

Hobbes's critique of religion undercuts every major tenet of traditional theology. First of all, there is no absolute good, and even if it should exist it is clearly unknowable. All the specific definitions men have proferred for the absolute good turn out upon examination to be merely personal preferences. Human reason not only does not reveal an absolute good, it does not reveal the existence of a universal ideal law binding on all of mankind. Natural law, in the sense in which Roman Stoic lawyers and Christian theologians had defined it, did not exist, and even if it did exist, it has had no visible effect on the conduct of mankind. There is therefore no absolute morality and God—who exists, but is quite material, albeit composed of a rather thin matter—does not appear to guarantee such a morality. If God can be used as a referent for anything knowable, it is only for power. Thus Hobbes deprived traditional metaphysics and theology of any meaningful content and reduced religion to the only thing left to reduce it to, the emotions.

Nothing illustrates this more clearly than Hobbes's famous definition of religion: "Fear of power invisible feigned by the mind or imagined from tales publicly allowed—*Religion;* not allowed—*Superstition;* and when the power imagined is truly such as we imagine—*True Religion.*" [10] One inference Hobbes did not draw from this definition, although one cannot but believe that he thought of it, was the conclusion that if true religion were not publicly allowed it would be a superstition. This, in fact, would be quite consistent with much that Hobbes said on the subject of religion. On the other

hand, he consistently refuted the charge of atheism, and was sometimes capable of discussing religious doctrines as if they were really
quite unproblematic.

Hobbes's views on religion have been a puzzle to his commentators. His system does not really allow for some of the more or less
conventional religious beliefs which he sometimes claimed to hold,
and Hobbes was much too acute a thinker to be guilty of the grossest forms of self-contradiction and inconsistency. Some of his interpreters have thought that he simply was prudential and did not
dare to express the full depth of his repudiation of traditional religious belief. Others point out that the Hobbesian interpretation of
the religious teachings he claimed to accept is often so heterodox
that he had no trouble in making the accommodations circumstances seemed to require. Given the brilliance of Hobbes's pioneering work in biblical criticism, the nature of his philosophical
principles, his contempt for the brutal intolerance of his age, his
courage in expressing views that were offensive to his pious contemporaries when even a Spinoza chose not to offend his Dutch
hosts and refused to publish—all this makes it probable that
Hobbes did not sacrifice conviction for mere expediency.

There is, however, another quite convincing argument for the
consistency and integrity of Hobbes's opinions on religion in spite
of apparent inconsistencies. F. A. Lange, the author of the classic
The History of Materialism suggested that when Hobbes spoke "directly" from his philosophical system, he viewed religion merely as
a superstition, and his brilliant analysis of the origins of religion in
the twelfth chapter of *Leviathan* rests unequivocally on such a
viewpoint. On the other hand, when Hobbes apparently accepts
some traditional religious doctrines, when, for example, he mentions some of the biblical miracles as actually having happened, he
is simply sacrificing to the great "Leviathan" of the state. Hobbes,
quite consistently with his political views, was a loyal citizen, and
since he postulated that the state determines what religion is, what
inherently obscure doctrines must be believed in, Hobbes accepts as
a *subject* loyal to his sovereign and to his own political principles
what he rejects as a metaphysician.[11]

Such a position is not as self-contradictory as it may seem to be at first sight. Hobbes, in effect, had revived the old classical, pre-Christian conception of a twofold theology, a rational one and a civic one. The civic theology was a matter of custom and law. It was not an intellectual matter at all, and Cicero, for example, could hold philosophical opinions concerning the nature of the divine which were incompatible with the beliefs and practices of popular official religion at the same time that he was willing and able to carry out various priestly duties without in the least sharing the popular belief in their efficacy. Paganism had no heresies, and an educated man could always respect popular religion as custom or, if he wished to take it more seriously, he was quite free to give a philosophical account of its presumed "esoteric" meaning while leaving the multitudes to the practice of the "exoteric" faith.[12]

Christianity, of course, also had a twofold theology, but the distinction in this case was between a natural theology and a revealed one. Since Hobbes lived in a Christian country and the state upheld a religion which demanded intellectual assent to its dogmas, Hobbes could not revive the classic concept of civic theology in all its purity. He nevertheless made his original and heterodox accommodations to the official faith, primarily in terms of a civic obligation.

One conclusion, however, is absolutely certain about Hobbes's views on religion: he was convinced that it is based on fear, whether it is true or false, good for mankind or bad. It is not only derived from fear, it is also sustained and disseminated by fear. Certainly a major motive in Hobbes's revision of traditional theology is his desire to diminish the fears of mankind, whether a fear of religious teachings or of religious fanaticism. Some of his major theological opinions seem to have this end in view. Thus Hobbes proposed that both God and the angels are corporeal. This, Hobbes seems to imply, would eliminate much of the current controversy over the nature of God. He reduced the Trinity to Moses, Jesus, and the Apostles, presumably to eliminate all of the numerous wars between the orthodox and heretics such as the Socinians and neo-Arians. All of them could name a Trinity of one kind or another.

Hell and heaven became terrestrial abodes and, while the saved will live forever, the damned will finally be annihilated after having endured a finite amount of torture. I think we can detect in Hobbes's eschatological reforms the attempt to remove from Christianity a doctrine, that of the eternal damnation of the mass of mankind, which constituted the most fearful and terrible threat of ecclesiastical authority over believers and a most powerful weapon in its wars with the civil power.

One does not have to read widely in seventeenth-century theology and sermon literature to see how much sadism, cruelty, and coercion rode on the vehicle of this belief in hell. As usual, the really wicked were not greatly affected by such threats, but the damage to the susceptible was, if we may believe Robert Burton, considerable. He attacked those divines of his day, and they were numerous, for inducing religious melancholy in many of their flock by their emphasis on an implacable divine wrath which condemned so many to eternal torment.

Hobbes's suggestions for the revision of traditional theology were thus pretty bold. There is, however, evidence that he may have been somewhat guarded in expressing his opinions in spite of their unorthodoxy. Aubrey reports that when Spinoza's *Tractatus theologico-politicus* appeared in 1670 Hobbes remarked that Spinoza "has cut me to a bar's length, for I durst not write so boldly." Aubrey is not always very exact and, in any case, prudence is not necessarily the same as dishonesty or self-deception.

It seems odd, on the other hand, that Hobbes should have felt that Spinoza had been so much bolder. It is true that Spinoza made no attempt at all, however sophisticated, to accommodate himself to religious teachings on the philosophical level. However much they may sometimes serve to inculcate morality, they have no positive intellectual content. On the other hand, Hobbes continued to publish views which the public opinion of his time found utterly outrageous and he spent years in polemic with eminent ecclesiastics and theologians such as Bishop Bramhall.[13] Oddly enough, the Church of England, which early in its history had been strongly Calvinist, had become the stanchest of advocates of free will, and

Hobbes was execrated by its spokesmen, especially Bramhall, for his determinism quite as much as for his other heterodox opinions.

There is not much point in going into Hobbes's controversies in detail or, like Milton's fallen angels, we too will find ourselves "in wandering mazes lost." The debate with Bramhall was perhaps the most famous one and Leslie Stephen caught much of the tone of it when he pointed out that Bramhall has all of the manner of the philosophical expert lecturing a coarse, untutored ignoramus on the subtleties of divine philosophy, much as "profound" nineteenth-century Hegelians lectured the disciples of John Stuart Mill or Herbert Spencer.[14]

One of Bramhall's arguments is of curious interest, however, and reveals something of the shifts in moral sensibility which were taking place in the seventeenth century. The learned Bishop maintains that men must be free because there is a hell where the wicked go to be eternally tormented. If they are not free, and are predestined to their respective eternal destinies, then we would have to believe that God is grossly unjust. Hobbes was particularly shocked by this argument of Bramhall's using the belief in eternal damnation to argue for free will. As we have seen, he had rejected an eternal hell on moral grounds and was surprised to find Bramhall arguing its existence on moral grounds. On the other hand, it is clear that Bramhall, although he accepted the notion of eternal punishment, was not entirely comfortable with it. He certainly could not bask in the Calvinistic notion of the predestination of the reprobate, and had to justify his God in some degree. Such discussions of eternal torment were a major theme in seventeenth-century theology and some of the best minds of the age, Hobbes, Newton, Leibnitz and Bayle were concerned with this problem. Among such men, the belief in eternal damnation began to wane because it began to be a moral problem. The most sensitive minds of the time could not accept such a vindictive conception of justice and were too responsive to the sufferings of others to worship a divinity with an endless appetite for suffering.[15]

On the whole, Hobbes's pious enemies read him right. There was no doubt that he made religion finally irrelevant, from an intellec-

tual point of view, however much he recognized its practical force.
Yet they were seldom fair enough to him to acknowledge that although he taught an egoistic psychology he did not derive an egoistic ethic from it. He was almost universally accused of fostering
gross immorality through his teachings in spite of the fact that he
never tired of pointing out that civilized life rests on the practice of
restraint and even renunciation.

The crown of Hobbes's work is his political philosophy, and his
masterpiece, *Leviathan*. With this book, Hobbes contributed a
classic to English prose and made a permanent addition to the
world's stock of ideas and insights. Men of any and every political
conviction have been able to learn from him. However much some
of his readers have disagreed with his conclusions and his remedies,
Hobbes's delineation of the fundamental political problems which
men are called upon to solve remains unrivaled. We might begin
our consideration of his political thought by placing him in his own
particular tradition of political philosophy.

There have been three great perspectives for the organization
and interpretation of political phenomena. One tradition, the main
one in Greek political philosophy, exemplified by Plato and Aristotle, employs two fundamental categories of interpretation: reason
and nature. In this view, the state is a "natural," rational phenomenon. It does not stand apart from or against the individual man.
There are, to be sure, bad or defective states, but man is *by definition* a political animal. His citizenship is, in a sense, as much a part
of his essence as his rationality, and whatever rights he possesses
flow from the "natural" fact that he belongs to a particular community. While no particular kind of polity is necessarily established
in nature as preferable to all others, some kind of polity is an indispensable requirement for man if he is to be human. We need only
contrast the miserable condition of the man without citizenship we
find in Sophocles' *Philoctetes* with the relative felicity, based on
personal resourcefulness and ingenuity, of Robinson Crusoe or
Deerslayer to grasp how impossible it was for a classical Greek to
conceive of the "apolitical" man. Man in the wilderness was man in
unutterable savagery and misery. Indeed, the wilderness is not even

nature in any meaningful sense of the word for it obscures that order which makes nature intelligible.

The *polis* was the very sphere of ordered nature and therefore of freedom, the place where man realized his true, "natural" humanity, where he found reason and liberation from the inchoate, subterranean furies of tribal laws and family guilts. Greek political ideals were not only enshrined in their philosophical thought but in their literature as well, and the great civic pageant at the end of Aeschylus' *Oresteia* represents, in imaginative terms, the triumph of reason and ordered nature over unstructured and irrational existence.

The good state, whatever its particular form, reflects the rational order of nature, of the cosmos, and permits man to actualize to the full his powers of reason, themselves part of nature. Below *physis* —nature as intelligible—in the order of things lies a realm of "nonbeing," or "chaos," the realm of blind impulse, striving, and disorder. Much that we might call nature, wild forests, jungles, savage mountain landscapes, would perhaps have struck a classical Greek as subnatural, as that realm of *chaos* awaiting the shaping hand of the demiurge to transform it into *cosmos*.

Another, and the most modern, tradition of political thought rests on the notion of the Rational Will and originated in the political theories of Hegel. I will not attempt a protracted analysis of Hegel's difficult political philosophy, but it might be summed up as a highly sophisticated and secularized version of the old pious proverb: "Man proposes and God disposes." For Hegel, the relation between Will and Reason was such that all of the irrational and private passions of men were transformed by the historical process itself into great public, rational structures, into institutions and cultural creations, and often in ironical ways. Indeed, the historical process is nothing more than the transformation of subrational individual desires into public intelligible meanings. The "cunning of Reason," in Hegel's own phrase, works to use men's energies for its own ends. Of course this is not the particular reason of a single individual but an impersonal, immanent World Reason.

An example at this point may help us to penetrate the obscurity of Hegelian terminology. The architects of the French Revolution strove to create liberty, equality, and fraternity, but finally, by a process which now seems perfectly intelligible, produced Napoleon. Napoleon, in turn, strove to create an international European order, but brought about a great intensification of German and Italian nationalism. These results are ironic if we consider them from the point of view of the will and intention of the individual actors on the stage of history, but are perfectly intelligible and coherent when seen from the point of view of the philosophical historian who comes after the events and discovers their rational concatenation. Individual reason may make the most logical plans to achieve its intention and be flawlessly rational in executing them, but the results of its action may be quite different from anything it expected and yet be no less "rational."

Hegel's is quite the opposite of a psychological view of history. The private motives of the movers of history are secondary to the manifest historical result, and the latter possesses a rationality which is not to be found in the realm of anyone's particular psyche or conscious intention. Moreover, history is not repetitive or recurrent. All that recurs is the human will, desiring and striving, but its fruits are determined by Universal Reason as it unfolds itself in successive stages of its own self-realization.

The tradition to which Hobbes belongs, and of which he is the greatest exponent, polarizes political thought in terms of the concepts of Will and Artifice. Language, religion, myths, symbols of one kind or another, are to be understood on the analogy of things made. They are in a sense "conventional," while what is fundamental, powerful, "real," and "natural" is passion or will. Therefore, reason and passion, state and subject, the one and the many, stand out against each other. In modern terminology one might state this view accordingly: With language or symbolization, that imperfect creation of his nervous system, man leaves the purely biological sphere and enters the sphere of culture. However, he carries with him his oldest and most powerful endowment, his emotions and drives, and carries them into an essentially "artificial" world, the world of civilization itself. In this new environment of culture, his ancient and primary endowment is, to some degree, excessive or inappropriate. It is of course true that man needs culture to secure his biological continuity more effectively. Nevertheless, the burden of culture is heavy in the controls it places on aggression, greed, and sexuality, so that man pays a price in biological freedom, as it were, in order to secure a more certain biological survival. The reader will recognize echoes of the thinking of the grimmer social Darwinists and of Freud's *Civilization and Its Discontents* in this brief account, and indeed such thinkers are close in spirit to Hobbes.

Man enters the realm of culture, in order to escape the tyranny of fear, but fear pursues him into culture too. He invents religion to conquer his fear of the unknown by specifying it, but, since there is ignorance even beyond his imaginary certitudes, fear re-enters by the window after having been cast out the door. The re-entering fear may even be greater than the one cast out, for man's ignorance truly appears limitless only after he possesses some knowledge, and the candle lit in the dark may also disclose how deep the dark really is. Language, religion, the state, are all collective human constructs, "artifices," whose function is to protect man from the shapeless fears and terrible dangers of the "state of nature," that state of *bellum omnium contra omnes* in which life, if it could survive at all, would be so savage and brutal that it would scarcely be worth living.

In the state of nature, Hobbes tells us, all is given unto all. There are no limits on the limitless will of each individual. The natural man in a state of nature is overtly and unrestrainedly competitive, distrustful, and ambitious for glory. Even without overt conflict such a condition is not peace but a state of war, and war of the worst kind, for it is not between groups and nations, but between each individual man and every other. Only a common power which keeps them all in awe and fear can impose peace. Even after men establish peace, bending their wills in obedience to a common object of will, the sovereign, the state of war remains latent, for war is a permanent psychological and moral condition before it is an overt act.

Hobbes does not insist there actually was such a time of war of all against all, or that there was an actual contract to obey a sovereign which marked the end of this condition of war. On the other hand he argues that such a "myth" truly describes the human condition, as we can tell by considering the life of the savages in the New World or simply by glancing at the warlike posture that kings and sovereigns have continually maintained toward one another in the civilized world.

But though there had never been any time, wherein particular men were in a condition of war one against another; yet in all times, kings, and persons of sovereign authority, because of their independency, are in continual jealousies, and in the state and posture of gladiators; having their weapons pointing, and their eyes fixed on one another . . . which is a posture of war.[16]

To understand this passage we must bear in mind that only kings or other persons with sovereign power retain the unlimited rights that each individual possessed in the state of nature. They alone can, without inhibition, gratify their lust for power and glory, they alone can elicit fear in other men and so rule them. Thus Hobbes finds the clue to the original condition of mankind in the behavior of contemporary sovereigns, the clue to relations between men in a state of nature in the actual relations between sovereign states. Whether or not the state of *bellum omnium contra omnes* was ever a historical fact, such a state exists *latently* in any civil society and *actually* in the conduct of international affairs. Force and fraud, which governed man in his uncivilized state, still govern the relations between nations and their rulers.

Fortunately, there are some passions which incline men toward peace, even if the weight of human energy tends toward anarchy. They are fear of death, desire for those things necessary to "commodious living" and the hope of obtaining such things by effort. Given these constructive impulses, reason suggests "convenient articles of peace, upon which men may be drawn to agreement."

This is Hobbes's version of a great paradox which recurs over and over again in the history of political thought: Man is born anarchic but cannot survive without order. Spinoza, for example, recognized it but felt, unlike Hobbes, that the contradiction was not necessarily a permanent aspect of man's condition. It was, rather, the result of the failure of most men to realize their truly rational nature. The passions are simply a natural endowment, neither good nor evil in themselves, and they created trouble only when they affected the processes of logical thought by substituting emotional and associative links between ideas for rational ones. The goal of every man is to replace such emotional and primitive processes by rational ones. Men do not need to resort to the remedy of universal coercion in order to regulate themselves. They can accomplish this end through the achievement of rational self-awareness and self-consciousness. To be sure, it is a task which is difficult and, perhaps, not for the majority of mankind, but the state should make it possible for those who can to achieve it. Hence Spinoza's great concern for the establishment of freedom of thought, for it is through thought that mankind will triumph over its lower nature.

Most Christian thinkers, following St. Augustine, traced the roots of the conflict between the one and the many, and the many with each other, to the fall of man and the consequent corruption of human nature. Man is, in a sense, ill, according to this view, and no longer possesses the perfections and abilities he once had. His mind is now clouded and he is prey to the strivings of a corrupt will. There are no real remedies for him in the natural order, for thought cannot save him, nor can coercive order do more than rescue him from the worst consequence of the fall, savage anarchy. The law of the state is the law of concupiscence and ambition. Whatever order it achieves is fragile and its laws, no matter how good, are truly unjust when measured by the law of love.

Ideas of salvation, whether derived from traditional religion or, like Spinoza's, ultimately derived from the contemplative ideals of ancient philosophical thought, are of little importance in Hobbes's universe. Like Spinoza, he does not condemn the rapacity of the natural man, but he has little confidence in man's rational or erotic capacities. Man is primarily a selfish will. His capacities for love and his capacities for rational thought are not the hegemonic powers of his being. For Hobbes, each individual is in essence solitary, a discrete bundle of strivings, unable to establish a true community with his fellows, if we mean by a true community one integrated by love or reason. If all men could live in solitude, there would be no problem. Their difficulties arise from the fact that they must come together, and human rapacity, not a defect as such, becomes one only in the collision of those bodily structures in motion which are mankind.[17]

In Hobbes, the political paradox possesses multiple facets. For example, Hobbes posits the beginning of civil society in a "contract" by which men irrevocably surrendered their rights, their freedom to exercise their absolute will in an unlimited way, to a sovereign, real or "fictitious," whom Hobbes calls an "artificial man." This sovereign need not be a single person and, even though Hobbes was a monarchist by preference, he was by no means a legitimist, for impotent rights are not rights at all.[18] A powerful oligarchy is better than an impotent king.

The state thus comes into being by a contract which creates the "artificial man" who gives laws, "artificial chains," and who possesses powers of succession, "artificial eternity of life." "Leviathan," the total structure of the state, is thus a "mortal God." The "artificial man" has rights which are natural, those rights of absolute willfulness which all other men surrendered to him, while his subjects have no more than those "artificial" rights that the "artificial" man is willing to grant them.

Of course, the sovereign has obligations, such as the primary duty of keeping the peace, and to do this he must make the necessary laws. Indeed, in spite of the fact that the contract is irrevocable it can, so to speak, "lapse" precisely when the sovereign can no longer fulfill his primary task of being an effective lawgiver. Such circumstances as the abdication of a sovereign or the loss of his realm to an enemy render the contract void since both these events also render the sovereign's will impotent. His sovereignty is thus nothing more than his right to make and enforce laws through the exercise of his will. Without the effective possession of authority and power, those rights are lost which the sovereign alone possessed. Will is prior to law and obligation as well as to reason.

On the other hand, no subject is asked whether or not he accepts the contract or the sovereign's authority. He accepts it by the simple fact of entering the world a subject. Society would simply fall apart if each individual were free to accept or refuse that obligation enjoined upon him by the contract. The sovereign, in fact, is the source of all obligation, himself obliged to none and, as we have seen, his only duty is to be an effective "artificial man." Nevertheless, although the sovereign is the only source of obligation, some rights remain vested in the individual. For example, Hobbes argues that any subject has the right to defend himself from being murdered or injured, and this is so in spite of the fact that the sovereign possesses the right of taking the life of or injuring his subjects. We then have the paradoxical situation in which a condemned criminal agrees, in a sense, that he shall be justly executed according to the "contract" but he cannot or need not agree that he should not try to escape execution. What Hobbes tells us in effect is that every act of the sovereign is to be taken as done by his subjects even when those very subjects resist the act.

We must bear in mind that Hobbes uses some traditional terms like "law of nature" or "natural right" in a very untraditional way. Historically, these terms derived from ancient Stoic philosophy, especially from the Stoic interpretation of the Roman *jus gentium,* that part of their law which applied to all the different peoples of the empire in spite of the fact that they frequently were also governed by their own special codes of law. When St. Paul protested that he was a Roman citizen, he was asking to be judged by the Roman law instead of the Jewish law, to which he was also subject.

According to Roman legal philosophers, law ultimately had a divine origin. It was visible in the universe as a whole and in the mind of man as "right reason." The proper use of the mind will uncover those natural, universal moral principles which are the ultimate basis of the *jus gentium.* In a way, they are natural principles precisely because they are universal. Of course, such an argument is not really very convincing and the notion of universal validity is not equivalent to "natural."

For Hobbes, natural law and natural right are not actual laws or discoverable in actual laws. They are, in fact, ideal constructions which refer to a condition of human existence *before* men contracted to create the state and, therefore, *before* the existence of any positive law at all. As we have seen, only sovereigns possess natural rights and are governed by natural law. Thus, for Hobbes, law does not express natural right but limits it, and this limitation is imposed by the one man who can exercise natural right, the sovereign.

Also, when Hobbes refers to the natural equality of all men he does not have reference to any legal status, for again, the reference is to the condition of men before they entered the civil condition. All he means is that no individual is endowed with sufficient power and intelligence—however much men, in fact, do differ in natural endowment—to *ensure* his safety and prosperity in the original state of *bellum omnium contra omnes.*[19]

The law of nature, the way Hobbes uses it, leads to another facet of the paradox of the condition of man in society. Reason—although not "right reason"—does discover the law of nature in that it discerns what men are like and how they find themselves situated. One such law of nature is the right each man has to use whatever resources he possesses to preserve his life. Nature, in a way, forbids him to do otherwise. On the other hand, each man has a right in the state of nature to everything he desires and can get hold of. How could it be otherwise, since the state of nature is antecedent to law and to the sovereign power? In such a state everybody owns everything and therefore nothing, and power of possession is all the law there is. This same right to everything derives from the very instinct of self-preservation, for this instinct is not, in principle, limited by the needs of others to preserve themselves or by their existence. On the contrary, it is absolute. We therefore reach a paradoxical position. In order for man to obey the natural law or instinct of self-preservation, given the natural equality of men in their weakness, man must depart from the state of nature by abrogating that very natural law derived from the law of self-preservation, i.e., that he has an unlimited right to all things. The contract is little more than this surrender of the right to all things, the surrender of a single natural right, in order to enjoy another right, the more fundamental one of self-preservation from which, paradoxically, the relinquished right originally derived.

From this peculiar condition whereby the rights of sovereigns and the rights of subjects are radically different, and their duties radically different, we derive the inevitable dilemma generated by the clash between the one and the many and between individual and political morality: it is legitimate for the state to do things which would be culpable in a private citizen. The brilliant and tragic paradox that Hobbes gives us in effect states that civil society is instituted by allowing the sovereign to continue to be barbarous while his subjects accept civilization. But the renunciation of right also leads, paradoxically, to the enjoyment of right, renunciation of the limitless exercise of the natural law of self-preservation leads to actual self-preservation, the acceptance of "chains" leads to a life worth having, to peace.

To lay down a man's right to any thing, is to divest himself of the liberty, of hindering another of the benefit of his own right to the same. For he that renounceth, or passeth away his right, giveth not to any other man a right which he had not before; because there is nothing to which every man had not right by nature: but only standeth out of his way, that he may enjoy his own original right, without hindrance from him.[20]

To have peace men must therefore relinquish their rights to all things to a sovereign and allow each other as much freedom of action as any single individual would care to see exercised *against* himself. The fundamental law of civil society is the relinquishing of man's natural right to follow the law of nature, that law which puts no limits to his will.

Society therefore rests on a "will not to will," but since a simple and universal agreement of this sort would lead to the extinction of the race, there must simultaneously be the agreement to give over the function of willing to a single representative. The sovereign will is the only unifying principle in the state. Hobbes does not envisage the possibility of political order through a harmonizing of individual wills, through the creation of a common will directed toward a common good. The only political order comes through replacing the wills of the many by the will of one.[21] However various the forms of the state, however various its rationalizations, this is the basic fact of political order wherever such order is found.

Hobbes acknowledged that the development of morality, as distinct from the bare minimum of order achieved through coercion, implies a certain degree of consensus among the members of a given polity. But until such a consensus is attainable, the sovereign should not try to inculcate an ideal morality among his subjects. It is not only impractical, it may even be undesirable, for men are always going to pursue private aims at variance with the common good. They will never be like ants and bees who live in organized communities governed by instinct, and they cannot be made to behave like that by imposing a strictly uniform morality on all of them. Human cohesion is "artificial" and derives from that initial rational act which prompted all men to give over their wills to the sovereign will. It is sufficient if men, allowed to vary in pursuit of their private goals, obey the sovereign will in all matters of importance to his state.

Hobbes has sometimes been misunderstood as an absolutist, as one of the fathers of the modern totalitarian state. Perhaps only Machiavelli has been as grossly misinterpreted in the history of political thought. Hobbes certainly stressed authority and deeply believed in it, but this does not make him an absolutist. He was of course not a libertarian, but he did not believe that the role of the state involved imposing a uniform on the mind and spirit or, for that matter, on the body. "He perceived the folly of his age to lie in the distraction of mankind between those who claimed too much for Authority and those who claimed too much for Liberty." [22]

Modern totalitarians are, after all, great "rationalizers" of life, malevolent utopians, who are not satisfied to have a peaceful civil society, to confine their control to acts of public disorder. "Big brother" wants not only external obedience but love, devotion, and utter submission. Those vast areas of privacy, individuality, and even eccentricity which Hobbes excludes from the political realm are precisely the ones invaded by totalitarians. Authority is a necessary part of any state, but Hobbes defines authority in terms of the genuine needs of the citizenry. He never claims, like the modern totalitarians, that the state's authority must be great enough to ensure the happiness of all in return for their submission. No authority would be great enough for that impossible task. Moreover, although the sovereign's authority is in principle unlimited, Hobbes does not imagine that the one man in the state who could do whatever he pleased would have much reason, most of the time at least, to exercise that authority in a stupid, cruel or irrational manner. He may have been too sanguine about this sort of sovereign restraint, yet even the modern totalitarians cannot seem to use terror as an instrument of policy forever.

In the last analysis, authority arises from the problems of political life that the sovereign must solve. He must make those laws which guarantee the life, security, and safety of his subjects, fulfill those fundamental needs which are the very reason for the hypothetical contract. Hobbes's strictures on libertarianism derive from the fact that all contending parties in the religious and political wars of his time and country claimed rights in such a way that they were destructive of the peace and security which had been achieved by the surrender of natural right. Moreover they were also inclined to press their "rights" to the degree where they infringed upon the rights of others.

Hobbes, in fact, was convinced that the cry for liberty all over the land was largely hypocritical nonsense. What those who cry for freedom really want is dominion. Even Milton, that eloquent defender of liberty, had to agree that the "new Presbyter" was really the "old priest writ large." Liberty, in fact, was an ambiguous term for Hobbes. Did it mean the right to make laws? Did it mean freedom from too much or too harsh legislation? Did it mean no laws at all? The people who shouted loudest did not seem to know. Hobbes felt that meaningful liberty rested on the effective existence of a single, supreme ordering authority which, although supreme, would not be all-encompassing. Indeed, he was inclined to feel that the good state would interfere as little as possible with its subjects.

Political authority, to be effective and to guarantee that liberty which consists in the protection of the lives, honor, and property of its citizens, must be single. Much of the disorder of the time arose from the political claims of churches and sects. As long as the church claims any share in making laws and governing, it must be completely unified with the state and the sovereign or there will be a fatal splitting of authority. Although Hobbes makes a display of extensive biblical references to show that civil and religious authority were always united, his essential argument is that religion is simply a matter of law. Religious teachings are so ambitious, not to say irrational, that the only definition they can receive is a legal one. The sovereign decides what religious truth is in the same way that he decides what the law is. The church is an arm of the state, and its theology a branch of the law. Hobbes does not advocate religious persecution in the name of political uniformity. Individuals may, indeed must, believe what they can believe, but the only religious beliefs to be publicly professed and disseminated are those allowed by the law.

Hobbes was in favor of absolute religious toleration and it was with reluctance, one feels, that he advocated a single official public religion. His horror and disgust at the bloody and fanatical religious controversy of the age with each sect often aiming at the annihilation of its rivals left him with no other practical alternative. The paramount consideration was public order, and even in his theological speculations he tried to make peace between various Christians by reducing the essential Christian doctrines to few and allowing for some flexibility in their interpretation.

He was strongly opposed, moreover, to the extension of the power of the state into the realm of private belief, privately and peacefully held. The only interest of the state is peace, and it will not want to seek out and destroy heretics as long as they do not raise public quarrels or seek to subvert the state. In Hobbes's day the state was less given to bigotry and persecution than the church, and the practical solution was an established church firmly under the control of the more tolerant secular power.

Hobbes's conception of authority is not one of pure force. The obligation of subjects to obey the sovereign is finally moral. The hypothetical contract by which the sovereign assumes authority is the same contract by which the subjects assume a moral obligation. Morality flows from the surrender of the will to authority, an authority created in the very act of surrender. There is a contract and, therefore, moral obligation, even if the contract was not a historical event. Force alone does not constitute authority, nor does self-interest alone, which may even collide with the subject's moral obligation to his sovereign. Hobbes's theory of political obligation is a special mixture of physical, rational and moral forms of obligation, as indeed any theory of political obligation must be. Every state can coerce, every state must indulge some of the self-interest of its subjects, every state obliges its subjects by defining what is moral conduct.

Hobbes treats the state and society as a massive construct, a dynamic mechanism, created out of fear and out of that small amount of prudential reason which prompts men to limit rapacity in the interest of survival. His portrait of mankind is too atomistic, perhaps, too neglectful of the permanent human need for a shared emotional life even in political society. Social cohesion has other elements at work than those few benevolent passions he discovers. Nevertheless, between all the insoluble tensions governing the relations of the individual and the collective, and between each man and every other man, Hobbes sought to find some islands of peace where mankind might enjoy a durable "felicity," no matter how modest and unheroic such contentment, in the nature of things, was destined to be.

Notes

*

1 For an excellent account of Hobbes's relation to scientific thought, see J. H. Randall, Jr., *The Career of Philosophy: From the Middle Ages to the Enlightenment* (New York, 1962), the chapter on "Thomas Hobbes: Rational Calvinist and Empiricist," pp. 532-559.

2 For an interesting account of Newton's historical and biblical investigations see F. E. Manuel, *Isaac Newton Historian* (Cambridge, Mass., 1963).

3 *Leviathan,* chap. 3.

4 *Ibid.,* chap. 8.

5 *Ibid.,* chap. 4.

6 *Ibid.,* chap. 2.

7 Cf. *ibid.*

8 *Ibid.,* chap. 8.

9 *Ibid.*

10 *Ibid.,* chap. 6.

11 F. A. Lange, *The History of Materialism,* trans. E. C. Thomas (3rd ed., 1925), Book I, Section 3, pp. 284-285.

12 Cf. the introduction to Michael Oakshott's edition of Hobbes's *Leviathan* (Oxford, 1960), p. lxii. This remarkable essay is indispensable to any student of Hobbes's philosophy.

13 For a recent study of Hobbes and his attackers see S. I. Mintz, *The Hunting of Leviathan* (Cambridge, Eng., 1962).

14 Leslie Stephen, *Hobbes* (Ann Arbor, Mich., 1961). This brilliant and witty book is still the best general study of Hobbes.

15 See the excellent study of D. P. Walker, *The Decline of Hell: Seventeenth-Century Discussions of Eternal Torment* (Chicago, 1964).

16 *Leviathan,* chap. 13.

17 Cf. Oakshott, pp. liv and lv. Oakshott makes the interesting observation that Hobbes anticipates the romantic doctrine of personality in his emphasis—in a secular framework—on the opposition between personality and rationality. Personality is a function of the individual will and therefore men are radically separated from one another. Reason alone would unite them, but reason is weak, and agreement is not reached by the achievement of common understanding but by the surrender of one man's opinion to the opinion of another. In ancient times Boethius had defined the person as an individual substance of a rational nature. A subsequent emphasis on reason led, in the seventeenth century, to the Cartesian view of personality, and an emphasis on substance to the Hobbesian.

18 There were different forms of social-contract theory in the seventeenth century. In one version, advanced largely by the Huguenots, the influence of biblical theology, Roman law, and feudal tradition is dominant. Whatever the specifications of the contract it was between subjects and rulers. Hooker introduced another version of the contract theory whereby the contract took place between the members of a contracting group. Hobbes makes the contract a total and irrevocable surrender of individual rights to the sovereign, while Locke, as well as political theorists of the Commonwealth, thought of the contract as limiting the sovereign, with the lion's share of political power remaining with the subjects. According to Locke, all that the social contract really meant was that the people did not govern themselves *directly* but through dele-

gates. In this view, the legislature may be the highest power in the realm in a practical sense but does not really possess sovereignty. That remains with the people.

19 Cf. Stephen, pp. 182 ff.
20 *Leviathan,* chap. 14.
21 Oakshott, p. lvi.
22 *Ibid.,* p. lvii.

VI

THE IDEA OF PROGRESS:

Science and Poetry

No single idea has dominated Western civilization in modern times more than the idea of progress, and perhaps none is more elusive, in spite of the universal conviction that we know what we mean when we speak of the progress of the human race. It is, in fact, more than a single distinct idea. It comprehends a number of related notions, ideas, beliefs, and attitudes, all more or less expressive of the conviction that the processes of social and cultural change we see about us are taking mankind in a desirable direction *in the long run*. This last phrase is obviously important, and no sensible believer in progress ever denied that we would suffer at least a few minor setbacks in what he assumed was man's otherwise steady ascent from his origins in barbarism to a golden future.

The notion of gradual, continual progress, with no discernible limit, in a more or less linear ascent from an inferior condition, was unknown to mankind before the seventeenth century. To be sure, some ancient thinkers were much interested in change and development. Aristotle, for example, advanced some interesting views about social institutions and their derivation from specific properties of the human animal. For him, social and cultural life derived from those characteristics of man's biological and psychological endowment which make him a "political" animal, one who fulfills himself in society. Culture does not contradict man, in whole or in part, and man's progress from barbarism to civilization is the actualization of his psychobiological potential.

But such progress has a limit. The perfect result of social and cultural progress is the *polis,* the city-state, which has an optimum size of 50,000 inhabitants. Its social and political structure has reached its apogee if and when the wisest men, be they few or many, rule the city of which they are citizens. From an ideal condition of size and government the *polis* can only decline. The rhythms which govern its life are cyclical, however, so that from its decline it may rise again to its ideal condition. Indeed, the structure of social change, as Aristotle and other Greek thinkers conceived it, was identical with their view of natural processes. An organism is born, grows until it achieves its ideal state of development, and then declines. In Aristotelian terms, its essence limits its existence, so that when it has grown to the point of being a full embodiment of its species, it must decay. The city, of course, need not decline into death in the course of its cyclical changes. Like the species, it outlasts the individuals comprising it.

Christianity, of course, introduced what might be called an idea of progress, but the blissful future which it postulated had no reference to this world as we know it. Any new heaven and new earth which mankind yearned for would be a miraculous and supernatural act. It would come at the end of time with the general resurrection, and the temporal process preceding this eschatological event was by no means a gradual approximation of it. Indeed, human affairs would get much worse before God, acting beyond all human comprehension, would make them suddenly better. Meanwhile, life was a journey, a pilgrimage, leading from the miseries of this world to the bliss of the world to come for those fortunate enough to be numbered among the elect, and to infinitely greater eternal misery for those who were damned. The general resurrection and the Last Judgment would alter the personal fate of no man. It would simply bring history to an end and consolidate, so to speak, the many inscrutable judgments of God.

For classic Christian theology, progress could only mean progress toward salvation, toward a goal outside of space and time, and classic theology, if we take St. Augustine as a model, was rather pessimistic about the number of mankind which would be saved. Such progress would be available to the lucky few God had decided to rescue from the general doom. Of course most Christians, even

Christian theologians, went on living in the world and, like men everywhere, tried to gain what material advantages and improvements they could. Still, for the faithful, this progress was finally irrelevant. The true believer who thought himself elect was constrained to reflect that his journey from sin to salvation and from sorrow to joy, the way of true progress, led through the gate of death.

However pessimistic the Hebraic-Christian view of history was, the modern idea of progress is indebted to it for some of its features. Of course, before we could even begin to think anything like our modern notion of indefinite progress, we had to reacquire the outlook of classic Greek naturalism and its conviction of man's ability to progress, at least to some degree, through his own capacities and efforts, even if only from the state of barbarism to the state of civilization. The idea of an enormously desirable, virtually infinite, goal for progressive change, however, seems to have derived in part from a secularized version of the Hebraic-Christian expectation of a messianic kingdom or a future millennium, from the belief in some sort of future renovation of man and his world, however conceived.

Before the vision of a temporal utopian future could capture the imaginations of men, the supernatural paradise of religious tradition had to become a natural and human possibility. Perfection, however defined, had to be glimpsed as a purely human potentiality and not as a divine gift miraculously bestowed. The linear movement of time, from the Fall through the Redemption to the coming Last Judgment, had to be given a gradual and steady upward direction. History, which existed only because God gave some men a second chance, and which would end as soon as all the elect had been winnowed out from the mass of the reprobate, had to become the story of man's gradual, incremental conquest of knowledge, virtue, and felicity.

This imaginative transformation of religious beliefs began in the Renaissance, and it is a necessary although not a sufficient condition of the modern idea of progress. Some further beliefs had to be added to the dream of a utopian finale for human history brought about by human effort. What sort of effort, after all, could achieve such an end? What sort of mechanism, so to speak, would encompass such a hope? The answer lay in a new attitude toward knowledge and its uses. The beliefs which complete the idea of progress state that man can achieve knowledge of nature such that he will gain power over its operations, that such knowledge and power have no discernible limits, and more important still, that the power to dominate nature and make it serve man will increase the happiness of mankind.[1]

The elusiveness and ambiguity of the belief in progress rests essentially on this last assumption, that progress in knowledge of a certain sort, at least, will increase the happiness of mankind. It does not clarify things much to say that social and cultural change is gradually and over the long pull bringing mankind closer to its heart's desire. The heart desires many things and frequently enough they are incompatible one with the other. Or different men desire different and incompatible things. There is no guarantee that the increase in knowledge or reason or even in freedom will, as such, make mankind happier. At the present time it seems clear that technological knowledge may well have outrun our capacity to use it for the benefit of all men, although a grim necessity may help us learn to do so. The diffusion of rational modes of thought to more and more of the human race may well make men saner but not necessarily happier. Freedom, too, may bring with it such anxieties as to lead men to flee from it, if some of the political disasters of the twentieth century have anything to teach us.

Determinedly buoyant optimists and bleak pessimists, by selecting some evidence and suppressing or minimizing other evidence, can present persuasive arguments to support the opposing views that civilization is or is not moving toward the goal of a happy existence for most, if not all, men. Understandably enough in the light of the history of the last half-century, spokesmen for an "unreconstructed" version of the belief in progress are not to be found among the major thinkers and artists of the twentieth century. Indeed, the notion so crucial to the moral character of the idea of progress, the notion of happiness or felicity, has become one of the important intellectual problems of our age. We are now perhaps more concerned with the problem of the good life than any other age since the ancient Roman empire, when various philosophical schools and a bewildering variety of oriental cults vied with each other in purveying some sort of felicity. Indeed, we have even gone beyond the assumptions of that age and have become more critical of the notion of happiness than any of the ancient sages. Is there a more fundamental criticism of this hope than Freud's brilliant and paradoxical thesis that happiness is always the fulfillment of a childhood wish? Such wishes, Freud tells us, are so atavistic that the pursuit of happiness cannot be the goal of anything we could call civilization. Comfort, money, success, knowledge, cannot therefore truly gratify men or detach them from their persistent desire to return to their origins.

Others would argue that even if the psyche is somehow inevitably self-contradictory and ambivalent, it is not, or need not remain, unalterably in excessive conflict with itself. Men can learn to make peace with themselves and with each other, difficult as the task may be. Culture, after all, does offer opportunities for gratifications as well as denials, it can actualize love as well as hatred, and its constructive possibilities may be made to increase. New knowledge may teach us how to manage the knowledge we already have wisely and well.

There is really no final conclusion to be drawn from this debate over the future. The answer, if any, turns on a deeper knowledge of human nature and of the workings of the mind, a knowledge we are only starting to acquire. How much can men change? How much of what we see in the world and are tempted to despair of is truly unalterable? If we learn how to change things for the better, for the inner as well as the outer man, will we be wise enough to use that knowledge constructively? However problematic these questions are, the fact that we are asking them has a most important bearing on the ideological legacy of the belief in progress. As secular as the belief in progress may seem at first glance, it conserved and drew life from a large residue, albeit disguised, of wishful thinking, from deep traces of its origins in religious, philosophical, and historiographical myths and speculations which had originally expressed some of the deepest hopes and aspirations of mankind.

Few men today would dare, like Comte in the nineteenth century, to base their optimism concerning human progress on the presumed existence of a law of nature which is inevitably taking us toward the millennium, on a hypothesis which has little but scientific window-dressing to differentiate it from the old idea of divine providence. And even our contemporary Marxists have had to modify their "theology," their unshakable faith concerning the goal and purpose of history, to take some account of the possibility of race suicide. As radical as the modern critique of the myths and legends of happiness is, our conviction grows that no law of nature or of history, no natural or supernatural plan, should be invoked to guarantee a better future while we relax and calmly watch its presumed operations on our behalf. The possibility of progress, the hopes for its continual realization, have come to rest upon our own efforts, whatever over-beliefs of a providential character, theological or scientific, men may also adhere to.

Under the present circumstances, a passive trust in extrahuman agencies would simply amount to a denial of our own responsibility. Indeed, such an attitude would contradict a fundamental category of the idea of progress itself, for the notion implies not that progress is automatic—the Comtians were pretty muddle-headed about this—but that continual progress can be assured because it will come about as the direct result of the application of human intelligence and energy to the problems that beset us. Only humans, if anyone, can assure human progress beyond the caprices of an extrahuman will or the purposelessness of impersonal processes. We may be in some degree deluded about all this but we should be clear about the assumptions on which our hopes for progress rest.

I have attempted to give a brief survey of the idea of progress before proceeding to a more detailed examination of the idea itself and of the great alternative accounts of social and cultural change which came before it. It is in the last analysis a theory of change and development, a vision of history in the broadest sense of the word, and it can only be defined fully against its predecessors. We might now return to antiquity, trace out the evolution of various theories of change with greater care, and so untangle the complex cluster of attitudes and beliefs, by no means homogeneous, which went to make up the ideology of progress.

If the philosophers of a people do reflect, in however refined a form, that people's convictions and assumptions about life and the world, then we can say that the Greeks were inclined to value the unchanging over the changing, the immutable over the mutable, the shaped and measured over the indeterminate.

Among Greek philosophers change was not, in itself, very desirable, for half the time it was likely to be for the worse instead of the better. In fact, the idea that there had been progress out of barbarism was contained within the more inclusive pattern which posited the existence of a truly golden age in the past from which mankind had declined. That age of simple bliss was, in the opinion of most men, not to be reached again. Progress simply meant that man had been able, through civilization, to mitigate the worst consequences of his loss of primal innocence. No Greek thinker thought that more inventions, for example, or different modes of economic and social organization would, if protracted, carry men closer and closer to a renewed golden age. Progress was relative and finite, and advances were defined against an over-all scheme of the degeneration of the human condition. Some thought that when the course of decay had reached its limit the whole world-process would begin again. For Plato this took place every 36,000 years, the "great year" which measured the endless cycles of universal change. This was the overarching cycle of change and all the lesser cycles—natural, historical, and political—imitated its encompassing rhythm on a lesser scale.

However inconsistent this fusion of a theory of cyclical change and a theory of decay, it dominated the thinkers of antiquity. The enormous political changes in the ancient world which culminated in the Augustan empire produced a few modifications in it for a time. Polybius maintained that the Roman hegemony and its mixed constitution had broken the political cycle, and Virgil suggested

that Rome had ended the historical cycle. According to some recent interpretations of his famous fourth *Eclogue,* Virgil believed
in a coming return of the golden age. Nevertheless, even the optimists under this scheme of things did not feel that the future would
be better than the highest point mankind had ever reached in the
past. In general, the optimists in antiquity contented themselves
with the idea that the future would preserve the blessings of the
present when, as in the case of Polybius, the present represented
more or less the maximum of human progress. Others expected
nothing but decay, and still others, although convinced of decay,
hoped for improvement at that time in the future when the cycle of
change turned upward again. "The best condition was already
achieved, either now or in the past; and the future, though it might
offer something better than the present, would offer nothing better
than both the present and the past." [2]

It is important for us at this point to distinguish between attitudes concerning progress of a social and cultural sort and progress
in knowledge. The idea that knowledge increases and that each
generation might make its contribution to it was well known to the
Greeks. Indeed Thales, the earliest of the pre-Socratic philosophers
of whom we have any knowledge, said that "truth is the daughter
of time." Hippocrates consoled his disciples over the shortness of
life by reminding them that the art of medicine is long and that
their posterity would be able to accomplish much that they would
have to leave undone, and Aristotle, in the first book of the *Metaphysics,* developed his own philosophical position on the contributions of the predecessors.

The atomists and their successors among the Epicureans placed
especially high value on the increase of knowledge, which they saw
as contributing to the elimination of magical and superstitious
practices. It was also knowledge which, in their view, had led men
upward from a barbarous and savage condition to civilization,
knowledge which had made useful technological discoveries and
helped to create institutions for bettering the lot of mankind.

The atomists and Epicureans, in fact, believed that a kind of
moral enlightenment had taken place through the growth of natural

knowledge and, unlike the Stoics who believed in the general moral decay of mankind from a golden age in the past, Epicurus and his followers were certain that increased knowledge of the workings of nature had liberated man from a crude, rustic, fearful and above all, ignorant past. Nevertheless, this progress neither could nor should continue indefinitely. Or rather, the important truths which lead to human liberation were known. When, for example, man finally understood his place as a configuration of atoms in the universal falling and swirling of the particles which constitute the universe, he had achieved the maximum that knowledge could provide for his inner freedom and tranquillity.

Moreover, among the doctrines which they taught was one marking a definite limit to the possibility of progress: the time would someday arrive, and perhaps at no great distance, in which the present structure of the universe would dissolve. Created by the concourse of atoms hooking each other as they swerve in their fall through infinite space, it would come apart to reorganize itself further down in its descent. Man's intelligence had taken him toward enlightenment through his own efforts, but his intelligence also told him of a coming dissolution of all things.

The Epicureans, in some respects, resemble those of our contemporaries whose intellectual outlook is made up of balanced proportions of scientific materialism, temperate hedonism, and what we usually think of as "enlightened" views of man's nature and his history. They appear quite different from their modern counterparts, however, when we realize that their interest in natural knowledge was not for the sake of controlling the external world but for the sake of liberating man in his inner world.

In general then, although the Greeks set a very high value on knowledge, they did so for rather specific and limited reasons. It could help man to govern himself and to create good forms of government. It could help him to distinguish right from wrong, reality from illusion, and promote the achievement of his true "good." It could help him to achieve *apathia, ataraxia* or whatever form of beatitude the various philosophical schools posited. But no Greek thinker thought that the growth of knowledge, whether as an individual or collective possession would, *pari passu* with its accumulation, increase the happiness or virtue of mankind. The leaders of the great philosophical schools of antiquity all seem to have assumed that the solution of the problem of life lay in *praxis,* in a kind of action, in self-reconstruction and a radical alteration of conduct. It did not take vast learning or endless researches into the mysteries of things to bring this about. It was a question of learning a new moral and psychological discipline. While knowledge and the attainment of moral or eudaemonic progress were related, the relation of knowledge to virtue was complex. Knowledge, as Aristophanes and Plato seem to have thought, might easily corrupt. It could destroy sound moral traditions and offer nothing comparable in their place. It might be used by unscrupulous men to further evil ends, to compound injustice and intensify social evils and misery. The growth of freedom or goodness or felicity or wisdom was not —and in this all the Greek thinkers and writers seem to have been united whatever differences in emphasis they might have made— simply and directly related to the growth of knowledge. To a certain degree knowledge of both a practical and a moral kind obviously fostered moral and social progress but at some point, often difficult to determine, it would either become useless in the service of truly human ends or even detrimental to the achievement of those ends.

The Greek distaste for the unlimited and the indefinite, their awareness of the ambiguities of knowledge, was part of their profound belief in moral limits. *Hybris,* prideful transgression of those limits brought its *nemesis,* an automatic retribution. Originally administered by divine agencies, *nemesis* came to be regarded as the inevitable "natural" consequence of human transgression of that fixed order of the universe which went by the name of *moira.* While *moira* has some affinities with the idea of fate, it refers less to a blind fatality presiding over the affairs of men than to a moral order as exact and rigorous in its way as the physical order is in its. *Moira,* man's allotted "portion," in fact was identified by the Stoics with *pronoia,* the rational, purposeful ordering of things by the divine mind immanent in the universe.

However ambiguous, this cluster of ideas of moral limit implied that the human condition cannot be radically altered whether through knowledge or action. The idea of unlimited progress would, to many Greeks, have seemed hybristic, rash, and bold, an idea appropriate to a god, perhaps, but not to a man.[3]

The growth of Christianity prepared the way for new conceptions of history, a different vision of the goal and purpose of life, and a different valuation of knowledge in its relations to virtue and felicity. It is very risky to generalize about what the Christian position was on any of these matters, for even within the sphere of orthodoxy one might point to the harsh pessimism of the aging St. Augustine or to the generally buoyant and humane temper of a Clement of Alexandria or a Gregory of Nyssa. Nevertheless, it is true to say that all Christian thinkers were committed in one way or another to the notion of history as the history of salvation. It would end when the plan of salvation had been completed and when each individual composing mankind had come to his final reward or punishment. There was no collective destiny for the species as such. Its empires and its achievements would sooner or later crumble to dust. There was no correlation between temporal success or temporal felicity and each man's eternal destiny. The rain falls on the just and unjust alike and God gives empire to the good and the bad alike. The meaning of history lay in the drama of salvation and that, in its essential lineaments, had been revealed. All mankind was waiting for the last act to take place and for time to give way to eternity. Such a reading of life did not always, as in the case of St. Augustine, generate a gloomy otherworldliness. Men, even deeply religious men, did not always use eternity to undercut the value of things temporal. But the meaning of life and the meaning of history lay, in the last analysis, outside of time and space, outside of the processes of change in which we are embedded.

Knowledge, which had been highly valued by the Greeks even if they did not expect too much from the growth of knowledge, took a different place in the Christian scheme of things. The notion that Christianity was itself responsible for the decay of ancient learning is a grossly distorted version of the truth. Opinion among the Fathers on classical culture ranged from the contempt of Tertullian who asked what Athens could have to do with Jerusalem, to the Alexandrians who saw in Christianity the capstone of the whole tradition of Greek *paideia,* the completion of the best in their pagan tradition. Nevertheless, there is no question that Christianity did reverse the classical estimate of the relations between reason and belief. From Plato on, the main assumption of Greek thinkers was that reason was superior to belief or opinion, however authoritative, and that reason was the guide in the questions which mattered most. For Christianity, it was precisely the most important truths, the ones which could decide a man's eternal destiny, which lay beyond the grasp of reason and of knowledge in any ordinary meaning of that word. St. Paul's statement that the Greeks seek after wisdom and that the Cross is foolishness to them was both accurate and influential. Even the most learned and rationally inclined of the Fathers and doctors of the church would not have been able, or even have wanted, to deny the superiority of belief to reason in this sphere of things.[4]

This transvaluation of the relations between belief and reason had the consequence of making irrelevant the whole classical concern over the uses of knowledge and its role in the acquisition of virtue or felicity. The joys and virtues of the Christian may well have been better than anything available to the most fortunate of nonbelievers, but he did not get them through knowledge, nor did they have any direct relationship to his temporal condition or his degree of intellectual cultivation. Knowledge did not and could not serve to make history or to alter its course. Patristic and medieval thinkers, in the last analysis, saw the history of the race and the individual as structured by divine actions. "If humanity had been left to go its own way it would have drifted to a highly undesirable port. All men would have incurred the fate of everlasting misery from which supernatural interference rescued the minority."[5]

The long-term optimism of Christian thinkers, at least about the transtemporal goal of history, was tempered by their acceptance of the Hebraic notion of the decay and degeneration of mankind. The grand and glorious hopes for the next world were balanced by few if any happy expectations about this one.

Interpretations of the Renaissance are perhaps more various than interpretations of any other period of history, and evaluations of it vary from those who hail it as a great liberation of mankind from the shackles of medievalism to those who deplore it as the beginning of a decline of Western civilization into all of the moral and social problems which plague us today. Indeed, a man's views on that cultural revolution we call the Renaissance are frequently a very good index of his religious and political opinions, and often tell us more about him than about the Renaissance. Nevertheless, all students of the period will agree that to one degree or another in the fourteenth and fifteenth centuries there came about a progressively greater secularization of culture. This does not imply that religious values and theological questions were not important, or ceased to capture the passions and the intellectual energies of men. It does mean, however, that matters religious were argued in a far richer and more diverse cultural context than had existed during the Middle Ages.

The so-called revival of learning which began in the fourteenth century accelerated the whole process of the recovery of ancient learning which had been going on during the Middle Ages at a slower rate and in a more selective way. The authority and prestige of ancient learning was enormous both during the Renaissance and the Middle Ages, but the vast increase in the knowledge of antiquity which marked the Renaissance was being diffused in a different Europe, in one whose social and economic structure was rapidly changing. The new culture was in great part the possession of secular, middle-class intellectuals, although ecclesiastics participated in the new movements and were numbered among the great humanists and classical scholars of the period. By the seventeenth century the return to antiquity and the recovery of more and more of the legacy of the ancient world had profoundly altered the cultural map of Europe. Europe had become more pluralistic than it had been since ancient times. The cultural choices with which we are familiar—atheism, one religion or another, one great philosophic system or another, naturalism or supernaturalism of different kinds and degrees—all of these had found great imaginative expression by the first quarter of the seventeenth century. Every great philosophical school of antiquity had been brought to life and had found a new leader: Lipsius for Stoicism, Valla for Epicureanism, Ficino for Platonism, Montaigne for Pyrrhonism, not to mention the various ancient forms of Christianity revived in the course of reformation after reformation. The return among the intellectuals to freer and more varied antique models in art, in political theory, in medicine and science, had vastly expanded the intellectual base for further thought and inquiry at the same time that it also served to enthrone new authorities for those that had captured the hearts and minds of men of the Middle Ages.

Among the many strands of thought which make up the complex structure of the Renaissance we can isolate a few that are of the first importance for the evolution of the idea of progress. If, on the one hand, there was a neat devaluation of the powers of human reason from quarters as diverse as Montaigne and Calvin, there was also a much greater gain of confidence in the power of rational human effort to accomplish great things on earth.

We can find an early and illuminating example of this general trend among those Italian historians of the Renaissance who restored the Greek theory of cycles to historical thinking and set themselves the task of writing national rather than universal history. The idea of cycles eternally recurring may strike us as rather depressing, but if it is juxtaposed to the idea of inevitable decay and dissolution of all things temporal, it can seem at least fifty per cent more cheerful than its alternative. The new history of men like Bruni and Machiavelli was based on the clear conviction that the Roman empire, whether holy or not, did not really exist any more. History was not the story of mankind, nor was it the story of God's dealings with mankind. It was, rather, the tale of the gain and loss of human liberty in one's own city and state. It was an exemplary tale of the actions of men insofar as they succeeded or failed in the great political challenges of peace and war. When they looked to the ancient past they looked to it for guidance concerning their own specific problems, for clues to action which would enable them to master events and achieve political progress. Hence they studied not the history of the Roman empire but the history of the Roman republic, the history of the politically creative progress of Rome from a community of farmers and soldiers to a great world power. That history was truly useful to the newly emergent city-states and even, to some degree, to the emergent monarchies.

These fresh tendencies of thought and fresh impulses to action come to their fullest expression in the thought of Machiavelli. He places his instructions for action in the frame of a theory of cycles of growth and decay, rejects all supernaturalism and providentialism from his thinking about the doings of men, and emphasizes to an extraordinary degree the power for creative political change that even a single individual might possess.

This reorientation of attitudes toward the past and its practical utility rests on the assumption that men can use knowledge to effect great social changes and this belief is reflected in the new historiographical categories. There are periods which furnish useful knowledge for action and others which are useless for this purpose, indeed, which are examples of intellectual cul-de-sacs. Thus it is in the Renaissance that the tripartite division of history into ancient, medieval, and modern first comes into being. Although the term "Renaissance" did not establish itself firmly in our historical thinking until the work of Michelet and later Burckhardt, the notion of a modern period of "rebirth" of the arts and sciences began to achieve currency in the seventeenth century.

Oddly enough, this threefold division of history into periods of light with an intervening period of darkness contributed to the development of the idea of uniform progress at the same time that it was inconsistent with it. After all, if the "dark ages" so-called were really dark, how could there have been steady progress? This question was not really raised until the eighteenth century, and all during the seventeenth century the emergent idea of progress, precisely because it had not been completely thought out and its full implications developed, found its adherents among those who also accepted the new historiographical divisions. This will seem less like another example of human inconsistency if we remember that both views of the past express a common impulse to devalue at least part of the past in order to free men to generate a better future.

There is, needless to say, a crucial distinction in temporal orientation between those who look to part of the past, classical antiquity for example, to serve as a model for the present and future, and those who see all of the past as simply a preparation for the present, as the childhood and adolescence of the human race, however conflated these different attitudes may have been at various times. A third possibility, the utter denigration of the historical past in its totality, the view of the past as a series of blind alleys into which mankind has ignorantly wandered, had to wait for twentieth-century primitivists and an occasional self-styled "existentialist" to find its spokesmen.

The great widening of knowledge which took place from the fourteenth through the sixteenth centuries, during what we have come to call the Renaissance, served on the one hand to free men from the immediate past of the "middle ages" and, on the other, to bind many of them tightly to the more remote past of antiquity. The great prestige antiquity enjoyed in the Middle Ages did, in fact, become even greater. The momentous changes in life and thought which occurred during the Renaissance were changes *sanctioned* by the past. Of course, in imitating antiquity and appealing to its authority, the men of the Renaissance were frequently doing something quite new and different. Modern opera begins as a self-described revival of Greek tragedy, and the sculpture of Donatello expresses a world of perception which can scarcely be called antique. If men could not escape the weight of the past neither could they escape the present.

The idea of progress with its insistence on futurity requires a more massive reorientation toward history, a more ruthless determination to reject the faith in a presumed ideal society or authority of the past, than any thinker possessed before the seventeenth century. Even Bacon, the first great figure to repudiate elaborately and thoroughly the authority of the ancient world, places his *New At-*

lantis in a geographically distant but contemporary locale, a sign that the idea of futurity as the realm of progress was not, even for him, the dominating category in his thinking about cultural and social change.[6] We have only to contrast our modern Utopias with those of the Renaissance to grasp the significance of this fact. For us, the perfect society is not only located in the future, but we think of it as resulting from the inevitable, or at least logical, consequences of possibilities inherent in the life of the present. The true utopian is inclined to confer on progress a necessary character and to view the illimitable future with as much certainty about what it holds for us as most men will give to tomorrow.

If Bacon was not this sanguine, he nevertheless did more than any other single individual to effect this reorientation toward the future by his eloquent denunciation of the notion of "ricorsi," of cycles. Where the Renaissance historians had found hope in the notion of a continual rise and fall of civilization, Bacon found a cause of hopelessness or passivity. There was, in his eyes, no greater single cause for the failure of learning to advance than belief in cycles. Man had failed to understand the strengths and weaknesses of the mind, had failed, on the one hand, to use it correctly and, on the other, to use it on its proper object, the world of nature itself.

His historiographical divisions of the past reflect a completely different evaluation of antiquity from that of the humanists. The first age of man, for Bacon, is preclassical, the period from which the oldest myths and legends descend. Apparently Bacon felt that in that very remote preclassical past men had possessed some accurate and useful knowledge of nature which had since been lost. His own ingenious scientific interpretations of ancient myth would seem to reflect this conviction. The next division of time was that of Greek and Roman classical antiquity, followed by a modern period which includes what we call the Middle Ages. Classical antiquity had had some science, but it was, after a couple of centuries at most, overwhelmed by those great "idols of the theater," the massive philosophical systems of ancient Greece and the medieval Scholastics. Our own time too had seen a few generations of scientific achievement but, according to Bacon, its results were uneven and its methods and procedures uncertain.

It is clear that Bacon's criterion for his historiographical divisions is not political or artistic grandeur, but whether or not an age had advanced in that sort of knowledge of nature which promised to be useful. The criterion of useful scientific knowledge differentiates the historiographical view of Bacon from that of the humanists and also of others, like Bodin, who shared Bacon's hopes for the advancement of learning, given a proper reorientation of the attitudes of men and a proper use of the intellect, but who did not emphasize useful scientific learning in their programs of renovation.

Bacon, like his original contemporaries, was willing to grant that the ancients had greater natural gifts, but he insisted that modern superiority over the ancients would come about in due course if the proper methods of intellectual inquiry were finally adopted. To encourage his contemporaries, he points out that modern times had witnessed three great discoveries which were unknown to the ancients: the compass, the printing press, and gunpowder. They had revolutionized navigation, education, and warfare. They were, moreover, the product of chance, not the result of any systematic self-conscious attempt to produce them. What then might modern men not expect once they develop the right theoretical understanding and practical procedures for making discoveries and inventions? Men must overcome the pernicious conviction that the ancients had discovered everything that could be known, and learn those methods of inquiry which would more than compensate for the imperfections of the mind itself as well as for any presumed inferiority of modern man to his ancestors.

Bacon's hopes for the increase of knowledge were not unlimited. He did not foresee an endless future of vast and unimagined increase of useful knowledge. On the contrary, he felt that the "new philosophy" would reach a complete state, once men embarked on the right track, in a relatively short time. Not in his own lifetime or even within a few generations, to be sure, but completeness was certainly not an ever receding goal.

Bacon's radical departure from tradition lay in his placing the amelioration of the human condition on the acquisition of useful knowledge, on the growth of man's mastery over his external environment. He thereby shifted the relations between knowledge and man's quest for happiness by redefining the kind of knowledge that men needed. Ancient sage and Christian saint had both agreed that man in one way or another had to know himself if he was to be happy. This could be the work of reason or revelation, or both, but the inner revolution which would bring felicity was a revolution in self-understanding. Bacon treats all such problems as settled. Indeed, he congratulates antiquity on its achievements in the ethical, political, and moral spheres. What men must really do now to better their lot is to master nature. Whatever happiness man would conquer lay in the manipulation of his environment, lay in another kind of knowledge, a kind which henceforth acquired more and more prestige and was essentially unchallenged in its promise until Rousseau's massive attack on the corruptions and ambiguities of civilization itself.[7]

Bacon clearly foreshadowed all the eighteenth-century theories of an emerging utopian state of mankind as a result of the increase of scientific knowledge. In spite of his belief in providence, Bacon was nevertheless able to view the historical process as a natural whole, its structure and direction given by the extent to which useful knowledge had been acquired at any particular time. He was able to shake the hold of antiquity on the imaginations of men by showing how poor the ancients were in useful knowledge and by proclaiming that, if truth is indeed the daughter of time, then we are the ancients. By this he meant that time itself has made us wiser by demonstrating the sterility of so much of the legacy of the ancient past and by bringing some new knowledge to birth. The ancients had inscribed *ne plus ultra* on the pillars of Hercules, but the moderns had gone beyond and opened the door to a vast new world. Thus, the ancients had erred. The new motto on the Gibraltar of the mind was to be *plus ultra,* just as moderns had made it the new motto on the geographical limits of antiquity.

Descartes, as different from Bacon as he is, contributed to the idea of progress by emphasizing more than Bacon two of the great postulates of scientific thought which they shared. One was the supremacy of reason over authority. Like Bacon, Descartes did not wish to apply this principle in political and religious matters, and rightly feared that its effect might be to weaken the role of traditional authorities in other than the scientific sphere. The second axiom was that of the invariability of the laws of nature. Nature had always been the same, had always followed the same laws. Since man, whatever else he might be, was also a part of nature, the analytical and empirical methods of the new philosophy, whether in its Baconian or Cartesian version, could in principle be applied to history as well as nature. Knowledge meant the discovery of those laws, always the same, which govern phenomena. If knowledge of the human sciences was to advance, it too had to rest on the assumption that there are permanent regularities in the course of events. These implications of Cartesian and Baconian principles were not fully drawn in the seventeenth century, but the new philosophers had done their work and it was only a matter of time before a thinker of the stature of Hobbes would try to bring the new scientific rigor to the study of human nature and society.

The proposition that nature had always been immutable and that it was somehow uniform, not only in space but also in time, profoundly altered man's attitude toward both the past and the future, and eventually served to sweep away all providential conceptions of history, whether optimistic or pessimistic. More important still, its immediate effect was to undermine the widespread and debilitating belief in the decay of nature. Although this thesis was primarily a religious one, it entered into all of the growing seventeenth-century controversies over the respective merits of ancients and moderns, of classical and contemporary civilizations.

In seventeenth-century England the debate over the decay of nature crystallized in the so-called Goodman-Hakewill controversy.[8] This debate began when, in 1616, Godfrey Goodman, the Queen's chaplain, published a book called *The Fall of Man, or the Corruption of Nature, Proved by the Light of our Natural Reason*. It was published again in two years, and a third time thirteen years later, ample witness to the liveliness of the subject for Goodman's contemporaries.

Goodman's approach to his subject was essentially theological, but he attempted to adduce many bits of scientific or pseudo-scientific and historical evidence for his thesis. Thus the presumed greater size, health, and wholesomeness of our remote ancestors is used as evidence for the steady postlapsarian corruption and decay of mankind. Life, in every respect, moral, physical and mental, was better long ago. It was not only better but simpler, and better precisely because it was simpler.

Goodman should not be misread as eulogizing the noble savage if only because he does not attack civilization itself as the root of man's evils. On the contrary, civilization, with all its imperfections, is a remedy for the worst consequences of the fall of man. Goodman's "primitivism" is really in the venerable tradition of praise of a presumed arcadian or pastoral past which mankind has lost. His version of this blissful time of long ago is a conflation of classical Arcadia with the Christian Garden of Eden. The Queen's chaplain, in fact, is a splendid example of a *laudator temporis acti,* a man saturated with a nostalgic yearning for times gone by, a seeker for a paradise once enjoyed and now lost.

The seventeenth century did not develop the perfect specimen of the utopian, the man who seeks to bring about in the future something like that golden age which Goodman placed in the past. Nevertheless, as the century went on, it would have been possible to divide the thinkers and writers, if I may borrow a formulation René Dubos applied to seekers after health, into arcadians and utopians.

George Hakewill, who was provoked by Goodman's book into a defense of the modern age and an attack on the theory of decay, did not, as we shall see, offer the theory of continual progress as an alternative to the theory of continual decay. His *An Apologie of the Power and Providence of God in the Government of the World,* first published in 1627, again three years later, and which had a third edition in 1635, did not, in any of its revisions, propound a theory of linear progress. Hakewill in fact duplicated in a religious

context quite alien to it the essential argument for a cyclical theory
of history used by secular historians of the Renaissance against the
historiography of Christian tradition.

> There is (it seemes) both in *wits* and *Arts,* as in all things besides, a
> kind of *circular progresse:* they have their *birth,* their *growth,* their
> *flourishing,* their *failing,* their *fading,* and within a while after their
> *resurrection,* and *reflourishing* againe.

As we have seen, the recovery of the cyclical theory of history
was the work of the Renaissance Italian historians, such as Bruni
and Machiavelli, who found in this pagan notion of cycles a qualified optimism about possibilities for successful political action in
their own times. To the notion of continual decay, or the theory
that God had ordained four ages or four world-empires, the last of
which was Rome, and that men therefore lived in the end time of
the world, they opposed the notion that modern men could achieve
great things in politics simply because decay was the correlative of
growth. There is, to be sure, corruption, but there is also generation, and no man should assume that he can know his exact place
on the curve of his cycle. Hakewill, drawing on this tradition, applies it to the recurrence of human genius—"wits" too can renew
themselves—and to the renewal of the arts and sciences.

Along with his cyclical theory of cultural change, Hakewill apparently adopted the notion of "compensation" so important to the
thought of Machiavelli and Guicciardini. This theory might be said
to interpret change as a kind of "steady-state system." It is true
that parts of the universe, whether in the realm of nature or culture,
are decaying, but those who reason from part to whole are in error.
While one part is decaying another is growing, while part of creation dies another is coming to birth. In the last analysis, men find
universal decay because they want to, perhaps out of the same motives which prompt old men to bemoan the present in secret envy of
those who are now young, or out of sloth, or perhaps out of simple
ignorance of the true state of affairs.

Hakewill's defense of the moderns was not tepid. Some of his
contemporaries had been fond of saying that the moderns, if they

surpassed the ancients in anything, did so only because they had the ancient inheritance to build on. The moderns, in a widely used image, were dwarfs who could see beyond the ancients only because they stood on the shoulders of those bygone giants. Hakewill completely repudiates this image of the relations of moderns to ancients. All men, at any time, are of a single condition. Intellectual ability is more or less uniformly distributed throughout the human race in any given era. Moderns had allowed themselves to be psychologically inhibited by their belief in the erroneous theory of decay.

Hakewill adduced ample evidence of modern achievement and progress, and urged men to bestir themselves, to set to work, promising them that, if they do so, they will be able to achieve all kinds of great and worthy accomplishments. His optimism was based not only on a rational theory of cycles but on the theological argument that God's providence, his goodness, is inconsistent with the idea of continual decay. While his religious arguments are not very convincing, that standpoint enabled him to take a universal view of history and to include all varieties of human achievement in his evaluation of the past. Thus, he was concerned with moral and social progress as well as progress in the various branches of learning. Modern men, according to Hakewill, not only equal the ancients in poetry, for example, and even excel them in a number of other branches of learning, they also have a superior individual and social morality. This last is a most important notion and is perhaps the earliest attempt to unify the idea of moral progress with that of intellectual progress.

While Hakewill's particular kind of religious orientation allowed him to be hopeful and to interpret the doings of providence optimistically, even as far as this world is concerned, it also checked any soaring vision of the future. The world, in fact, would end in a universal conflagration even though the course of history so far shows a generally upward movement in spite of the retrogressive moments which are inevitable in cyclical change.

Where classic Christian historiography was deeply pessimistic about this world, Hakewill transferred some of its hope about eternity to time, and he was able to do so by an interesting adaptation of a pagan theory of cyclical change! The history of ideas is filled with many such ironies simply because the same idea can inspire such different kinds of sentiments, provide the motive for so many different sorts of actions, depending on the context. Many years later, when Nietzsche revived the classical theory of cycles, of eternal recurrence, he saw in it an abysmal and maddening vision of the human situation, a vision of terror fully the peer of the old Christian hell in which he did not believe. When cycles replace decay, they are grounds for hope, but when they replace progress, they are just as surely a cause of despair.

As we have seen, the modern idea of progress rests on a number of assumptions, the most important of which is the belief that knowledge will steadily and continually increase and that this knowledge, if it is to promote human welfare, will be of both a scientific and a utilitarian character. An implicit part of this conviction about the advancement of learning is the awareness, at first dim and later explicit, that scientific knowledge has unique properties because it is verifiable knowledge, the kind of knowledge which provides a steady foundation for continual increments. Of course the ancient world made enormous and invaluable contributions to scientific thought and method, but as the spiritual condition of the ancient world changed and the great thinkers sought salvation through moral discipline or ecstasy rather than inquiry, what science they had became more and more the mere underpinning of various quasi-religious systems of redemption.[9]

In the seventeenth century, science first truly came into its own. Only then did science mark itself off *distinctly* from the sort of speculation characteristic of philosophers and theologians, the sort of speculation which finally by late antiquity absorbed Greek science. Only then did scientists become *thoroughly* aware of their own view of knowledge and of their own characteristic methods and results. Science became an organized form of social activity, and scientists began to constitute a society governed, in Bronowski's phrase, by "the habit of truth, not as dogma but as process." [10]

It was the model of the kind of knowledge which was not only faithful to fact and tested in action, but which can grow steadily, continually yielding new understanding and new powers over nature. In a manner which was never fully developed in antiquity science became knowledge in a new temporal mode, that of the future. That the truth was to be found, not given, was an ancient belief. But in the seventeenth century, the realization grew that men not only needed new methods but that the truth was to be found by a society of men working together, a society, moreover, perpetuating itself into future generations, for the truth would be the slow work of time. Since the truth they would uncover was also power, their inquiry would transform the future even as the future revealed new truths. The prospect of the future is obviously a crucial ingredient in the idea of progress, but that future must be a future which man can determine, at least to some degree, and it was the new science with its promise of new truths and new inventions which placed the lever of history in the hands of mankind.

Not only was science oriented toward a future of progressive change, but its triumphs and the faith which its achievements inspired in its methods encouraged the belief that science would continue to grow irrespective of the work of any particular individual. Both Bacon and Descartes played down the role of the individual genius and emphasized the all-important role of correct method. Thus it was to be expected that Fontenelle, later in the seventeenth century, would be able quite plausibly to maintain that even if Descartes himself had not existed someone would have done his work. The Baconian and Cartesian belief, that with the correct methods the growth of knowledge would be inevitable, came to be extended to a general theory of the growth of knowledge that made it a matter of historical necessity. Descartes, Galileo, Bacon, and the other heroes of scientific thought thus became part of an inevitable series in a historical process leading to the development of modern science.

By making progress in knowledge a historical inevitability, Fontenelle completed the particular vision of scientific knowledge and its inevitable growth that was needed for a fully developed notion of progress. He was also of great importance in popularizing science itself as well as the mythology and ideology that was developing around it. This popularization of science—some would say it really was a vulgarization of science—was of the greatest importance in creating that scientific or quasi-scientific ideology which, for better and for worse, has been the vehicle of so much subsequent social and political change. For it was not only the technological changes which science brought about that were to be so influential, it was scientific ideas themselves and the hopes and values which had come to be attached to them that were to move men in unprecedented directions, challenging old moral and social ideas. Sometimes, to be sure, these ideas reached a wide audience in very diluted and distorted forms as, indeed, they do to an even greater degree today. Nevertheless, a good deal of more or less sound scientific knowledge and some awareness of its implications was pretty widely diffused among people of power and influence by the end of the seventeenth century.

In 1686 Fontenelle published what is the first masterpiece of scientific popularization we have, his *Conversations of the Plurality of Worlds,* a charming work in which he undertook to explain the new astronomy and cosmology to the ladies. The work is notable not only for the soundness of its exposition but because of the attention its author gave to the implications of the new picture of the universe. Fontenelle, like many of his contemporaries, found the idea of a plurality of worlds more challenging to the imagination than the simple facts of the heliocentric astronomy. The possibility that these other worlds might be inhabited was infinitely more of a challenge to the anthropocentric assumptions of traditional Christianity than the displacement of the relative positions of the planets in relation to the sun. If there were men elsewhere in the universe, as seemed likely, since the number of worlds appeared to be infinite, were they like us? Had they gone through the great drama of Fall and Redemption? Were there as many Christs as there were inhabited worlds? Indeed, as educated men familiarized themselves with the new science they considered just those questions which have again become of popular interest with the beginnings of the space age.

The triumphs of the new science did not, however, go unchallenged. Indeed, scientific advances served to sharpen the great debate over the respective merits of ancient and modern cultural achievement which marked the transition from the late Renaissance, with its new tyranny of classical precedent, to the modern era.

This debate over the relative merits of ancients and moderns gave rise to a considerable literature of a polemical character which is most familiar to English readers as "the Battle of the Books." Although it was the new philosophy and the new science that really accentuated the contrast between classical and modern cultures, the quarrel was most intense over the relative merits of ancient and modern writers, especially the poets. This is quite understandable when we bear in mind both the imperishable greatness of the best of ancient literature and the fact that the general educated public, then as now, could lay little claim to making authoritative judgments on scientific matters.

The terms of the debate and its literary focus were first given by the celebrated Italian writer and critic, Alessandro Tassoni, the author of *La Secchia Rapita,* "The Stolen Bucket," a widely admired mock epic which continued to be read into the eighteenth century and may have influenced Pope in his composition of *The Rape of the Lock.*

Tassoni was strongly on the side of the moderns and he attacked not only classical writers of the stature of Homer but even those authors closer to his own time, such as Petrarch, who had been incorporated into a canon of modern classics. His general attack on the authors of the past was presented in the first nine books of a work later to be called *Ten Books of Diverse Thoughts* (*Dieci Libri di Pensieri Diversi*). These first nine books were published in 1612 and the tenth book, the comparison between ancients and moderns which was to touch off the great controversy, appeared together with the previous nine in 1620.

The starting point for Tassoni's comparison of ancients and moderns was provided by the controversy over the nature of the epic which centered on Tasso's *Jerusalem Delivered.* In its simplest form the argument of Tasso and his defenders amounted to a defense of romantic epic on the grounds that it offered greater variety than the classical epic. True, its episodic structure and proliferating form seemed to sacrifice unity, but this lack of unity was more apparent than real, for the unity of the whole poem, in spite of its diversity, was provided by its hero. In a properly constructed romantic epic, all the events, subplots and episodes would finally refer to the central figure of the hero even if some of them were, in themselves, somewhat remote. Thus modern epic did something different and did it well. It gave rich variety within its own principle of unity. A bold defense in the light of the weight of antique precedent on what an epic should be like!

Throughout his work, Tassoni comes out effectively on the side of the moderns, and his argument is an interesting one. He accepted the assumption of his opponents that the arts are not capable of indefinite development and that when any kind of artistic genre or form has been carried to its maximum development it must decline. The usual conclusion from this assumption was that the ancients could not be surpassed. But Tassoni argued that the moderns had shown that the ancients had not, in fact, carried everything to perfection. Indeed, moderns had improved, in some cases at least, on the literary legacy of the past and had even developed some new forms of their own.

Throughout the seventeenth century in Italy, those literary critics who sought to defend the moderns against the ancients would, like Tassoni, point to romantic epic, Ariosto or Tasso, as distinctively modern achievements of the highest order. Some critics even added to the rival modern canon of classics the new poets of wit, such as Marino, whose extravagant conceits and verbal pyrotechnics had no parallels in antiquity.

The controversy over ancients and moderns spread from Italy to other countries in Europe. In England, the first important contribution devoted exclusively to the debate over ancient and modern classics came in Sir William Temple's *An Essay on Ancient and Modern Learning* in 1690. In this work Temple came to the defense of the ancients. While there is little in Temple's essay which is either original or very persuasive to a modern reader, it elicited in 1694 a reply from William Wotton of considerable interest.

In his *Reflections upon Ancient and Modern Learning,* Wotton argued that the thesis of ancient superiority, in those fields where it was clearly established, need not rest on the assumption that the ancients were more abundantly endowed with talent. Moderns have quite as much natural ability, are as fully endowed with intellectual gifts of various kinds, as the ancients. The causes of ancient greatness must be sought in the character of classical civilization, in some of the features of its political and social life. Thus eloquence and skill in debate were practical necessities of Greek and Roman political organization, and the magnificent achievements of the ancients in oratory were a result of the response of gifted individuals to the special necessities and opportunities of their times. Moreover, Wotton argued, we should distinguish between achievements in the arts and achievements contributory to the growth of knowledge. There has been an indisputable advance in knowledge of all kinds since ancient times. The arts, however, not only do not have an incremental character, but are further distinguished from knowledge in that they lie in a cultural sphere in which different reasoned judgments and evaluations may all be valid. Diversity of opinion is a valid principle in our dealings with works of art, while true knowledge demands universal assent.

Like Fontenelle, Wotton recognized the difference between artistic achievement and the slow growth of knowledge, but neither of them really examined the question of development in the arts. The idea came to be suggested in contemporary critical circles that since the moderns had a broader experience of the world—the legacy of a longer history—and therefore a more penetrating grasp of the complexities of the human soul, so they had developed a literature of greater psychological complexity than the literature of antiquity. Nevertheless, no one made a clear formulation of the difference between aesthetic progress, a possible progress in artistic value, and progress in the sense of the invention of new artistic techniques or the discovery of new subjects for artistic treatment.

Before we think of this debate over artistic progress as of merely historical interest we might look at some of the best modern literary criticism where we will find some similar confusions and problems. Few critics would, I suppose, maintain that it is possible to say, in some absolute sense, that Shakespeare is a better *poet* than Homer, or Dante than Shakespeare. Yet the evaluation of figures of somewhat lesser rank seems frequently to be based on some notion, more or less covert, of ideological or moral progress. In fact, artistic achievement has consistently evaded the attempts of theorists of progress to find a uniform pattern for both cultural and intellectual development. To be sure, literature and art have been studied as reflections of complex historical and cultural dynamisms and events, but no reader fresh from the magic of Homer's *Iliad* can find such data immediately relevant to what has in fact transpired in his consciousness as he read the poem, to what he has learned from the poem *qua* poem.

Both the defenders and attackers of the idea of progress frequently failed to distinguish between the kind of knowledge which is incremental and the kind of knowledge given to us by poets, artists, and speculative philosophers. Most if not all the beliefs and aspirations of Dante, for example, are obsolete, the dead freight from the past which, to many readers, seems to clutter the poem. Yet we read him because he has much to say to us that is relevant to our deepest concerns. In some way, we learn from him, for he still can sharpen our moral vision and throw a brilliant light on the darkest corners of our experience. Art in its deepest meaning, as that activity which comprehends and takes cognizance of human experience in all of its complexity remained and still remains unassimilable to the category of intellectual progress.

In a way, this contrast is a special case of a larger contrast between knowledge and wisdom, *scientia* and *sapientia,* the public and personal uses of knowledge. The knowledge men need to make themselves happy may and often does differ from the knowledge that satisfies their curiosity or gives them power over nature. It differs not necessarily in the concrete content but in the kind of relation it bears to the desiring and willing self. A man may be largely ignorant, live among physical discomforts, and yet be wise and happy, or he may be a genius, live in luxury, and find life unendurable. I have permitted myself the expression of this uttermost truism precisely because it is so commonplace a bit of collective human wisdom that we need to remind ourselves of it. The most divergent conceptions of man and the world have served to liberate individuals from misery at some times, and to compound their miseries at others. Lucretius rejoiced in freedom from the supernatural, while Dante sought and found therein the highest felicity. Dante's world, to Lucretius, would have seemed, viewed as knowledge, a massive illusion, but he would have been forced to conclude that even illusions can make some men happy, or at least less unhappy.

All of this, I suppose, is so obvious as to seem trite, yet the history of the idea of progress is filled with obscurities concerning distinctions of just this order. Still, the theorists of progress were by no means as naïve as this might seem to imply. The most sophisticated form of the faith in progress, as we might find it in Condorcet or Comte, did not blink the many concrete challenges to optimism that surrounded it. If the growth of scientific knowledge and technological power had brought problems as well as benefits in its train, more knowledge and more technology could uncover the causes of the problems and eliminate them. It is at this point that we of the twentieth century must pause and reflect. We have had too much experience, not simply of the destructive uses of the scientific control of nature, but of seeing how difficult it is to use the new technology to do what is actually possible to alleviate misery. As John Plamenatz has pointed out:

Knowledge, power and will are closely related to one another, and related in many ways, both in the individual and in society. Unfortunately, they are not so related that we can assume that, as knowledge accumulates, it will be so distributed among men that it comes to those who have the power and will to use it for the common good.[11]

Rousseau's arcadian fantasy of primitive freedom and virtue is a myth, but he used it to point directly and indirectly to some truths. The growth of civilization, its increasing complexity and dynamism, the loss of traditional habits of life which made for security

—all of these, according to Rousseau, had generated destructive passions. He correctly perceived that the growth of one kind of knowledge, the kind which lies behind the great differentiation of the skills so vital to life in complex societies, the kind which makes the comforts and security of civilized life possible, would generate the need for an increase in self-understanding, in a discriminating kind of intelligence whose growth would inevitably lag behind the need for it. The less simple and traditional society becomes, the more men will experience confusion and anxiety, the less they can live by simple habits the more they will have to develop the very difficult art of flexibility and discrimination in thought and action.[12] The need for the second kind of knowledge may become so great that political and social disasters as well as individual miseries of an unforeseen sort will overtake civilization.

The political and social power of the idea of progress did not derive from its most refined and subtle versions but from the belief, stripped of qualifications and nuances, that knowledge is valuable in direct proportion to its practical utility. The emotional and volitional power of this idea has largely spent itself insofar as it generated what now seems like a fatuous optimism about the short-term future among the leaders of thought and the wielders of power. It does not make much sense to replace it, as some would, with a senseless despair of the present or modernized versions of a golden age in the past. Technology, with all the problems it presents, is not only an essential factor in the growth of scientific knowledge, it is the hope of that majority of mankind which still lives on the verge of starvation. A distinctive product of Western civilization, it has proved to be more exportable than any other aspect of our cultural and social heritage. Some form of the idea of progress, however inconsistent and heterogeneous a cluster of ideas it may prove to be upon analysis, will persist as long as poverty and disease remain the overwhelming problems of most of the world. An idea, after all, is not just a logical matter or a rational act. It is, as Hobbes tells us, a scout of desire.

The idea of progress, especially in its more naïve forms, can be understood as a religious idea, the mythology of the religion of discontent with one's position or one's lot. The great historic religions at one point or another preached resignation, and there often may be nothing else to do. But the key to the life of an idea or a religion lies in the sphere of the psyche, and early or premature resignation no longer seems to be a widespread human trait, or an option that men are willing to take before having exhausted all possibilities. Technology has generated possibilities for the imagination as well as actualities. It has awakened desires where none had existed before and strengthened desires that had once limited themselves. Insofar as the mind of man is a sum of hopes and expectations, it has changed its character forever. It has given rise to hope, both realistic and extravagant, and channelized the major portion of human energy in the modern world. Along with its corrosive effect on some of the great traditional human values it has also, at times, been ethically creative, and has fostered the commendable tendency to equilibrate conflicts by adjusting them rationally.

Ideas are indeed the scouts of desire, but they in turn may serve to moderate desires and channelize them. Their use is a function not only of what men want, but of what men can or ought to have. Knowledge may serve to make our needs seem infinite or to pare our needs down to those which are truly human.

The post-Renaissance conflict between utopians and arcadians, new and old philosophers, utilitarians and contemplatives, proponents and opponents of the belief in progress, the lovers and haters of technology, is rooted not only in temperament but in a different reading of life and of the relation of knowledge to living. I have tried to express that difference in terms of the classic differentiation between *sapientia* and *scientia,* the truth which sets you free and the truth about man and the world. It is obvious from this formulation that much that is *scientia* may become *sapientia.* It all depends on whether man is able to use the truth about things in the service of moral self-awareness.

The arcadians were those who felt that the essential part of wisdom, if not of learning, had been enshrined in one religion or another, or in one philosophical discipline or another, and there was much to substantiate their claim. But it is true, that beginning in the Renaissance, even for many of those who sought "wisdom," the old authorities, faiths, beliefs and disciplines came to seem less and less relevant. And the mass of exegesis which increasingly surrounded the sacred and near-sacred texts of antiquity did not make the implementation of whatever wisdom they might contain any easier. It was in the seventeenth century that the terms of this conflict over the uses and kinds of knowledge were set, and we might view it advantageously as a conflict between science and poetry, or science and what we may call the "humanities." The conflict, with all the confusions and false antitheses between scientific and so-called "humane" learning, persists into our own time where it has been revived with more heat than light at a level of thought and discourse far below the magnificent contributions of Mill, Huxley, and Arnold in the nineteenth century.[13]

It is of course true that science, like any other cultural phenomenon, has had its influence on imaginative writers. From classical times to the present, poets and writers of the highest order have responded to the scientific ideas of their times. We have only to think of Lucretius and Dante who found in the scientific thought of their time—its limitations are irrelevant to the matter of influence —part of the focus and frame for their magnificent visions of the human condition and of human destiny. Science, like philosophy, has always furnished men with images and patterns of order, and some men will always respond to these images with passionate intensity and in an imaginative mode.

It is significant that it is impossible to find in modern literature, especially in the literature of the nineteenth and twentieth centuries, any equivalent kind of imaginative grasp of the available body of scientific knowledge. Some reasons for this state of affairs are obvious. The sciences have progressed at a staggering rate and the languages of science, especially mathematics, and scientific ideas have come to be more and more removed from the language and experiences of that ordinary world in which we do most of our living, less relevant to the world of common moral experience which the imaginative writer seeks to render, interpret, and specify.

Scientific discourse has itself been fragmented into a plurality of carefully defined "sublanguages," intelligible to a relatively small number of carefully trained men, while literary discourse, in the very nature of the literary activity, must remain deeply rooted in the common language of men, even if it is always at some distance, far or near, from the undisciplined language of the many.

A Dante or a Lucretius could not only command the scientific knowledge of his time, but this science came to him as part of an integrated body of knowledge. The traditional system of liberal arts included mathematics, astronomy, and what was called "music," a study we would call acoustics or proportion, actually, and the ancient legacy of science, however erroneous it may have been, was at least the common possession of all educated men. Moreover, the ideals which permeated the study of science in antiquity and the Middle Ages were of an ethical or contemplative character. Science, like philosophy from which it was not sharply separated, was virtually unrelated to technology, and the study of science, like the study of all liberal subjects, was presumed to lead not to the mastery of the world but to the mastery of the self.

For Lucretius, scientific knowledge of nature could help to liberate mankind from the terror of the supernatural and from the fear of the unknown. For Dante, the workings of nature revealed the purposes and intentions of the Creator and helped man to live in harmony with the divine order. Matthew Arnold thought that the finest line in the *Divine Comedy* was "In His will is our peace," and I think he was right, for the will of God is nothing other than the order of things, that order into which man must insert himself if he is to achieve whatever harmony may be his lot.

As opposed as the intentions of Lucretius and Dante may have been from the point of view of religion, they both agree on the importance of exact scientific knowledge of the workings of nature. Such knowledge will contribute, as much as knowledge can, to human felicity. It can help to make men more human by telling them of their true possibilities and their valid limitations, and it can make them more humane by replacing illusion with truth and irrational fear by that courage and freedom which accompany the intuition of order. The idea that the study of astronomy or physics, for example, was somehow less liberal, less humanizing, less edifying than the study of rhetoric or poetry would have struck either of these two great poets as nonsense.

Nevertheless, however commendable and exciting their commitment to science may have been, it is precisely in those aspects of their work in which they were most abreast of the thought of their time that they have now become most obsolete. Dante may well have felt that his poem would live because he had made it a veritable encyclopedia of all that was known, but it lives because of his marvelous poetic power, the extraordinary control over the resources of language which makes it possible for him to express the widest spectrum of human experiences with the maximum of discrimination and particularization. Like all great poets he, miraculously, can make language do what it really should not be able to do, name the concrete particular and make unique human experience intelligible in all of the complexity, but without the obscurity, it has in life. His beliefs and his knowledge, those statements in the poem which can be abstracted from the great drama which unfolds before us, which can be removed from their context in the consciousness of an acting, wondering, judging, choosing human being, live on for the most part as myths. Ironically, we find ourselves trying to understand a good many obsolete scientific ideas in order to enhance our understanding of the poem as a poem.

It is true of course, that some great scientist-poet of the present or future will probably not have his work as ravaged by the further advance of science. An allusion to the flight of galaxies in our expanding universe will never sound as archaic to our descendants as an allusion to the epicycles of the Ptolemaic system sounds to us.

Nevertheless, this fact should not obscure for us the radical difference between the way in which the scientist or the philosopher looks at experience and the way in which the poet or artist does. I do not wish to deny that at some very profound level of mental functioning, creative work of any kind may emanate from processes which are fundamentally similar or that, in the final analysis,

Shakespeare and Newton may be closer to one another than either of them is to lesser luminaries among poets or physicists. I rather think that in the Elysian fields the master spirits of humanity from whatever field are more likely to be talking to each other than to ordinary mortals. It is melancholy to speculate on the possibility of anyone spending eternity simply conversing with his own colleagues. Indeed, I wonder if this is not a perfectly good definition of hell.

It is for us now an elementary fact, but one of the highest importance, that the arts do not progress in any meaningful sense of the term, and the same may be said of those great works of history and philosophy which in some sense approach the conditions and value of works of art, works of the order of Thucydides' *History of the Peloponnesian War* or Spinoza's *Ethics*. It is still valid to argue that Homer is, after all, the greatest of poets precisely because he is, of all the major poets, the least interested in ideas about life or theories about it. We seem to get from him more of the texture and substance of recognizable human experience than we do from any other writer. I do not mean to say that works which are permeated by philosophical or scientific ideas may be less valuable as poetry. It is simply that such ideas, where they do occur in works of art, are not there primarily for informing us. We do not read *Julius Caesar* to learn about Stoicism from Brutus. On the contrary, we may learn about Stoicism in order to discover what Brutus' ideas can tell us about him.

In fact ideas finally have a double reference. An idea of whatever sort may be not only a statement about the world but at the same time a statement about the self. Thus the abstract content of Hamlet's great soliloquy, "To be, or not to be—that is the question," is a tissue of rather platitudinous speculations on whether or not a man should take his own life. But in the words that Shakespeare wrote, it is a deeply moving moment in the drama of Hamlet's self-revelation. The poet breaks through our wall of habitual response and makes us perceive a rather common sort of experience as if it were unique, as, in a way, it is. For when we are under the poet's spell we understand the words of Hamlet as if they were being uttered for the first time, and understand his anguish as if it had never happened before to any man.

Much of the effort of literary criticism is an attempt to explain why this sort of thing happens in great poetry, and numerous useful explanations can be given. One interesting if not exhaustive way of looking at this phenomenon is to consider the function of metaphor. Metaphor may be a more or less useless adornment of a thought—and it is in bad writing; or it may be—and it is with good poets—the way in which a particular experience became fully intelligible with all of its nuances.

It is simply because Hamlet thinks not only of suicide but of taking arms against a sea of troubles, because he wonders what dreams may turn the sleep of death to nightmare, that we come to know not merely *what* he thought but *how* he thought it, what complexities of perception and feeling cluster around that thought. The metaphors of the soliloquy thus serve to give a complete statement of the particular state of consciousness of the protagonist.

Science has its metaphors too, and if they serve, unlike the metaphors of poetry, to guide research, they are often like poetic metaphors in stating a set of complex relations which we would not otherwise be able to grasp. Think of how marvelously illuminating Darwin's metaphors like "natural selection" and "the survival of the fittest" were! Of how many apparently heterogeneous facts they were able to make immediately intelligible! Of course, further explanation is indispensable, and it will involve technical descriptions of operations and results, fresh observations, experiments with the ultimate intention of making predictions, the search for latent mechanisms or microstructures which support and explain the phenomena that Darwin first identified. Nevertheless, the metaphor will not pass out of existence as long as it remains a way of briefly referring to the evolutionary process or as long as it remains a vital starting point for explanation or the guidance of observations.

The nature of scientific explanation is a complex subject with a rapidly growing literature,[14] and I cannot pretend to any expert knowledge of it. Three recent contributions to the subject have served, however, to help clarify for me the role of metaphor in scientific explanation and discovery.

J. Bronowski, in his *Science and Human Values,* gave a penetrating criticism of the theories of science advanced by operationalists like Bridgeman, or logical empiricists like Russell, and defended the indispensability of analogical and metaphorical thought in creative scientific work. More recently, G. G. Simpson and Warren Weaver, writing in *Science,* have attempted to differentiate among various kinds of scientific explanation appropriate to different purposes or different branches of science.[15]

Warren distinguishes between what he calls "horizontal" explanation, analogical explanation in terms of the more familiar, a form of explanation which tells us little or nothing new, and "vertical" explanation in terms either of substructures and microstructures, or of supporting axioms and principles. This latter kind of explanation, unlike analogical explanation, is in terms of less familiar concepts. Simpson, on the other hand, distinguishes between reductionist explanation, which I take to be the equivalent of Weaver's "vertical" explanation, and what he calls "compositionist" explanation. Reductionist explanation is sufficient in the physical sciences and in the physico-chemical side of biology. But biology needs the further category of compositionist explanation, which makes a cautious use of teleological metaphors, in order to account for "the adaptative usefulness of structures and processes to the whole organism and to the species of which it is a part, and still further, in terms of ecological function in which the species occurs." [16]

Now these accounts of scientific thought, like most such accounts with which I am familiar, suggest that there is more than one kind of scientific explanation and that the relations between them are complex. They seem, however, to obscure the differences between what we might call the psychology of creative thought and a logically rigorous philosophical account of the process and its results. Nothing is more striking about the study of the history of

ideas than the extraordinarily improbable ways in which some of
the greatest thinkers hit upon their insights and made their great
discoveries.

Kepler, if I may use Bronowski's example, believed in astrology,
in universal cosmic sympathies of a magical sort, in Pythagorean
number mysticism, and these beliefs doubtless furnished him with
those metaphors and analogies, however false or fantastic, by
which he moved toward the formulation of the laws of planetary
motion. Nevertheless, his beliefs have no logically strict or rational
connection with those laws. They were psychologically important
and psychologically prior to them, but they were not logically important or prior. They expressed a passion for order and symmetry
which at times have served to close men's eyes to the actual structure of things because of their eagerness to find too ready an explanation. If Kepler had not been the great observer and mathematician that he was, if he had not possessed a great "feel" for the facts
and for plausible ways of putting them together, he would have
been a museum piece in our cultural history. Yet we can also say
that without his mysticism, without his openness to even excessive
forms of analogical thinking, he might never have been impelled
toward his discoveries.

I don't think then that it will do to write off analogical explanation as really not explaining anything. It may or may not, depending on whether the analogy will serve to guide and stimulate research, or whether the root of the analogy is planted in the solid
soil of fact. Indeed, scientific hypotheses frequently begin as analogies. Newton began his work on planetary motions by an analogy
which in effect extended Galileo's law of falling bodies to extrater-
restrial motions. He then was able to reduce one set of phenomena
to another. The initial analogy worked as a lever to pry open the
door of a second kind of explanation. Sometimes a valid analogy
will be premature. Aristotle correctly grasped the homologous
character of lungs and gills but, since he did not know the function
of respiration, he guessed that lungs served to cool the organism.
Kepler's mystical metaphors and analogies, on the other hand,

were in themselves objectively useless even though they were some-how indispensable to him.

In the last analysis, analogical or metaphorical thinking is no more than the discerning of identity in difference. Not every such act of discrimination and unification is valuable, needless to say, yet Aristotle's praise of the metaphor-making faculty need not be confined to poets: ". . . by far the greatest thing is metaphor. That alone cannot be learnt; it is the token of genius. For the right use of metaphor means an eye for resemblances." [17]

This ability for discerning identity in difference is perhaps the most important distinguishing mark of all the most creative kinds of intellectual activity whether in science or in literature or philoso-phy. The process of creative thinking, as distinct from a logical structuring or interpretation of the results of creativity, inevitably involves metaphorical thinking. Indeed, what we think of as literal language is nothing more than the repository of dead metaphors, analogies once fresh which have lost their force through daily use or which have entirely taken on the abstract meaning they were meant to point to. Creative thinking has its random, undisciplined, virtually autistic moments, moments of rich and often disordered productiv-ity. This is, at another point in the process, balanced by the disci-pline of logical thought or, in the case of science, also by experi-mental verification.

Not only is metaphorical thinking an essential part of creative thought, but the value of such metaphorical thinking oscillates be-tween private or public uses of the insight it incorporates. Thus Kepler's metaphors of cosmic sympathies and correspondences convinced him of order and helped him, and him alone as far as I know, to formulate new laws of the universe. Darwin's, on the other hand, are still indispensable in our discourse and guided the observations, the thinking, and the researches of the generations of biologists since his time.

Metaphor is very frequently the way in which fresh experience first becomes intelligible, the form in which new insight states itself. Whatever kinds of subsequent rethinking or investigation may follow it, no thinking man, in whatever of the pigeonholes of knowledge he may occupy, will replace metaphor as long as he uses language or as long as he seeks fresh understanding.

These views on metaphor are, of course, little more than a few reflections on an enormously complex subject, one which reaches out indefinitely in every direction. The study of the symbolic process is the study of thought itself and such investigations place us in the peculiar position of thinking about thinking, of using language to examine language. Whatever its peculiar complexities, there is a rapidly growing literature of modern studies on symbolization and communication, and just as vital contributions to it have been made by scholars from the most varied branches of learning—from mathematics and philosophy, from linguistics and literary criticism, from psychology and anthropology—so these various contributions are, I believe, creating a point of view from which we can perceive the unifying aspects of disparate kinds of intellectual activity. We are, perhaps, on the threshold of establishing firm links between scientific and other kinds of knowledge, and bringing into fruitful relation that which was sundered in the seventeenth century.

Before that "century of genius" great writers either responded directly to the scientific knowledge of their time and incorporated it into their poetic vision of experience, or they ignored it altogether as irrelevant to their themes and purposes. The seventeenth century marks the great dividing point in the nature of the influence of science in literature. At that time, the influence of science begins to become more complex, more problematic, more varied, and most important, progressively more indirect. Science had, with Bacon, redefined itself as an activity which produces useful knowledge, and with Descartes had defined the truth as that which approaches the conditions of mathematical statement. What these two great methodologists had in common, in spite of the great philosophical distance between them, was an intense mistrust of language— although they were both excellent writers—and especially of metaphorical language. If they did not, like Jeremy Bentham, come to regard poetry as equivalent to the game of pushpin, their influence, on its negative side, served to generate the conviction that what we call the humanities may afford men pleasure but can give them little if any truth.

The process of somehow making a radical cleavage between scientific and other modes of thought took place gradually and extends into our own time. Of course, zealous and articulate utilitarians appeared among the Baconians right away, and a few of the more radical Puritan reformers wanted to change all the schools of England into some sort of combination of Bible college and trade school. On the whole, however, thoughtful men among scientists and humanists remained in some degree of vital and significant contact with one another. While it is true that the seventeenth century witnessed a growth in scientific knowledge so extraordinary that it was gradually less and less possible for laymen to keep abreast of scientific change and to judge it, cultivated men had not yet lost the traditional belief in the unity of knowledge. It was still possible for laymen to grasp the implications of the new science, even if its details escaped their comprehension in many cases, and the range of intelligent response to the discoveries of science was just about as remarkable as the discoveries themselves.

The new astronomy had shattered the crystalline spheres of the heavens which had cradled the earth, silenced the music they made as they glided against each other in their eternal circlings, and opened man's gaze into a universe which was endless. Ptolemy's bandbox universe had exploded into infinity. And how various were the reactions to this new vision of things! The thought of infinite space which terrified Pascal was exhilarating to the poet Traherne, who found in infinite space, as did Newton himself, an image of the divine.

The microscope revealed the infinite in another direction and, again, men were either shocked at the fantastic variety of minute forms of life it revealed or found cause for rejoicing in the ingenuity of their Creator, whose wisdom and marvelous fecundity were revealed in his creation of such a wealth of living forms. The new discoveries, the enormous extension to experience given by the revelations of the telescope and microscope, gave to science a particular prestige which has grown with time. However men reacted to the new knowledge—some welcomed it as liberating knowledge, others saw it as a threat to the old pieties and values—no one ignored it. We should not assume that men of letters were necessarily suspicious of it. The Royal Society, from the beginning, included writers in its membership, and its meetings brought together luminaries of quite diverse intellectual tastes and interests. Moreover, the influence of Bacon had given a particular direction to the development of science in England because of his eloquent criticism of the pitfalls to the advance of learning inherent in the nature of language itself. The cause of experimental science and the cause of the reform of language came, in England, to be intimately associated with one another.

The most significant example of the fusion of these two interests and of the misconceptions it generated is afforded by Thomas Sprat's *History of the Royal Society* (1667). This work is not only a history of the Royal Society but a defense of the new science against a variety of assorted political and religious fears. Sprat, moreover, has two interesting suggestions to make in regard to matters literary and linguistic. On the one hand, as a good Baconian, and to some degree a Cartesian, he advances the Society's program for a reform in language which will bring style and expression as close as possible to mathematical plainness and simplicity. On the other hand, aware that the language of poetry is not identical with the language of an ideal scientific prose, he suggests, in an appendix entirely concerned with the "benefit of *Experiments*" to writers and "wits," that the new experimental philosophy will be a boon to poets. It will, in fact, give them a new source of metaphorical material, a new and ever increasing fount of images, drawn from the data provided by new experiments and inventions.

Sprat, in fact, was proposing not simply a linguistic reform in the interest of greater clarity of style and expression, but a new system of poetic allusion, a new mythology and a new set of conventions to replace the gods and goddesses, the shepherds and shepherdesses, the courtly lovers and ladies, of poetic tradition. Both of these tendencies in Sprat's thought spring from a common impulse, the desire to bring all expression in whatever mode closer to the truth, but the truth defined as the new scientific cosmology of Descartes and Bacon conceived it.

The term "wit" in the seventeenth century, among its multiple meanings, had served to signify that gift for making metaphors which Aristotle had thought so highly of. But Sprat is one with Hobbes and others among the new philosophers in changing the notion of wit from the faculty which discerns identity in difference, which traces out the unity of being in unsuspected places, which generates a bold inventiveness of thought, into the faculty which gives men the immediate reflection of fact. By fact, Sprat would have meant the data that scientific observation and experimentation uncovered, and he seems ardently to have wished that poets would firmly anchor their similitudes in fact so conceived.[18] He says:

> To this purpose I must premise, that it is required in the best, and most delightful *Wit;* that it be founded on such images which are generally known, and are able to bring a strong, and a sensible impression on the mind.
>
> The *Sciences* of mens Brains are none of the best Materials for this kind of *Wit.* Very few have happily succeeded in *Logical, Metaphysical, Grammatical,* nay even scarce in *Mathematical Comparisons;* and the reason is, because they are most of them conversant about things remov'd from the Senses, and so cannot surprise the *fancy* with very obvious, or quick, or sensible delights.

Literature, in the last analysis, had to conform to the true nature of the universe as science was showing it to be, and Sprat's vision of what the new science said about the world was that the world was both minutely factual and mathematically severe.

Curiously enough, Sprat's thesis that poets should root their imaginations in scientific fact had already been put into effect earlier in the seventeenth century. Donne and others of the so-called "metaphysical" poets had drawn heavily on the scientific and philosophical ideas of their time as well as on homely and technical imagery for making new metaphors. They had banished the ancient gods and goddesses from their poetry, had scrapped the elaborate conventions of pastoral, the conceits of courtly or Petrarchan love poetry, for the sake of a greater fidelity to concrete experience and of greater psychological realism, whether in the sphere of love or the sphere of religion. George Herbert's *Pulley,* the alchemical and astrological metaphors of Donne, the ideas of Hermetic medicine in the work of Vaughan—all would seem to have been the implementation of the very wishes of Sprat. Of course, the trouble was that their science and their learning had been largely made obsolete by the new science. They seemed to Sprat, I expect, what they certainly seemed to Dr. Johnson in the next century: unfaithful to nature and perversely learned. Sprat's ideals of thought, language, and expression, like those of Bacon and Hobbes, were congruent with the emergent neoclassical approach to literature which marks the middle decades of the seventeenth century in England and which becomes dominant in the Restoration and eighteenth century. The new science and neoclassical ideals joined to create a new taste in literature which relegated the "metaphysical" poets, the poets of wit and bold metaphorical imagination, to the category of extravagants in literature.

What, in the last analysis, did Sprat want? It would seem that he was asking for a poetry with up-to-date allusions, for a new poetry which would reflect the new learning, the new ideals of order and relation which the scientists of his own time were revealing to the world. He would have said that the learning of Donne was false, that the ingenious and witty analogies he employed did not reflect the structure of reality. We might easily reply to Sprat that it is not the job of poets to orchestrate the ideas of scientists, and that if the passage of time had served to make Donne unfaithful to the truth of external reality, he was nevertheless faithful to the internal reality of his own experience. The artist, after all, is not bound to the world of fact. Sprat would, on a theoretical level, have acknowledged this truth but, like Hobbes, he was against giving fancy—we would say imagination—too free a reign. Judgment, the sober ordering faculty of the mind was not, I think, for him the critical power which, in the artist, helps him to shape artistic materials to aesthetic ends, but the voice of common sense and empirical reality. The right of the artist to transform reality, to view it in personal and oblique ways, is precisely what Sprat would have denied him.

It is truly astonishing to find Sprat's view of the relation of scientific discovery to poetry reflected in a distinguished scientist of our own time. Alfred J. Lotka, at the conclusion of his book, *Elements of Mathematical Biology,* suggests the possibility of a revolutionized future for the arts when they come to give full imaginative expression to the discoveries of science.

Men have gained much knowledge, but as yet they have scarcely had time to realize what they know, and the grandeur of the new truths. It is not enough to know; there must be a vivid imagination presenting to the mind's eye for contemplation at once the many facets of the glittering gem. When men shall have learned not only to know but to appraise the esthetic value of their knowledge, when they shall be filled with the glory of it all, surely a new era must dawn for the poetic arts. Wordsworth says:

Poetry is the breath and finer spirit of all knowledge; it is the impassioned expression which is the countenance of all Science. . . . If the time should ever come when what is now called Science . . . shall be ready to put on, as it were, a form of flesh and blood, the poet will lend his divine spirit to aid the transfiguration, and will welcome the Being thus produced as a dear and genuine inmate of the household of man.

It is, presumably, with such thoughts as this, that he writes in his "Prelude":

> . . . The song would speak
> Of that interminable building reared
> By observation of affinities
> In objects where no brotherhood exists
> To passive minds. . . .

And Renan, in *L'Avenir de la Science,* shows similar sentiment:

Disons donc sans crainte que, si le merveilleux de la fiction a pu jusqu'ici sembler nécéssaire à la poesie, le merveilleux de la nature, quand il sera devoilé dans toute sa splendeur, constituera une poésie mille fois plus sublime, une poésie qui sera la realité même, qui sera à la fois science et poésie.

We may well ask: If the simple Hebraic myth was competent to inspire a Haydn to compose an oratorio of the Creation, what tone poem shall adequately celebrate the new meaning, in the mind of the modern astronomer, of the words

> The Heavens declare the Glory of God
> The Wonders of His power proclaims the firmament.[19]

This noble passage by a scientist of brilliance and high cultivation is eloquent with the liberating power and imaginative splendor of scientific thought. Doubtless it was a similar vision of scientific and philosophical truth which inspired Lucretius, Dante, and Goethe, to list Santayana's "Three Philosophical Poets." Nevertheless, I think there is a fundamental misreading here of the nature of poetry. To many readers, the ideas—philosophical, religious, theological, and scientific—of Santayana's trinity are in great part obsolete. Each of them wrote their poems to convey the truth which saves in a quite uncomplicated sense, but what still draws the modern reader is not the ideas *qua* ideas of these poets, but the recognizable life and variety of experience which their ideas enabled them to comprehend, interpret, and order. Their ideas are the vehicles of a vision of reality in all its particularity and concreteness. Moreover, the reality the poet perceives is common reality, not the reality, if I may echo Renan, which lies under a veil of appearances and which is apprehended by pure thought and inference.

It is common reality but not, I should add, commonplace reality. It is, as Wordsworth suggests, common reality perceived as uncommon. The veil that poetry strips away is the veil which all of our stock responses, the necessary habits of living, impose on our perceptions. Metaphor in poetry is not essentially explanatory, nor is it a guide to the operations of a microstructure supporting appearances, nor does it demand external verification of one kind or another. It is, rather, illustrative of the specific quality of a particular experience. To the extent that science uses metaphor it uses it to explain. This use of metaphor is primarily cognitive and directly referential to some objective reality. Metaphor in poetry elucidates, specifies, and interprets. Thus, if I say with Burns, that "My love is like a red, red rose," I have explained nothing but have said a great deal about the specific mode of my experience. The first man to make this now commonplace comparison must have surprised and pleased his audience. Some of them must have said, "I know now exactly what he means. Somehow she really is like that."

Recently, the nightingale has, surprisingly enough, been the center of the contemporary debate between self-appointed spokesmen of what is vaguely called the "scientific" culture, on the one hand, and the "humanistic" culture, on the other.[20] Apparently, the nightingale has been thrust into the thick of the battle only because of its role, hitherto believed to be quite innocent, in one of the great poems of the English language, Keats's "Ode to a Nightingale." We are told—and by a writer and literary critic—that the famous bird is emphatically not, as Keats thinks, pouring out its soul in ecstasy, nor does it really sing of love and death. It is, in fact, as biologists well know, establishing a territory, shooing off males and inviting females. The moral of this observation, if I understand it correctly, is that it would be a good thing if poets knew more about science. Now this is probably true but, I would submit, it is irrelevant to the poet *qua* poet.

This truly extraordinary argument assumes that the subject of Keats's poem is an actual nightingale. The biological facts about nightingales may well be the subject of a poem, but it would not be the poem by Keats we all admire. The nightingale of his poem is an imaginary one, and its imaginary song seems to symbolize to the poet all the energy and power of life itself, a splendor and vitality whose true measure is death. The song of the bird is the occasion for a set of complex reflections, in the mode of the imagination, on the relations between love and death, life and art, immortality and extinction.

No one, I think, in his right mind, ever read Keats to find out the scientific truth about nightingales, and no one, I hope, is so unresponsive that he would, on looking at a beautiful landscape or hearing a bird sing, inhibit the emotions and reflections it would generate, however "unscientific" or untrue to fact. I don't want to go on whipping this dead horse, but I would like to point out that there is in this sort of argument a radical failure to understand what we might call intellectual indirect discourse, a flagrant example of intellectual bad manners. If I tell a friend not to hide his head in the sand like an ostrich, I do not expect him to reply that ostriches do not in fact hide their heads in the sand. One characteristic of schizophrenic thinking is precisely a form of concrete literalness of response which makes it impossible to communicate anything even remotely metaphorical.

Now the poet will always, wherever he may begin, return to common reality. He will nevertheless sometimes do this by a detour and use any or all of his learning and experience en route, whether his mind is erudite or simple, whether his ideas are extraordinary or commonplace. In other words art, if it is to do its work of freshening perception, must frequently be oblique. If the common realities of mortality and love are to be made uncommon we may have to go the long way round and talk about them in terms of imaginary nightingales with imaginary properties. This is one way of breaking habitual response, the way of placing old undiscriminated experience in a new context, in fresh relations to data, real or imaginary, with which it is not customarily associated. As Marianne Moore suggested, in order to talk about real frogs you may have to put them in imaginary puddles.

The true stuff of the greatest poetry is remarkably commonplace after all: a tiger, a lamb, a rose, a soldier stricken in battle and falling as a flower bends in the springtime when it is heavy with dew, a bird arching the air with great ecstatic soarings. We might say that science and philosophy in different ways explain, but that poetry and art unmask. Unmask what? The object? Perhaps not. In the final analysis it removes the mask of habit from our perception. As I have said, ideas in the sense in which scientists and philosophers understand ideas may be and often enough are the occasion for poetry, and for some of the greatest poetry we possess. But they are not the life of poetry, and poetry has outlasted and even embalmed many great speculations and powerful beliefs which have intrinsically lost their hold on mankind.

The old conflict between science and poetry—we should here comprehend poetry in a broad sense as including the traditional humanistic and moral culture—was a fateful antithesis bequeathed to us by our seventeenth-century ancestors and which we are now only beginning to transcend. It was, however inevitable, based on a number of misconceptions: on too sharp a distinction between literal and metaphorical statement, on too rigid a set of distinctions between literal truth and other indirect ways of making valid statements, on a confusion between the psychological and logical order of thought, on claims which were too exclusive. The student of this controversy will witness a blind desire for innovation and utility in conflict with a rigid and lifeless conservatism maintained with an equally blind snobbery. The Puritan zealot who would have abolished humanistic learning found his opposite counterpart in those whose attitude was much like that of the nineteenth-century professor of Greek in England who began his course with the following defense of Hellenic learning: "Gentlemen. A knowledge of Greek will permit you to look down from the heights of scholarship upon the vulgar, will enable you to read the oracles of God in the original, and can sometimes lead to positions of considerable pecuniary emolument."

The most pervasive form of the quarrel between science and poetry, and the one which still has a lot of life in it, in spite of the confusion it engenders, rests on the assumption that scientific language is clear while poetic language is ambiguous in some pejorative sense of the term. This formulation is really rather primitive but it does point to a confusion of thought over kinds of discourse, kinds of precession, kinds of reference, in which Sprat and other kindred spirits since his time have shared.

All living language is, of course, both inherently ambiguous to one degree or another and, except in virtually monosyllabic utterances, also redundant. A syntax which did not express some essential category of meaning—tense, gender, or reference, for example—more than once in ordering a sentence would simply be unintelligible. We would lose the beginning of a train of thought before we got to the end. Depending on the structure of the particular language involved, some category of meaning will be stated in the noun and verb, or in the verb and adverb, or in some combination or other of different sentence elements. This property of reinforcing meaning through semantic and syntactical repetition is a compensation for a contrasting property of language, its ambiguity. By ambiguity, I refer to the fact that only when we are using words as a kind of code, not as the symbols they are, can we single out one meaning of a word as the stock use. What, for example, is the meaning of the preposition *on* in English or the preposition *epi* in Greek? They are used in so many ways, with so many verbs and phrases, that we cannot even think of their meanings as constituting a sum but only as a continuous spectrum.[21]

In the language of poetry, redundancy, as a structural and semantic property of any viable language, is at a minimum. The formal "tightness" of a good poem, and frequently its difficulty, derives both from the artistic necessity of saying as much as possible with as few words as possible, and of using words to particularize experience. Paradoxically enough, the quest for poetic precision and economy makes poetic language more ambiguous. Ambiguity, of the normal kind inherent in language itself, is the basis of some poetic virtues. The poet accepts it, controls it, and turns it into an asset insofar as he can use the ambiguity of language to convey complementary or contrasting configurations of meaning, what we might call alternative *Gestalten,* formed by starting with one or another of the multiple meanings of a word or image as the focus of attention. Analogously, we view a painting in a number of alternative ways, depending on which feature is taken as the base of perception. The mind cannot make all of these alternative constructions at once, but it does make them serially. Hence there are, as Wotton dimly grasped, multiple valid interpretations of works of art.[22]

The difference between scientific and poetic language does not rest on the presence or absence of ambiguity. Both kinds of language are ambiguous, but the forms of scientific inquiry enable the investigator to deal with the ambiguities of his language whenever they, so to speak, "get in the way." The poet, on the other hand, exploits ambiguity to realize some of his intentions. Let me insist at the risk of repetition that ambiguity in a poem does not mean imprecision. On the contrary, the poet uses ambiguity to give a more exact representation of complex states of perception and valuation.[23]

All language, after all, communicates by eliciting responses in us and these responses are, to one degree or another, configurations of meaning rather than discrete, atomistic, utterly singular, units of signification. Even mathematics is free from ambiguity only as a purely formal structure of internal relations. When used to describe phenomena it is "no more precise than the terms which give it empirical reference. We can give an absolutely exact count of the number of objects in a class only if the class itself is defined with absolute precision.[24]

It has been maintained now for a long time that the spread of scientific modes of communication is serving to make poetry more and more difficult to write. Keats, in one mood at least, bemoaned that science had "unweaved" the rainbow, and Blake's criticism of Bacon, Locke, and Newton has often been quoted to demonstrate how the poets of more recent times have felt both about the scientific demythologizing of the world and about that other great axiom of scientific thinking since Galileo, the subjectivity of secondary qualities. Blake had far more complex views on science than some of the people who quote him, however, and so did Keats. Nevertheless, there is no doubt that in some quarters science has been regarded as the enemy of poetry. Those who hold this view seem frequently to confuse two distinct questions. One is whether the scientific view of the world and of experience somehow make it difficult or impossible either to write poetry or to read it with pleasure. The other is that scientific language—identified with the singular language of truth, it would seem—is changing our habits of thought and expression so radically that we are losing the skills of poetic discourse while acquiring the skills of scientific discourse.

All the evidence we possess would indicate that both views are wrong. First, we have had a series of great poets throughout modern times. One has only to think of Keats and Yeats, of Goethe and Rilke, of Baudelaire and Valéry, of Leopardi and Montale, to know in fact that science has not extirpated poetic gifts. It is true that most modern poets and men of letters have been critical of contemporary civilization, and some of them have been hostile to science because of the social and cultural problems created by scientific technology, the "dark satanic mills" of industrial society and, more important, the bland "scientism," surprisingly wide-spread at one time, whose spokesmen were so fond of telling us that men are "nothing but" a rather simple sum of chemical elements. Whatever the attitude of men of letters to science may have been, the great poetic achievements are there.

As for the supposed pernicious effect of science on linguistic habit, this is simply nonsense. The enemies of the honest users of language, whether poetic or scientific, are not really in the laboratories but in the advertising agencies, television studios, and government bureaus, if anywhere. The language of science is not a code, but part of the symbolic system of language itself. The scientist who writes clearly and well about his work, whether for his colleagues or for a wider audience, is adapting language to one of its legitimate purposes, to convey certain kinds of information as accurately as possible. He may limit the inevitable associations and overtones of words in order to achieve his particular ends, but he does not destroy the poetic possibilities of language in so doing.

The same words he uses in a technical, abstract, and logical mode will be put together differently and for different purposes by the poet, and this can even include his technical vocabulary once it enters the main stream of human conversation. One of the great linguists of modern terms, Karl Vossler, had the following remarks to make about language, which are illuminating for us:

> The language of prehistoric times was no whit more naïve, not a particle more natural, neither more poetical, nor more pious, nor less logical, nor less practical than the most developed literary languages of art or intercourse of the present day. The opinion of sentimental Philistines, that the poetical and the natural are gradually dwindling away in favor of the intellectual and the technical, should find no further encouragement in science.[25]

I would suggest that the enemy of poetry—and I now mean by poetry something far-ranging, similar to what Coleridge meant when he defined poetry as the best words in the best order—is jargon, whether it is the result of simple confusion of mind or the result of one kind or another of political confusion or commercial chicanery.

At a more fundamental level this pseudo-conflict—for that is what it was—arose out of the profound change in the temporal outlook of Western man which found expression in the idea of progress. The representatives of humanistic culture from the Renaissance on all too frequently looked to the past with an extraordinarily narrow and frequently authoritarian view of its possible uses. The new science, on the other hand, looked to the future and, after Bacon, it possessed a vision of that future filled with hope for mankind. Generous spirits among the formulators of the idea of progress, beginning at this time and continuing to the present, tried to find the law of progress—and therefore of hope—in all of the achievements of culture. However, the application of some version of the idea of progress with its attendant values of practical rationality and utilitarianism to the great works of speculation and imagination which were our legacy from the past introduced a serious distortion in our understanding of the distinctions between different kinds of spiritual and intellectual activity. By trying to fit all the works of the mind into one developmental series we lost our sense of the morphology of knowledge, our feeling for the different kinds of precision appropriate to different subjects, for the different methods of inquiry different phenomena demand. Unconsciously, we have marked off the branches of knowledge from each other in terms of some more or less narrow notion of utility, or we have blurred the distinction between that kind of knowledge which is cumulative and that kind of knowledge which has to be rewon generation after generation. Worst of all, we have lost the classical distinction between the public and the personal uses of knowledge, between *scientia* and *sapientia*.

The answer to this legacy of confusion concerning the different kinds of learning and their uses certainly does not lie in compelling the humanist or the poet to acquire a specific bit of scientific information, even if it is the second law of thermodynamics, or making a scientist learn the structure of a Pindaric ode, although such knowledge would doubtless enhance the one and the other. There is nothing inherently unpoetic about the second law of thermodynamics or about the structure of a cell. It is simply that such facts, as mere facts, cannot easily be brought into relation with that general reality in which we do most of our living and whose inexhaustible diversity and rich particularity literature and art attempt to disclose to us. The Pindaric ode is a marvel of variety within order, of complex symmetry, but it has no immediate relation to the images of order by which the scientist organizes his experience as a scientist. Nevertheless, as thinking men, neither the humanist nor the scientist will remain unmodified by his understanding of the work of the other, nor should we presume to judge what use the mind will eventually make of mutual understanding.

The imagination has many mansions, even terrifying ones, and they all lead into each other even if only through labyrinthine ways. It is at the root of nightmare, but it is at the root of all creative thought. It has not only the function of grasping new relations, or the interrelations of new facts, it can quicken old truth and old experiences, raising them to a new life. In regard to new discoveries, it has the function of acclimatizing them, of making them meaningful to us now, in the very immediacy of our existence.

This I think is what Wordsworth meant in his hope for a time when what we now call science will put on flesh and blood. I don't think he means that this will be simply a matter of vocabulary, of making the great ideas and methods of science the common possession of cultivated men, and of bringing scientific terms and concepts into more general circulation. This is important and even indispensable.

I think, however, that he looked forward to a time when the great ideas and procedures of science will be so stated and presented to us that they will throw light on the world we live in as willing, thinking, and desiring beings, when these ideas will come to cultivated men as liberating, transforming ideas. The scientist operating exclusively as a scientist makes an abstraction of himself for the sake of his work. He looks for facts and in order to get at them must pretend that there is such a thing as fact without value. But this is a fiction, albeit a useful one. The great discoveries of science tell us finally about man, some more directly and immediately than others, but all of them serve to elucidate his nature and that of his environment. To the extent that they shatter our conventional assumptions about the world and our place in it, they are moral ideas of an explosive and revolutionary character.

From this perspective, the sciences and the humanities unite, for both orders of knowledge, whether of the workings of nature or of the records of human experience and perception, should, if properly apprehended, change the way in which we look at ourselves and the world about us to make it more consonant with the way things are. Neither scientific knowledge nor knowledge of past experience of mankind need be comfortable or comforting knowledge. The anxiety that some men have experienced upon the introduction of new knowledge, whether in the Middle Ages with the recovery of Aristotle, in the Renaissance with the recovery of all the diversity of ancient thought, or in the seventeenth century with the new cosmology, is finally a symptom of man's radical unwillingness to surrender his sense of his own omnipotence. Yet the faith of all creative endeavor, in science, in scholarship, or in the arts is that the truth, however unexpected or frightening it may appear at first, will finally set you free by helping you to live with things as they are. Illusions may make men felicitous for a time, and some men have even been able to cherish them until they died. They have, however, one fatal weakness, that of collapsing at the first breath of reality.

Whatever the ultimate scientific value of Freud's researches may prove to be, it is no accident that he has had such a striking influence on the arts and the humanities, an influence comparable only to that of Darwin and Frazer. Of course his theories were comprehensible to educated laymen in a way that was impossible in the case of the work of Einstein or Planck, and there is no doubt that they suffered some gross distortions in the process of being disseminated. It is also probable that Freud's candid study of sexuality had a good deal to do with some of the popular interest in his work. Nevertheless, the greatness of his influence lies in the fact that the material he dealt with is in great part the material of common life and common experience, that same dimension of experience which is the concern of the artist and the final focus of humanistic inquiry.

He validated the brilliant perception of William James that the mind of man is ineluctably poetic and broke down the walls between the clinic and everyday life. This is one of the reasons for the impressive fact that the community of artists and humanists was ahead of the medical community in their willingness to entertain Freud's ideas when they were new and as yet unassimilated. Even if some of this intellectual interest, like popular interest, was motivated by a hankering after novel ideas or curiosity over that which had hitherto remained hidden, most of it was prompted by the human need to gain understanding of the darker corners of human experience and so to help liberate ourselves from the tyranny of the irrational.

Like his great model Goethe, Freud was both humanist and scientist, the detached observer of the processes of the mind and the brilliantly gifted writer in the personal idiom. What he discovered of the truth about things, his *scientia,* he also simultaneously experienced as *sapientia.* In this, he was faithful to both sides of his greatly gifted mind and to both poles of the oscillations of live thought between acts of objective interpretation and acts of personal appropriation. Perhaps this sort of fidelity to the rhythms of thought is easier when your subject is the mind itself. Nevertheless, all knowledge has this double aspect. The great ideas are precisely those which help us to define human possibilities and limitations, which finally tell us about ourselves. They may not always come into the world clothed with flesh and blood, but if they are to live outside of the minds of the few, they must be relevant to self-understanding, the most badly needed form of knowledge in our own time. Scientific knowledge has given us vast technological power and this has been used for good and evil, for the preservation and the destruction of life. As this ambiguous application of scientific knowledge grows—and it will—it becomes more and more imperative that science present its true face to the world, as an intellectual enterprise whose true purpose, like that of the arts and humanistic scholarship, is helping man to understand the world and finally himself. *Eros* and *thanatos* have always struggled with each other for the control of civilization, but merely to side with *eros* is not enough. True, *eros* is not blind, nor is it a subrational power. It must be what Platonists called the philosophic *eros, eros* saturated with intellect, love guided by the truth and continually seeking fresh knowledge.

Notes
*

1 On the idea of progress see the indispensable work of John Plamenatz, to which I am heavily indebted: *Man and Society: A Critical Examination of Some Important Social and Political Theories from Machiavelli to Marx,* 2 vols. (London, 1963), Vol. II, chap. 7, "The Belief in Progress," pp. 409-457. The classic work of J. B. Bury, *The Idea of Progress* (New York, 1955) should be read in the light of Plamenatz' chapter on the subject. On the relations between religious thought and the idea of progress in the seventeenth century see Ernest Lee Tuveson, *Millennium and Utopia: A Study in the Background of the Idea of Progress* (Berkeley and Los Angeles, 1949).

2 Plamenatz, Vol. II, p. 413. The idea of a "golden age" in the past and a successive decline through ages of silver and bronze to an "iron" present began as myth. It attained philosophical stature, however, and came to be a fundamental principle of Stoic thought in antiquity. Paradoxically enough, they believed that this general decline, by creating the opportunities for the manifestation of Stoic virtues, had led to moral progress to the degree that it had engendered Stoic sages. This interesting theory bears some strong resemblance to the Christian doctrine of the "fortunate fall" (*felix culpa*), whereby the drama of salvation is so glorious that it was somehow worth our expulsion from the Garden of Eden.

3 See the classic study of William Chase Greene, *Moira: Fate, Good and Evil in Greek Thought* (Cambridge, Mass., 1944).

4 See the remarks of Walter Kaufmann, *A Critique of Religion and Philosophy* (New York, 1958), p. 305. I realize that the conception of faith is not synonymous with that of belief, but there is no question that in practice and often in theory there is little to distinguish them.

5 Bury, p. 21.

6 Cf. Bury's interesting remarks on the choice of place and time in the literature of Utopias, in *op. cit.,* p. 61.

7 See the penetrating study of Rousseau in Plamenatz, Vol. I, pp. 364 ff.

8 The major study of this important controversy is in Victor Harris' book, *All Coherence Gone* (Chicago, 1949).

9 On the decline of Greek science see the study of George Boas, *Rationalism in Greek Philosophy* (Baltimore, 1961). It is interesting to speculate on the proposition that Greek science decayed because it had too little relation to technology, was too divorced from the needs of men. Compare the remarks of J. Bronowski in his classic *Science and Human Values* (New York, 1956), chap. 2, on the way practical needs influence scientific inquiry. Thus the importance of navigation and, ironically enough, astrology, in fostering astronomical study during the seventeenth century.

10 On the new forms of the social organization of science see the works of Martha Ornstein, *The Role of Scientific Societies in the Seventeenth Century* (3rd ed., Chicago, 1938), and R. K. Merton, "Science, Technology and Society in Seventeenth-Century England," *Osiris,* IV (1938), 360-632.

11 Plamenatz, Vol. II, p. 455.

12 *Ibid.,* pp. 455-456.

13 I refer, of course, to the Snow-Leavis controversy over the "two cultures." The documents are available in C. P. Snow, *The Two Cultures: And a Second Look* (Cambridge, Eng., 1964; also a Mentor book, 1964), which contains his original lecture and some afterthoughts about the controversy it generated. F. R. Leavis' attack on Snow's original lecture is now available in book form, *Two Cultures? The Significance of C. P. Snow* (New York, 1963). The most perceptive comment on the controversy was made, it seems to me, by Lionel Trilling, "Science, Literature and Culture: A Comment on the Leavis-Snow Controversy," *Commentary* (June, 1962). I do not feel that the work of Aldous Huxley, *Literature and Science* (New York, 1963), or Jacques Barzun, *Science: The Glorious Entertainment* (New York, 1964), especially chap. 1, or of Douglas Bush, *Science and English Poetry: A Historical Sketch, 1590-1950* (New York, 1950) are really as informed or as illuminating as the essay by Trilling or the well-known studies of Whitehead, Julian Huxley, and Bronowski.

14 Excellent anthologies of major writings on the philosophy of science are available in *Philosophy of Science,* ed. Arthur Danto and Sidney Morgenbesser with an introduction by Ernest Nagel (New York, 1960), and E. H. Madden, *The Structure of Scientific Thought* (Boston, 1960).

15 G. G. Simpson, "Biology and the Nature of Science," *Science,* Vol. 139, No. 3550 (Jan. 11, 1963), pp. 81-88; and W. Weaver, "Scientific Explanation," *Science,* Vol. 143, No. 3612 (Mar. 20, 1964), pp. 1297-1299.

16 Simpson, p. 87.

17 *Poetics,* xxii, 17.

18 See George Williamson, *Seventeenth-Century Contexts* (London, 1936),

for the decline of "wit" in the sense of imaginative and metaphorical boldness. For more recent studies, see M. H. Nicolson, *The Breaking of the Circle: Studies in the Effect of the "New Science" on Seventeenth-Century Poetry* (rev. ed., New York, 1960), and J. A. Mazzeo, *Renaissance and Seventeenth-Century Studies* (New York, 1964), the chapters on "metaphysical" poetry.

19 A. J. Lotka, *Elements of Mathematical Biology* (New York, 1956), p. 425. This book was first published in 1924 as *Elements of Physical Biology*. I provide a translation of Renan's French: "Let us admit then without fear that if the marvels of nature, when they shall have been unveiled in all of their splendor, will constitute a poetry a thousand times more sublime, a poetry which will be reality itself, which will be both science and poetry at the same time."

20 See Aldous Huxley, *Science and Literature*, pp. 112 ff., J. Barzun's review in *Science*, Jan. 3, 1964, and a letter by L. Berlowitz commenting on the review in *Science*, Mar. 13, 1964.

21 See on ambiguity in poetry the classic work of William Empson, *Seven Types of Ambiguity* (New York, 1931), and for some excellent modern essays on language from the philosophical point of view see Max Black (ed.), *The Importance of Language* (New York, 1962). This volume contains important essays by Gilbert Ryle, Friedrich Waismann, and Owen Barfield, among others. On how grammatical structures work to convey and limit meaning see the interesting study of Thorleif Boman, *Hebrew Thought Compared with Greek*, trans. J. L. Moreau (Philadelphia, 1961). On redundancy, see Colin Cherry, *On Human Communication* (New York, 1961), chap. 3, especially pp. 115 ff.

22 See on this question of ambiguity the brilliant work of E. H. Gombrich, *Art and Illusion: A Study in the Psychology of Pictorial Representation* (New York, 1961). See also Empson, *The Seven Types of Ambiguity* (pp. 102 ff.), who points out that ambiguity used to be predicated of the mind, which was supposed to clarify the ambiguity by picking the right one of a number of multiple meanings. He suggests that, as in recent atomic physics, the notion of probability, of weighing alternative interpretations according to their probabilities, has now come to be attached more to the object than to some defect of the mind. According to Empson, ambiguity in poetry, like probability in physics, does not necessarily imply the fallibility of the mind. If I am correct in interpreting him, Empson is saying that ambiguity and the uncertainties of probability both inhere in the nature of the object as much as in the nature of the mind.

23 See the excellent essay of Ernst Kris and Abraham Kaplan, "Aesthetic Ambiguity," in Kris, *Psychoanalytic Explorations in Art* (New York, 1952), pp. 243-264. On the difference between poetic and scientific ambiguity they explain: "They [i.e., ambiguities] occur in what Morris [C. Morris, *Signs, Language and Behavior*, New York, 1946] called "different modes of signifying" and serve different purposes. Disjunctive and additive ambiguities are more common in the designative mode, and arise when language is used as an instrument of discrimination and gen-

eralization; conjunctive and integrative ambiguities emerge in language embodying syncretistic and autistic thought. In the former case, where discourse is primarily "informative," ambiguity is a necessary evil; in the latter, where the functions of language are predominantly "valuative" and "incitive," a virtue is made of that necessity (p. 250).

24 Kris, p. 251.

25 *The Spirit of Language in Civilization* (New York, 1932), p. 94.

INDEX